Shelter and Shadows

An Awakening to Our Common Identity

By Raymond M. Keogh

Our Own Identity

Shelter and Shadows

An Awakening to Our Common Identity

Our Own Identity Ltd
Bray, County Wicklow, Ireland

Published by Our Own Identity in 2016

© Raymond M. Keogh

ISBN 978-0-9935652-0-5

Printed and bound by Lettertec, County Cork, Ireland

Cover by Ana Grigoriu, Books Design, Germany

A Product of The Gerald Keogh Identity Series

Decade of Commemorations (2012–2022)

Contents

Acknowledgements...iv

Preface...v

I. Indigenous Identity..1

    Awakening...1

    Domestic Shadows...3

    Blood Sacrifice..8

    Anzac Bullet Brings Shaw to Town..14

    At Odds with the Stereotype...20

    Cultural Shock...25

    Foreign Bride..30

    Kate's Curiosity...36

    Family Secret..44

    Trevelyan's Claque...48

    Decline and Recovery...55

II. A Forgotten Society...59

    Anthropology of an Urban Tribe..59

    Radically Inclusive...65

    The Merchant and the King..71

    Beginnings of Native Urbanisation..78

    Roads to Wealth...83

    Urban-Rural Links..88

    Native Upland Farmers...93

    Tribal Roots..100

III. The Wider Perspective...107

    Idyllic Illusion...107

    White Feathers...118

    Old English Identity..127

    A Dangerous Pastime..131

    Love of Enemy...136

    Destiny...141

    Bison Hunting to Bib Manufacturing..146

    Tip-toeing Round Eggshells...154

    The March of a Nation..163

    Universal Reunion..169

References...171

Relevant Dates in History..176

Author..177

Acknowledgements

Thanks are due to all who contributed to this book, including, amongst many others:

John Arden and Margaretta D'Arcy (actors) who helped me establish contacts with the second branch of the Keoghs of Ranelagh. Many details of this family were clarified by Ms Anne Dowden, Ms Margaret Baczkiewicz and Ms Germaine Greenwood, who supplied important facts about the family's involvement with the Irish theatre and the independence movement;

Niall Bergin, Supervisor, Kilmainham Gaol Dublin and Brian Crowley, Curator, Pearse Museum Rathfarnham—instrumental in casting new light on Irish Volunteer Gerald Keogh, who was killed outside Trinity College Dublin in 1916, and his brother Cyril who also took part in the Easter Rising;

Deirdre Larkin of the Parnell Society for information relating to the possible involvement of James Keogh—father of the Keoghs of Ranelagh—in Parnell's visit to the USA;

Lieut. Alan Kearney of the Irish Army's Ordnance Corps for information pertinent to the death of Gerald Keogh;

Anne Matthews for her clarification about movements of The Kimmage Garrison in 1916;

The National Art Gallery of Ireland for providing pertinent insights into portrait painting of middle-class Gaelic business families in Dublin by Charles Russell in the late nineteenth century. Special thanks are due to Andrew Moore, Library Assistant, in this respect;

Dr. Colum Kenny who supplied valuable insights into the life of John Keogh of the eighteenth-century Catholic Committee;

Lloyd Dunlap of The Library of Congress and Monsignor William Awalt of Saint Peter's Rectory, both of Washington City, for assistance in uncovering civil and church records belonging to private John M. Keogh, 40th N. Y. Volunteers;

Saint Patrick's Hospital in Dublin which has been singularly helpful in providing information about Thomas J. Keogh, particularly Mr Andrew Whiteside, Archivist, and Breda Ryan, Record Keeper—whose painstaking examination of the archives contributed to clarifying details of his life;

Dr. John Harbison, former State Pathologist, for suggestions in relation to the possible exhumation of subjects in order to clarify reasons for illness;

Damien Burke of the Irish Jesuit Archives for examining the details of Milltown Jesuit records to check for possible family connections with their property;

Michael Kelleher, Senior Library Assistant, Bray Public Libraries, for his valuable support;

William J. Hayes, Coordinator of the Restoration Project of Holy Cross, County Tipperary, for invaluable help in clarifying details about the roofing of the abbey. To Michael Mallin and those associated with the reroofing of the monastery, including Sean Campbell, Pat McCloskey and Dom Ryan, formerly of Irish Forest Products, for their valuable input;

Mauricio Pineda for providing information on particular cultural aspects of Latin America;

Henning Flachsenberg colleague and companion of the Orinoco expedition;

Deceased family members, especially Nanette and William Keogh;

Author Patrick McCusker for his candid advice, input and corrections to the text. I also thank Blanca McGarry and writer P. J. Cunningham in this respect; and to colleague Paul Clinch for his helpful suggestions in relation to an early edition of the work;

Hilary Johnson of Authors' Advisory Service, UK, for copy editing the text;

To Ana Grigoriu of Books Design, Germany, for the cover design;

Keogh Photography for cover photo.

Raymond M. Keogh

Preface

Shelter and Shadows reveals what it is to be born and live between two worlds that emerged from conflicting Irish traditions. In a lifetime quest to resolve his dilemma, Raymond Keogh traces the origins of his contradictory ancestral legacy. The outcome is the story of a hybrid family; its complex social histories; its interweaving genealogies; its genetic profile and its identity.

Coming to terms with ancestral conflict and cultural incompatibility awakens a revolutionary view of our common humanity. Ultimately, we are presented with an uplifting exploration of the meaning of human identity.

The account is divided into three:

Part I—*Indigenous Identity*—aims to affirm Raymond's paternal Gaelic roots in spite of personal discomfort that arose from his maternal Old English cultural background. Simple anecdotes, oral history, a search of written records and a candid treatment of sensitive family issues highlight the characteristics of the native society from which the author emerges. The account is interrupted by periods of fortuitous foreign service that helped him gain a wider understanding of the nature and diversity of human cultures outside his country.

Part II—*A Forgotten Society*—uncovers the social stratum to which Raymond's Gaelic family belongs. An unusual view of Ireland's past is revealed as the focus of attention is the country's little-understood native urban middle-class who lost their tribal lands to confiscations and plantations in the seventeenth century. Its roots are traced to the professional ranks of Gaelic society.

Part III—*The Wider Perspective*—shows the author's parental backgrounds in conflict with each other. These cultural contradictions are resolved by facing the issues that prevent the emergence of a clear understanding of the nature and meaning of identity. Human genetics reveals the true base of our distant ancestors. Our *golden threads of life* are found to have arisen beyond artificial geographic boundaries in a multitude of cultures across a series of wide spatial platforms and deep into the past, thereby raising questions about the true nature of who we are. This leads to a redefinition of what is meant by personal, family, cultural and national identities.

Shelter and Shadows is relevant to Irish society as it seeks for a clearer perception of itself during the anniversary period of its independence. Its conclusions are timely for a world in which multiculturalism and globalisation have become increasingly important. Ultimately, the conclusions provide a new way to comprehend the meaning of human identity.

I. Indigenous Identity

Awakening

The Irish are a contradictory race. They are moulded by a mix of opposing cultural influences. Declan Kiberd puts it well when he says: *there is no single Ireland, but a field of varied forces, subject to constant negotiations, and there is no unitary Irish mind, but many Irish minds ...*[1] These forces expressed themselves as cultural contradictions in my hybrid makeup which arose from two distinct sources: the Gaelic identity of my father's people and the *Old English* identity of my mother and her people. The Old English were pre-Reformation settlers in Ireland. This foreign dimension disturbed the purity of my native inheritance and gave me an uncomfortable feeling, when I was growing up, that I was not fully Irish. I even began to suspect the genuineness of my Gaelic roots.

But, in the early 1950s I was oblivious to many of these issues. Vivid memories from those years evoke my grandfather's redbrick terrace house at Beechwood Road in Ranelagh. It was the one location in Dublin where a sense of the past completely encased and impregnated the present. It contained a residual presence of former generations. I find it difficult to explain the nature of this "presence". Many different influences from the past coalesced to create an enchanted atmosphere and I was acutely sensitive and receptive to these stimulating ancestral leftovers. It was as if I had arrived late at a farewell reunion, was not informed about who had departed and could only garner vague notions about them from fragments of conversation and surviving memorabilia. The palpable void left by their absence drove me, over the following half century, to reconstruct the world of my forefathers.

It intrigues me that my most vivid early recollections call to mind happenings that occurred when I was less than four. I know this because many of these memories involve Bartholomew, my grandfather. I was born in 1947 and he passed away in 1951. My last memory of him is indelible. I looked back from the rear leather seats of our Morris Minor as he waved to me from the upstairs window of his sick-room in Ranelagh.

My elder brother and I visited this special place with our father every Christmas morning during the late '40s and early '50s. The drawing room on the ground floor had a roaring turf fire that burnt brightly in a cast-iron fireplace. A marble mantelpiece was decorated with an elegant clock and mirror; and twin statues—one of a Viking warrior and the other of a Roman soldier—standing sentinel over the hearth. A painting on the wall represented a platoon of soldiers resting before a battle during the Napoleonic Wars. Other paintings and photos reflected people and locations associated with the family.

There was always something exciting happening in the drawing room; it was full of surprises. I remember the hushed silence as Bartholomew shouted down the phone to my uncle in New York one Christmas morning. I felt a deep sense of occasion and perceived the dimension of the world increase.

---

1   Kiberd, 1996; p. 298.

The smell of cigars was strong when my grandfather smoked. I liked the smell but tobacco gave him a ferocious cough. He was a white-haired man in a dark suit and his gold watch-chain was draped across his waistcoat. He slept a deep sleep in his favourite armchair by the fire, facing the door with his back to the street window. The cough began in his sleep and worsened as he raised himself to get oxygen. His face reddened exceedingly in contrast to his white hair the more he coughed. I was terrified. He would surely burst or vomit. I ran out of the room. My aunt pursued me into the hall and ensured me all was well. She brought me back and I peeped round the door. My eyes were at the level of the door handle. Bartholomew was sitting up looking at me in amusement and some embarrassment. He had recovered and all the room was gazing at me and laughing.

Visitors were welcomed in the front room on Christmas morning and sat around on the settee and seats, and a host of odd chairs that were assembled for the occasion. Trays of cakes and lemonade and tea and bottles of Guinness were brought in amidst the opening of presents and the buzz of animated conversation. Boxes of chocolates and biscuits were peppered about on small tables. Faces I had not seen since the last year reappeared. Introductions were made and niceties exchanged. The cosiness of the place and the feeling of so many friendly people made it a warm cocoon. My uncles were there with their girlfriends or wives; some years later their children appeared. Other people would come and visit too and the atmosphere was as good as one could hope to expect anywhere.

My aunt made sure we were always entertained, and challenged us to complete a jigsaw puzzle or play a game of snakes-and-ladders. When all avenues were explored—or perhaps it was the last resort to keep order—the family album would appear. It was full of black-and-white photos, many of which had faded to sepia. My aunt would tell us about those who featured in it. It was stocked with people I knew, like my uncles, photographed in sports cars when they were young. However, there were others whom I had never met. Women wore long dresses and men were always presented as if bedecked for a special occasion. Cars were more boxlike than round like our Morris Minor. Whenever the album appeared the conversation turned to stories of men and women who were no more. These were real relations and friends that had existed and were known to those present. Accompanying anecdotes reinforced the ever-present sense of lost time and the fading oral memory caused by relentless bereavements. Lost time emerged repeatedly in that house and connected me intimately with the mystery of the past.

The wave that Bartholomew gave me from his sick-room as I looked back from our Morris Minor was our last farewell. I never saw him again. He carried with him the knowledge of his father's life and times, and that of his grandfather. A family secret was almost extinguished in his passing; mere threads survived. The past was almost laid to rest—but not quite. My desire to uncover the true story of his forefathers grew from a fascination into an obsession. In the years after his death, I began to follow—to their sources—all the paltry clues left behind in his enchanted house.

Domestic Shadows

Several shadows lurked within the domestic shelter of my home, including—as mentioned—the cultural contradictions of my parents' families. But, I also began to sense something sinister in the story of my paternal ancestors. A veil of censorship appeared whenever I attempted to delve into the lives of my forefathers in the generations previous to my great-grandfather, James Keogh, father of Bartholomew. Snippets had come through from behind a persistent obstruction but they were mainly vague and garbled.

Despite all obstacles, I followed each trivial clue, each anecdote, each snippet of oral history, each written record to make sense of the past. At no stage did the underlying drive subside despite many years of frustrated progress. Goals changed as new findings were made and as I grew older. I wove along an erratic course that began in a cloud of childhood memories and visions. Curiosity shifted from the family to the society from which it originated. Paltry progress along this twisted track was sweetened by a trickle of new discoveries, followed by the incessant pull of increasingly complex questions and the promise of ever-greater enlightenment. Family history turned into an obsessive quest to answer the ultimate questions of genealogy: Who are we and what is our identity?

*

In 1953 the evocative country-wide event—*An Tóstal*—an emotional celebratory festival of things Irish was held throughout the country. It occurred well before I began delving formally into family history. *An Tóstal* placed emphasis on nostalgia, sport, nationalism and history and left a strong impression on my young memory. It was an attempt to attract tourists to the country by the government of the day. It was also an opportunity to re-conjure the spirit created during the cultural revival movement of the late nineteenth century—called the *Irish Renaissance*—for a younger generation that had not experienced this romantic age. Flags lined O'Connell Bridge, Dame Street and the Liffey and brought the aura of ancient Ireland within the old city walls. The festival took place during the heyday of our family outings made through cities, towns and the countryside in our Morris Minor, and draped the land in Celtic imagery. Its attempts to impress the youth were successful, at least in me.

When travelling through the landscape, I watched it pass and become altered with each change in scenery. The view from the moving windows of the car linked the visible and the present with the hidden and the past. Residues from previous periods created an invisible presence round abandoned historical monuments. As with all memorials they can be ignored, but I allowed myself to be captivated by their tantalising magnetism. Faraway places, and incidents—disconnected in time—emerged and disappeared. The world transformed again and again in marvellous imagery, stimulated by sun, shadow and changing panorama. Wonderful visions ignited a mind already aroused with the glories of a heroic Celtic nation, where warriors lived in emerald settings and where they exercised their young and agile lives in the freedom of woods and glens and open fields.

What makes Celtic imagery, myths and legends so potent a force? Far from being a childish fetish, they were exploited in modern times by Irish revolutionary movements like the Fenians, and poets and writers like W. B Yeats and Patrick Pearse and politicians like Douglas Hyde and Eamonn de Valera. Gaelic symbols and literature were so evocative that they succeeded in gathering about them the men and women who ignited the independence movement. Even today, Celtic images are used as the symbols of free Ireland. Part of their fascination is the link they evoke between us and our primordial roots in the Irish countryside. Implied in this vision is a perfect bond between the early Irish and their natural environment.

Contemporary society may or may not consider the past to be an inspirational compass for current and future nationhood. Today we may regard Irish romanticism as archaic sentimentalism based on outdated myths, even though its power gave rise to a particular definition of Irish nationhood that influenced, in its turn, the shape of the early Irish Free State.

In the 1950s I was touched deeply by Celtic romanticism. As a result I became determined to affirm my Irish identity through my Gaelic surname. The most reliable fragments of oral history suggested that the family came from Leinster, probably County Wexford, where, it was said, we had owned property. If I could link my people to a specific parcel of land in the province I would be able to validate my identity as genuinely Irish and authentically part of the Keogh or *MacEochaidh* tribe of ancient Leinster. This became my fixation as a young adult, almost half a century ago. At the same time, I refused to acknowledge the stark cultural fracture in my makeup, caused by the contradictory traditions of my mother's people. I simply ignored them.

*

The accumulated memorabilia, conversations and experiences of life that I encountered in the houses of my father's relations in Dublin collectively amounted to a set of shared characteristics peculiar to a society that appeared to have few connections with the rest of Irish culture. The anecdotal snippets coming from past generations confirmed definite links with Irish history but they were somehow extraneous to the flavour of the past lauded by schoolteachers and commentators on Irish radio. It would take me many years before I clearly understood the nature of this divide.

Someone told me that at one stage in his life my grandfather, Bartholomew, rode a penny-farthing bike. Bicycles were becoming fashionable to such an extent that cycling organisations were formed. He joined one of these and there met Jenny McDowell. The couple began seeing each other for a time but broke off their dating. However, one day, while still convalescing after an illness, Bartholomew happened to be on a tram in Glasnevin. The story goes that he had a ghastly pallor. Coincidentally, Jenny had taken the same tram and didn't fail to notice him and his alarming appearance. They began to converse. This led to a renewal of their friendship and eventually, in 1911, they married.

Several years after Jenny became Mrs Keogh, the family moved to Beechwood Road. The anecdotes of this period become the oral history of my father's generation. Much of his awakening years were spent in Beechwood. He related to me the memory of a chest of drawers on the upstairs landing containing blood-splattered swabs—elements of the confusion and paraphernalia surrounding the birth of another child. In all, his parents had five children: four boys and one girl. The brothers were a wild bunch. Several of them carried wounds of old battles fought with wooden swords in the back gardens and lanes around Beechwood. There was a gruesome story told about them sitting round a table while one circled the palm of his hand over the point of an upright and large darning needle. Another suddenly slammed a fist down on the revolving palm, forcing the needle through the hand.[2]

Bartholomew created a tie-manufacturing firm called Bart & Sons in the 1920s. Being the managing director of the enterprise, my grandfather came to be known as *The Boss* by his children. But, the emphasis they put on the title was more a sarcastic jibe than a reference to his position. The business was a family-run affair. Despite the fact that ladies were not recognised in company titles, Jenny and her daughter Nanette worked there and it was often said that Jenny was the real force behind the firm.

My father left the family business because he didn't get on well with *The Boss*. He set up a bicycle repair workshop. Later he established a firm called JEKA Ltd, a Dublin manufacturing company that made children's clothing. JEKA grew behind the Republic of Ireland's protective tariffs and was located in Smithfield. In the 1950s the business was doing well and I remember being brought into town to be fitted out with new clothing every summer. The smell of brand-new leather sandals is a particularly vivid memory. My mother used to buy these clothes in Our Boys shop in Wicklow Street.

However, when the Taoiseach, Mr Lemass, decided to open the economy to free trade and eliminate protective barriers, the rag trade collapsed. My father recalled how establishments fell and how acquaintances of his died under stress. There was a strong feeling that similar support—psychological or otherwise—was not on hand from government, parallel to that given to the farming traditions. Diarmaid Ferriter makes reference to the veneration for the rural way of life in official thinking and cites a speech given by Charles Haughey in his capacity as Minister for Agriculture in 1966 where he stated that: ... *we must always think of farmers as people. We must not listen only to the economist and the bureaucratic planner who think of agriculture as simply another sector of the economy and who are concerned only with output, return or investment and so on.*[3] This type of comment exacerbated the sturdy perception in urban circles that business people, including those of Gaelic origin, were not viewed with the same reverence as those who inherited the land and this served to highlight the favouritism, on the part of government, towards those who were regarded as being *genuinely* Irish.

---

2   Ms Anne Dowden; personal communications, 2010.
3   Ferriter, 2005; p. 551.

The dismantling of protectionism really began after 1966. Among the industries most exposed to foreign competition were textiles, clothing and footwear. The cold winds of import penetration were felt most severely by such enterprises.[4] The response of my father to these economic ills was to keep JEKA afloat by designing and developing his own business machines, thus ensuring increased productivity and competitive prices. Before his creations emerged he filled single sheets of paper or blank corners of the newspaper he was reading with pencil-drawings and sketches of his ideas and inspirations. I remember visiting his premises in Smithfield where he housed the resulting gadgets. The factory was on the first floor. Access was by way of an old wooden stairway bordered by a smooth and unstable ebony banister-rail leading to what to me was a large room, laden with the smell of new cloth.

Long rolls of fabric lay on the floor; each contained a tubular cardboard core which was designed to allow the metal bar of the cutting machine to pass through before the large roll was set up for the operation. There were pressing machines that stamped the cloth into shapes and sewing machines that completed the finer details. Huge make-shift tables of plywood covered the available space of most of the room over which lay a structure of iron bars with attached cogs, wire ropes, flexible bands and circular disk-knives. When working, all parts moved in unison and with sudden loud clanging noises at the beginning and end of the operations. Out of all this chaos came aprons, pinafores, kiddies' bibs and bias binding. On these self-created machines and rolls of cloth we survived as a family.

Bartholomew's wife Jenny, who was born in Belfast, belonged to an urban Catholic class in Ulster equivalent to that of her husband's in Dublin. But, the nature of this class was not clear; little has been written about it in history.

Jenny's father, William McDowell, was a journalist. A feature article in a centenary supplement of The Irish News, dated 1955, revealed something of his professional background. William became editor of the Belfast Morning News in 1875. It was the only Catholic daily published in Ulster; the first penny-newspaper in Ireland and the first successful penny-paper in the United Kingdom. The publication engendered animosity. The Belfast Newsletter warned the people of the city that: *... it emanated from the Press which printed the Douai Bible and sneering at it as having been established on the street hawking system and having as its readers "servants, street-sweepers, pedlars and pot-hogs."*[5]

One would have thought that the working-classes ought to have been congratulated for their ability to read. However, reasons for this reaction were partly fuelled by the paper's success. In July 1856 its circulation was over 2,000 copies, more than all other Belfast newspapers combined. The outburst against the religion and class of its readership also shows that sectarian bitterness in Northern Ireland extended back at least to the mid-nineteenth century. Indeed, this intolerance has deep historical roots. In reference to the Protestants of the North, Roy

---

4   Kennedy, et al, 1988; pp. 241, 242.
5   Irish News and Belfast Morning News; p. 2.

Foster says: *At once austere, exalted and unbending, they were also cantankerous, febrile and prone to hysteria and conspiracy theories. Initially, religion had not been important indictating the unofficial Scots settlements of Antrim and Down; but settler defensiveness and intolerance fused with anti-establishment Presbyterianism to create a northern mentality ... Ulster people believed they lived permanently on the edge of persecution; they gloried in covenanting against 'tyranny'; and they were committed to a democracy that extended to the elect only. These attitudes did not moderate with time.*[6]

Oral history suggests that William McDowell was threatened for something he had written in the Morning News. He was told to leave Belfast or would be killed. As a result, he moved to the Freeman's Journal in Dublin but didn't continue in that newspaper. Once again he encountered trouble. There were rumours that he took an action against the paper. Whatever the circumstances, he opened a shop or several shops in Dublin and died eighteen years later in 1912, one year after his daughter Jenny married my grandfather Bartholomew.

At this time Ireland was about to enter the most transforming period of its recent history.

---

6   Foster, 1989; p. 78.

Blood Sacrifice

Four years after the death of his first wife, my great-grandfather—James Keogh, father of Bartholomew—married eighteen-year-old Mary Walsh of Cullenswood. Her father owned property in South Dublin and obtained an income from it. The Walshes originally came from County Kildare[7] and were of Norman or Anglo-Norman descent. James' marriage to Mary is an example of hybridisation between native and Old English lineages, though it seems that the cultural differences between the newly-weds were significantly less than those between my parents. The couple eventually settled in Ranelagh. They had ten children. The best-known of these are J. Augustus, who became manager of the Abbey Theatre in 1916, and Gerald, who was killed in action during the Easter Rising of the same year.

While browsing the internet I discovered an obituary, written by actors John Arden and Margaretta D'Arcy in memory of Finola Keogh, which appeared in the London Guardian in 2003. Finola was a grand-daughter of James' second marriage. In the write-up, reference was made to a special edition of Theatre Ireland to which John and Margaretta had been asked to contribute. They persuaded Finola to write a feature for the issue. She responded with a multi-layered and strongly polemical nine-page article, which traced the history of the Keoghs all the way back to the United Irishmen movement of the 1790s.[8] It is clear from Finola that the family withdrew from discussing their part in the 1916 Rising because they felt let down and betrayed by the Irish Government after independence and, for this reason, their story disappeared from history. Finola's article provides an insight into the offspring of her grandfather—James—and his two wives, which she collectively and aptly christened *The Keoghs of Ranelagh*.

In addition to business and manufacturing, acting became a major life-changing activity for the children of James and Mary Walsh. A flavour of the theatrical scene of Dublin shows the importance of the stage at the time. The average Dubliner was infatuated with theatre-going throughout the late nineteenth and early twentieth centuries.

Given the popularity of theatre, it is little wonder that playacting was a favourite pastime amongst Dublin's youth around the turn of the century. An often-cited example is that of the Sheehys at Belvedere Place where they had an open house on the second Sunday night of each month, to which James Joyce was a regular visitor. Republican leader Patrick Pearse, who became Gerald Keogh's headmaster and his mentor, was also infected by this playacting fad. Pearse had a strong imagination and, as he grew older, began to write plays for the younger members of his family. The source of inspiration for things Irish was his mother's octogenarian aunt, Margaret, who would tell him stories and sing patriotic songs about Irish heroes. She had spent her childhood in the countryside of County Meath and imbued the boy with a special reverence for the Irish language. As a result it awoke in him romantic notions of ancient Ireland, and the voice of the past seemed to come alive through it. However, skill

---

7   Germaine Greenwood, personal communications. 2011.
8   Keogh, 1992.

in the language was gained painfully through long periods of learning and the result ... *was scoffed at by native speakers.*[9]

Pearse spent some time on the western island of Arran in 1898 and the experience was novel and exhilarating. The Gaelic-speaking West was to be his favourite place of retreat and the main stimulant for his fictional writings during his short life. Like other Irish Renaissance followers and young republicans, Pearse found what he regarded to be the remnants of true Celtic Ireland in the native Irish-speaking populations along the western seaboard. He went as far as buying a small cottage at Rosmuc in Connemara where he spent his holidays.

Pearse, himself a teacher, developed his own school. The inauguration of Saint Enda's, an Irish lay-run establishment, was the realisation of one of his visions. It opened in 1908 in Cullenswood House, an old Georgian mansion in Oakley Road, Ranelagh, not far from the Keogh household.

An important activity in the school was the production of plays, which had grown out of an association between headmaster Pearse and his friend Thomas MacDonagh. MacDonagh brought him into closer contact with theatrical circles in Dublin. As a result, the pupils of Saint Enda's attended performances in the Abbey and it was not long before the school produced its own plays which were graced by large and distinguished audiences. Contemporary poets and historians like W. B. Yeats, Padraic Colum and Standish James O'Grady attended the school's first production in March 1909, which received excellent reviews in Dublin and London newspapers. Pearse was ecstatic when, immediately after the performance, historian O'Grady made a stirring speech.[10] O'Grady was responsible for making the exploits of the Irish hero Cuchulainn available in the English language to a national readership.[11] Pearse invested an even greater effort in a follow-up pageant about this Celtic hero, called: *The Boy-Deeds of Cuchulainn.*

Saint Enda's attracted the attention of the Keoghs of Ranelagh. When the senior school reopened on 11th January 1909 Gerald Keogh became a day-boy.[12] He was practically a next-door neighbour living, as he did, in Elmgrove. Gerald's entry in the school's account-book is in Pearse's own handwriting. Gerald joined in the preparations for *The Boy-Deeds of Cuchulainn* in which he played a minor role as a soldier. The play again attracted a glittering audience and favourable press reviews.[13]

But for Pearse this was more than playacting. He was now laying the foundation for his blood sacrifice for Ireland. Declan Kiberd points out that nationalist rebels like Pearse ... *followed the gospel which asserted "the triumph of failure", the notion that whoever lost*

9   Dudley Edwards, 1990; p. 89.
10 *Ibid*; pp. 104 ff.
11 Kiberd, 1996; p. 196.
12 Recorded in *An Macaomh* (school magazine of St Enda's). Midsummer, 1909. Vol. 1 (1); p. 83.
13 Dudley Edwards, 1990; pp. 123, 124.

his life would save it.[14] Pearse transmitted this outlook to his pupils stating: ... *when I said [to the boys] that I could not wish for any of them a happier destiny than to die thus in defence of some true thing, they did not seem in any way surprised, for it fitted in with all we had been teaching them at St Enda's.*[15]

In a note written in reference to 1909, Pearse states: *I dreamt that I saw a pupil of mine, one of our boys at St Enda's, standing alone upon a platform above a mighty sea of people; ... I felt an inexplicable exhilaration as I looked upon him, and this exhilaration was heightened rather than diminished by my consciousness that the great silent crowd regarded the boy with pity and wonder rather than with approval—as a fool who was throwing his life away rather than as a martyr that was doing his duty. It would have been so easy to die before an applauding crowd or before a hostile crowd: but to die before that silent, unsympathetic crowd!*[16]

Pearse's dream might be described as a premonition. It was certainly coincidental that it came to him in the year that Gerald—the only pupil or ex-pupil of Saint Enda's to die in the Easter Rising— joined the school. Gerald caught the infectious spirit of Pearse and became a member of the Fianna, equivalent to a nationalistic boy-scout movement. In 1911 he was a draper's apprentice. Later he enlisted as an Irish Volunteer and, finally, played a minor but fatal role in the real-life drama on the streets of Dublin in 1916.

Gerald's death was one of the most documented fatalities of the Rising. At least eight accounts were written by a variety of observers who were in and around Trinity College at the time. But, until recently, the nature of his mission was steeped in confusion.[17] We now know that he had been sent out from the General Post Office (GPO) late on Monday afternoon to summon a party of volunteers of the Kimmage garrison that had been left behind at Larkfield House, the home of Joseph Mary Plunkett.[18] This location was used as a training camp for the Irish Volunteers and consisted of Irishmen who had fled conscription in Britain or were on the run in Ireland. According to John Reynolds in a feature article in An t-Óglách: *About midnight Keogh brought a message from Comdt. Pearse ordering the party to come to him at the G.P.O. for further orders.* The group went to rebel HQ by way of Stephen's Green and Grafton Street ... *they formed into fours and in military formation crossed the city, passing Trinity College at 1.30 a.m., and reaching the G. P.O. without further incident.*[19]

How come they were able to pass Trinity unmolested but Gerald was not? A feature entitled *Inside Trinity College* written anonymously by "One of the Garrison" observes that: *The Anzacs had been above on the roof of the College since an early hour. Owing to the strict*

---

14   Kiberd, 1996; p. 201.
15   Dudley Edwards, 1990; p. 143.
16   *Ibid*; p. 143.
17   Bateson, 2010; p. 195.
18   Reynolds, 1926; p. 4; The Catholic Bulletin. 1916. *Events of Easter Week.* Vol. VI (II): p. 629 and Watts 1981; p. 125.
19   Reynolds, 1926; p. 4.

order received from the Irish Command not to fire until attacked, many chances of "potting" Rebels had been missed. But later in the morning this order had been withdrawn.[20] It would seem, therefore, that although Gerald and his companions left Larkfield at the same time as the Kimmage contingent, he was delayed somewhere along the way.

This suggestion aligns with the account written by Finola Keogh, Gerald's niece. Finola states that Gerald's errand was to bring a message from Pearse to Countess Markievicz in Saint Stephen's Green.[21] We know that Gerald left the Green with dispatches for the GPO two and a half hours after the Kimmage contingent passed Trinity. This allows plenty of time to have encountered Countess Markievicz or others who were about to take over the College of Surgeons. Unfortunate for him the delay meant that he undertook the final segment of his journey when the defenders were under a different set of orders.

Shortly after 4.15 a.m. in the dull light of dawn, Gerald lay dead on Grafton Street outside the College. The soldiers who were defending the buildings were made up of Anzacs (Australian and New Zealand soldiers) and other Dominion troops on furlough from front-line duties in France during the First World War. And these were aided by men of the Trinity Officers' Training Corps.[22]

It was claimed that Gerald was killed by rifle discharge, described as ... *a hard shot at a downward angle from a high window.*[23] On the other hand the Anzac, Corporal Garland, who actually fired on the volunteers from the roof of Trinity, described the scene as follows:

We got our first bag on Tuesday morning at 4am when three Sinn Feiners came along on bikes evidently going from Shepherd's Green to the G.P.O. The men on my left, as soon as they saw them coming, told us to mark the last man and they would get the first two. We all fired at once killing two and wounding the other. When they were brought in, the chap we killed, he had four bullet marks on him which meant that we all got him, and that he must have been killed instantly.[24]

Gerald's corpse was carried into the College grounds and laid out on the floor of a building next to the porter's lodge. Medical student Michael Taaffe, who was accustomed to the sight of dead bodies, tells us that: *He rested as quietly as any of the subjects in the dissecting-room, but he was new to death and looked as if he might get up off the flags at any moment and go about his business ... there was a small black hole in his temple.*[25] This seems to be at variance with Garland's description. Other accounts suggest that only one man was killed; a second was wounded but managed to escape with the third.

---

20 'Inside Trinity College by one of the Garrison' (Blackwood's Magazine, July, 1916).
21 Keogh, 1992; p. 59.
22 Kildea, 2007; p. 54 and Kostick and Collins, 2004; p. 36.
23 Kildea, 2007; p. 64.
24 Keane, H. June 23rd, 2013. *New Zealanders in the 1916 Irish Rebellion.* Irish Volunteers Commemorative Organisation site (< http://irishvolunteers.org/ > August, 2015).
25 Taaffe, 1959; p. 174.

Whatever about the details of the event, Gerald lost his life that morning. Elsie Mahaffey, daughter of the Provost of Trinity College, was another witness who wrote about Gerald. In her diary she stated that: *For 3 days he lay in College, in an empty room. When necessary he was buried in the Park and later, when quiet was restored was disinterred and sent to the morgue; but during the fortnight while he lay in College; though well dressed and from a respectable street, no one ever came to ask for his body.*

His friends must have seen him fall but apparently were too cowardly or too callous to come & secure him decent burial.[26]

The reasons why no one came for him may have been quite different. Gerald's brother, Cyril, also participated in the Rising and was part of the Stephen's Green garrison. He described himself as an actor when he was arrested after the general surrender and was subsequently sent to Knutsford detention barracks in England on 30th April. Two other brothers—Frank and Leo—were also involved in the troubles. Frank belonged to the same company and battalion as Gerald and was part of the GPO garrison.[27] Being either detained or on the run, they were in no position to recover the body of Gerald.[28] Besides, did they know he was dead? Patrick Pearse, writing to his mother in early May from Arbour Hill Barracks, stated: *All here are safe and well. Willie and all the St. Enda's boys are here. I have not seen them since Saturday, but I believe they are all well and that they are not now in any danger.*[29]

In the aftermath of the Rising, Cyril continued fighting in the War of Independence and went on a special mission to the US in 1918. As a result of such activities the Keogh household in Ranelagh was under continued surveillance and was raided repeatedly by British troops on the eve of independence. Cyril belonged to the 4th Battalion of the Dublin Brigade. He, along with his brother Frank, didn't approve of the partition agreement in the Treaty and left Ireland. Leo stayed at home for a time to run the Torch Theatre in Dublin which he founded with his wife Evelyn Lund in 1935.[30]

Undoubtedly, Patrick Pearse had a strong influence on Gerald's political outlook. Other influences that spurred Gerald's nationalistic drive came from his parents. It is said that his mother bore hatred against the English. His father was considered to be a Fenian and a Parnellite. It is difficult to gauge the strength of each of these separate influences. Circumstantial evidence shows that they cast a spell on his three other brothers who shared his outlook and were involved in the independence movement. Therefore, the Keoghs had strong nationalistic and revolutionary leanings, but these were largely confined to the four younger men who were born during or after 1889.

26 < http://digitalcollections.tcd.ie/home/index.php?DRIS_ID=MS2074_116 > Mahaffy, 1916; folio 28r (August, 2015)
27 Wren, 2015; p. 148.
28 Keogh, 2009; p. 33.
29 < https://en.wikisource.org/wiki/Patrick_Pearse%E2%80%99_Letter_to_his_Mother,_1_May,_1916#cite_note-4 > (August, 2015)
30 Torch Theatre Dublin < http://en.wikipedia.org/wiki/Torch_Theatre,_Dublin > (August, 2015)

J. Augustus, the eldest, learnt of the dramatic events in Dublin and his family's involvement in them. He lived in London where he was stage manager at the Royalty Theatre. He immediately made moves to return home.

Anzac Bullet Brings Shaw to Town

Finola Keogh's writings serve to clarify the character of the Keoghs of Ranelagh in the lead-up to Irish independence, but suffer from inaccuracies. For example, she states that J. Augustus was ... *a great deal older than his brothers.*[31] She is mixing him up with their half-brother, Bartholomew, who was eight years older than he. All the subsequent children of James and Mary Walsh were born in rapid succession, after J. Augustus.

In contrast to his younger rebel brothers, who participated in the independence movement, J. Augustus held an apolitical cosmopolitan outlook and became part of the delightful make-belief world of acting, which, as we have seen, was hugely popular in his native city. He trained at the Royal Irish Academy of Music in Dublin. He later became a professional actor and made his debut at the Gaiety Theatre, Hastings, in 1903. After this, he spent five years with a large Shakespearean Repertory, followed by a period in Grand Opera. He stage-managed thirty-two operas on tour and at the Lyric Theatre in London. Then there was a long engagement with Mrs Horniman's Company at the Gaiety Theatre, Manchester, in which he played in everything from Shakespeare to Shaw, and Greek tragedy to children's pantomime. He toured with Shaw's plays during 1912-14 and joined Vedrenne and Dennis Eddie at the Royalty Theatre, London, in 1915-16.[32] Here he learnt of the Easter Rising in which his brother Gerald was shot dead on the streets of Dublin.

Being aware of the trouble which was brewing in the Abbey between the board and its manager—St John Ervine—J. Augustus offered his services. His desire to become manager was clearly motivated by family problems, given that his widowed mother had to contend with the fact that Gerald was dead and her other boys were detained or on the run.

At a meeting of 14th July 1916, the reappointment of Lennox Robinson in place of Ervine was favored by W. B. Yeats but Lady Gregory resisted.[33] As a result, J. Augustus was engaged by Gregory for a six-month period.

J. Augustus was to begin his new role in September 1916 but, understandably, returned home early with the intention to produce, with his own company, a summer season of George Bernard Shaw's plays at the Abbey. A note from Shaw in the family records shows that, as early as August, the playwright wanted a formal contract with the theatre. It reads:

> *11th August 1916*
>
> *If Miss O'Neill will play Candida you may go ahead.*
> *G. Bernard Shaw*
>
> *P.S. If your enterprise goes on, we must have a regular agreement. I ought to have one with the Abbey Theatre anyhow.*

---

31 Keogh, 1992; p. 59.
32 Theatre Programme. The Irish Repertory Players; *Juno and the Paycock*. The Hecksher Theatre, New York. May, 1936.
33 Welch, 2003; p. 70.

According to Christopher Morash, J. Augustus ... *decided it was time that Irish audiences became better acquainted with Shaw, partly because he had a long history of involvement with Shaw's work, but also because he believed that 'Abbey acting is not acting at all', and he hoped that the discipline of playing Shaw would teach the company stage technique.*[34]

J. Augustus' decision to come to Dublin was fortunate for Shaw, who had protested against the execution of the 1916 leaders in the Daily News, stating: ... *an Irishman resorting to arms to achieve the independence of his country is doing only what Englishmen will do if it is their misfortune to be invaded and conquered by the Germans in the course of the present war.*[35] This kind of comment was not well received in London during the jingoistic climate of conflict. Shaw's box-office appeal in England slumped but Dublin audiences were swamped with his works. Of course, his reputation amongst Irish nationalists was very high at the time.

J. Augustus' formal assignment as manager of the Abbey was marked publicly by the opening of Shaw's *John Bull's Other Island* on 25th September. Then, on 16th October *Arms and the Man* was performed. J. Augustus continued to present Shaw's plays. The autumn season was enthusiastically supported by Gregory and Dublin audiences grew. A deluge of Shaw continued with *Man and Superman, The Inca of Perusalem* and *The Doctor's Dilemma*. Though few have made the connection, it is clear that the Anzac Bullet that killed Gerald Keogh created ripple effects that went far beyond its immediate impact. It resulted in a significant boost to Shaw's theatrical presence in Dublin in 1916.

Problems soon appeared on the horizon for J. Augustus. These are outlined in bitter terms in Finola Keogh's article. She claims that Gregory usurped a cultural development that already existed and was conceived by the Fenian movement. According to her, she: ... *took care ... to associate herself with her Protestant Ascendancy friends of the privileged landowning society of Co Galway. Together they set about the education of the local peasantry. This could be interpreted as a 'counter-political' programme to defuse Nationalistic agitation, or it might have been an insurance policy for the gentry to draw upon once the Irish people attained their freedom.* She continues with unconcealed venom: *The mind bobbles at the audacity of this Anglo-Irish landowning class so coolly setting about the re-education of the people whose lands it had stolen and whose culture it had deliberately attempted to destroy.*[36]

The real reason for Finola's diatribe is found in Gregory's journals. On 12th November 1916 Gregory visited Shaw in London and told him that, on her return to Dublin she was going to evict the Keoghs from the Abbey. Robert Welch records: *Ominously, in a journal entry of 23 December 1916 Lady Gregory wrote: 'Went to Dublin and did business; helped in the eviction of Keogh's two brothers from the Abbey.'*[37] The word *evict* was a particularly provocative term in Ireland, and coming as it did from an ascendency landlord, incensed Finola.

34 Morash, 2004; p. 158.
35 Redmond-Howard, 1916; pp. 118, 119.
36 Keogh, 1992; pp. 61, 62.
37 Welch, 2003; p. 73.

J. Augustus had employed his brother Leo to manage the congestion with theatregoers. Frank had also been drafted in as acting manager, though Finola does not seem to have been aware of this fact. According to her, Gregory concluded that nepotism was ... *a very 'Irish' thing to do...*[38] But, she accuses Gregory of having deeper motives for wanting to expel the Keoghs. In her view, the Protestant Ascendancy had received a severe shock from the Easter Rising in Dublin and, although Gregory expressed a sentimental sympathy for the Celtic tradition, she was alarmed that a republican family might take over the Abbey. The reality was that J. Augustus seems to have had little interest in the struggle for independence. On the other hand, many were aware that the Keoghs of Ranelagh had taken part in the Rising. If a republican take-over was on Gregory's mind it assumes that she didn't make the connection between J. Augustus and his rebel brothers when she first offered him a contract.

The reasons why J. Augustus finally left the Abbey in 1917 are suggested by an inveterate theatre-goer and critic Joseph Holloway in a letter to a friend in New York: *You will be surprised to hear that J. A. Keogh has got his walking papers from the Abbey; a love of Shaw and a hatred for Irish drama and Irish acting were, I am sure, the cause. Keogh from the first wanted to make it a sort of Shaw playhouse, and not caring a tinker's curse for the traditions of the little theatre ... As an Irish theatre, the Abbey reached its lowest ebb under the reign of Keogh.*[39] Old disagreements may have coloured Holloway's assessment. Finola, on the other hand, states that: *In fact J Augustus remained at the Abbey until April 1917, the end of the season for which he was employed.*[40]

This may have been the case. However, Robert Welch, who wrote a history of the Abbey, contends that he didn't go willingly. *Keogh was something of an entrepreneur; he continued to run his own theatre company at the Tivoli and elsewhere, and the directors were worried that his loyalties were divided, and that his energies were being dispersed. ... In fact Keogh's relations were also a problem, in that his brothers, who were part of the private company Keogh was managing ... spent a good deal of time in the Abbey (hence Lady Gregory's 'eviction'). Furthermore, he was enticing Abbey actors into his own enterprise, on lucrative short-term contracts.* Welch concludes that ... *Fred O'Donovan the actor, who had joined the* [Abbey] *in 1908, became manager on 25 May when the keys of the theatre were taken from Keogh in the office of Fred Harris, the Society's accountant, and handed to the new man.*[41]

After leaving the Abbey, J. Augustus established a theatrical agency and mounted touring productions. He set up a Shaw company and, afterwards, went to the US where he became head of the New York Irish Repertory Theatre.[42] He remained in American theatre for the rest of his life apart from a brief holiday home. Finola remembered this particular visit because, although she was only about five at the time, it was one of the few occasions she was invited into the inner sanctum of the drawing room of her grandmother's house in Ranelagh. The visit took place around 1927. About fifteen years later, in 1942, J. Augustus was killed in a car crash in Walnut Ridge, Arkansas.

---

38 Keogh, 1992; p. 66.
39 Hogan and O'Neill, 1967; pp. 192, 193.
40 Keogh, 1992; p. 66.
41 Welch, 2003; p. 73.
42 *Ibid*; p. 73.

Finola informs us that when independence finally came to Ireland: *Lady Gregory ended up as the High Priestess of the National Theatre, with Yeats alongside her just as she had planned. ... The British connections were maintained, the privileged lifestyle continued.* According to Finola, future Irish governments would protect her and her associates and acclaim her for her role in the revival of national culture but they would forget their own people. There was a residual bitterness in the family about the treatment it had received after the Rising and this is illustrated in the final remarks of her article. When Mary Keogh died, just before the Second World War, the family was asked if they wished to have a Republican funeral. They declined. Finola concludes that: *... like so many Nationalist families, the Keoghs did not benefit from the 19th century Fenian movement, nor from the 26 county Irish government they helped to put into power. ... The Keoghs had lost interest and didn't care much for the outcome of the 'Irish struggle' which had left such a bitter taste in their mouths and had broken up the family. Nothing about 1916 or the Treaty was every discussed in the Keogh household.*[43]

There was another side to the family. J. Augustus' half-brother, Bartholomew, was not known for a firm political stance. Both of these men differed radically in outlook from the four rebel brothers who were younger than them. But, Finola fails to mention another brother, John Baptist. The emphasis she places on the Keogh's role in the independence movement, without mentioning this man's involvement with the British Army, tends to distort the true nature of the family. To be fair, she was not trying to define the entire political leanings of the Keoghs of Ranelagh; her aim was to launch a broadside against Gregory.

John Baptist developed his political perspectives in sympathy with happenings in Britain and beyond. Just before the First World War, the Irish Parliamentary Party held the balance of power in the House of Commons and an Act was passed removing the veto of the House of Lords against Home Rule for Ireland. The Bill was signed into law in 1914. In other words, it seemed likely that the Home Rule would be accepted. However, events moved rapidly to weaken its implementation in full.

Fifty-eight British cavalry officers resigned their commissions rather than have to obey commands which might involve coercing Ulster into accepting the legislation and in April the Ulster Volunteers armed themselves after a consignment of 25,000 rifles and three million rounds of ammunition were landed at Larne in County Antrim. In July a Unionists' plea for the exclusion of the nine Ulster counties from Home Rule failed.[44]

At this stage, events on mainland Europe helped to diffuse North-South tensions in that the outbreak of the First World War provided a state of affairs that seemed, for many, to dwarf internal politics. The invasion of neutral Belgium by Germany challenged the right of small nations to exist. Britain declared war on Germany and Home Rule was put on hold until after the war. It was felt that the people of Ireland would not have long to wait for their parliament; hostilities would be over by Christmas.

John Redmond, leader of the Irish Parliamentary Party in Westminster and also head of the Irish Volunteers, became convinced that the need to support Britain was the overriding duty of his party and the Irish nation. His stance produced a split in the Irish Volunteers after he

---

43   Keogh, 1992; pp. 62, 67.
44   Ferriter, 2005; pp. 114, ff.

insisted that the organisation should ally itself with the British Army. A majority of about ninety-five per cent of members sided with Redmond. Many felt that by supporting Britain they would guarantee Home Rule for the whole island after the war.

John Baptist Keogh held the majority viewpoint and enlisted in the Second Battalion of the Royal Irish Rifles. His unit was part of the British Expeditionary Force (BEF) that was sent to halt the German advance through Belgium and Northern France. The Germans tried to secure a quick and decisive defeat of the allies at the outset of the war and overthrow the combined French and British armies. John Baptist's Second Battalion was part of the Third Infantry Division (Seventh Brigade).

The most pertinent event in which John Baptist's Division was involved—from the perspective of the Keoghs of Ranelagh—is described by Nikolas Gardner as follows: *As German attacks continued on the morning of 25 October, the battered units of 3 Division began to waver. After repulsing enemy attacks during the night, the Royal Irish Rifles of the 7th Brigade abandoned their trenches shortly before noon. As was the case the previous night, the 3 Division line was restored with the assistance of neighbouring units. Enemy attacks continued through the 25th, however, with no sign of abating.*[45]

Sometime during that fatal day John Baptist fell in action. He was one of the many casualties the British Army suffered by the end of October 1914. A memorial, rather than a grave in Le Touret Military Cemetery, is a reminder of his part in the War. His body was never recovered. Was his ultimate sacrifice made to ensure that his country would achieve Home Rule; was it to guarantee the liberation of small nations or was it that *others might live in freedom,* as his commemoration-scroll suggests? We will never know. His ideals are buried with him somewhere east of Neuve Chapelle. Home Rule never came; his views of freedom were not shared by all; rather than thanking him, he was regarded as a traitor by many in his own land. His sacrifice was ignored; then forgotten, even by his own family.

Looking back on this brief history of the Keoghs of Ranelagh, several family characteristics or memes are identifiable. The term *ancestral meme* is preferable to *family characteristic.* A "meme" is useful for expressing the reality of non-genetic influences including attitudes, concepts, religious beliefs or even poetry, songs, etcetera, which have been handed on from one generation to the next. It is a special category of inheritance. A meme hops or is passed on from one person to another and produces a behavioural response. The words of a song cause us to hum or sing it; a mealtime ritual prompts us to approach the event with a certain routine or derivative of that routine.[46] At the macro level the collective ancestral memes of a people is its living cultural heritage.

The ancestral memes of the Keoghs of Ranelagh included their tenacious association with business and the professions, be it the drapery trade, journalism or the owning of theatrical companies. At the same time, mixed political and apolitical views characterised the family and included the more-or-less neutral stance of Bartholomew, the cosmopolitan outlook of J. Augustus, the Redmondite attitude of John Baptist and the revolutionary ideals of Gerald and his rebel brothers who conserved the ingrained memories of a people who felt that they had

45   Gardner, 2003; p. 132.
46   Wright, 2001; pp. 87, ff.

been treated abominably in Irish history and acted upon these sentiments. It became clear to me that, although they belonged to the native middle-class, the Keoghs defied a simplistic definition of that social stratum. This serves to underline the complex character of urban society in Ireland in the lead-up to independence and in later decades and shows that the family didn't conform to unqualified generalizations. Further research into the family's past reinforces this picture many times over.

At Odds with the Stereotype

I was determined to press on towards my ultimate goal: that of trying to authenticate my Irish identity by demonstrating that real links existed between my family and their tribal roots in Leinster. My immediate task was to explore the world of my great-grandfather James Keogh—father of Bartholomew. James is commonly called the "father of the Keoghs of Ranelagh". As I began this phase of my quest, I learnt several lessons of importance. The first is that contemporary events can assist in making sense of our legacy of facts and random snippets of oral history. In other words, the collective story of a people or nation can facilitate the contextualisation of anecdotes and memoir.

Another lesson I learnt is that family research is about ordinary people. Most individuals that come into ancestral narratives are not well-known historic figures. In this respect everyone shares the same ranking. Family history has little to do with fame, fortune, outstanding achievements or attributes. So, when approaching the study of our ancestors, a change in mind-set is required. The value apportioned by individual forbearers is that they are directional arrows pointing towards our true identity.

When I compiled a resume of the life of James Keogh I immediately noticed several apparent contradictions. He was, according to oral history, deeply religious, charitable and a staunch follower of Charles Stewart Parnell, the leader of the Irish parliamentary party in Westminster. Politics in Ireland were dominated by the activities of Parnell and his party during James' adulthood in the late nineteenth century. Like most with a nationalist lean and a Gaelic surname, James was a Catholic. He participated in the Land League and had connections with the Fenian movement. It was even rumoured, incorrectly as far as I can tell, that he gave away several farms in Milltown to the Jesuits.[47] His overall religious-political profile was an odd mixture considering the antipathy with which the church held any organisation that would recommend force in achieving its aims and the apparent gulf between Parnell's constitutional stance and the philosophy of open rebellion of the Fenians. To understand the context in which my great-grandfather's life developed it was imperative for me to know something of the background of Parnell and the associated political issues of his time.

In 1800 a law had been passed which dissolved parliament in Dublin and, from then on, Irish matters were dealt with from Westminster in London and administered through Dublin Castle. Many, including Parnell, wanted the parliament to return to Ireland, though it was not to be run as a Protestant Ascendancy assembly as it had been in the eighteenth century. A different arrangement was envisaged; it would be more representative of the people but the precise nature of the institution was unclear. The overall aspiration was known as *Home Rule.*

During the final quarter of the nineteenth century, large landowners—the landlords—often charged their tenant-farmers high rents. If they could not pay then the tenants were evicted. Eviction, as mentioned, was a highly emotive issue and caused deep resentment, not only

---

47 Jesuit land at Milltown Park was purchased by Denis Redmond (who acted as an agent for the order) from a Mr Calvert Strong about 1858 (Damien Burke; personal communications Irish Jesuit Archives, April, 2009).

because it deprived a man and his family of an income and roof over their heads but also because of the fundamental feeling that the landlords had stolen the land from the legitimate owners—the Celtic people of Ireland. England was viewed as a satanic power that was responsible for putting the landlords in place.

It is understandable, then, why not everyone believed that freedom could be obtained exclusively through constitutional means. The Fenians—otherwise known as the Irish Republican Brotherhood—had many members who felt that the only way forward was a complete severance from England under a republic and this dream could only be achieved through force. Fenianism took its name from the Gaelic *Fianna*—heroic bands of Irish warriors that could perform magnificent feats of valour in idyllic Celtic landscapes, the stuff of ancient Irish folklore. The Fenians exploited the same potent Gaelic spell which enchanted many subsequent Irish generations and movements, both peaceful and revolutionary.

An unexpected occurrence provided Parnell a common platform with the Fenians. After several years of uncertain harvests, the catastrophic weather conditions of 1879 damaged agriculture in Ireland. The worst effects were produced on the western seaboard. Potato blight struck and generated unnerving flashbacks to the Great Famine of the 1840s which had killed about one million people. The West was threatened with hunger and it took the nation by surprise. The emergency brought together various segments of the Home Rule and nationalist spectrums in Ireland on issues concerning land.

In a rapidly changing political environment it was quite possible for my great-grandfather to have been staunchly religious yet support an apparently disparate variety of political options under Parnell's guidance. The Fenian connection with violent revolution was undeniable but Parnell gave the movement a somewhat constitutional gild.

The outcome of the 1879 emergency was a conference convened in the Imperial Hotel in Dublin in October of the same year, designed to create the Land League. The invited gathering represented tenant farmers, Fenians, a few priests and members of the Dublin business community. It may seem odd that the urban business population supported farmers through the Land League. However, this becomes understandable when it is realised that Dublin communities felt that they were more likely to achieve the reforms they wanted through agitation at the national level using rural grievances, than through direct pleas for more limited urban improvements. Parnell became the first president of the League and the most important decision taken at the conference was to tour America to raise funds for the organisation.

At this time James Keogh lived at Sackville Street, now O'Connell Street, opposite the GPO in Dublin where—until recently—Clerys store was located. It is significant that the Imperial Hotel was close to James' residence where the Land League held its first meeting. It is highly probable that he was well informed about the activities of the League and closely linked to the organisation.

James' personal life was marked with success and misfortune. He married Mary Jane Delaney, daughter of a deceased ironmonger. He held the position of cashier in a *shirt tailor, hosier and glovier* business located at his home in Sackville Street. The Dublin directories express the nineteenth-century motto for his enterprise as: *Gentlemen who appreciate the comfort of perfect fitting shirts.*

My great-grandparents seemed destined for a promising life after they married in 1875. The following year their first son, my grandfather, Bartholomew, was born. When James became joint owner of the business his fortunes reached a high point. He could now afford to move his family out of Sackville Street to Dartmouth Road—a large three-storey detached house in a respectable environment of tree-lined avenues and parks—south of the River Liffey. The business remained at Sackville Street.

Several photographs of James exist. One of these is a faded image of a well-groomed white-haired man with a trimmed Buffalo-Bill style goatee and moustache. He bore a high starch collar with an elegant bowtie and looks out directly and uninhibitedly at the camera. I also have a photo of his wife Mary Jane with her baby, Bartholomew. She wore a heavy full-length blue dress. Lines of blue silk cross the dress below the waist-line; large cuffs with big buttons complete the sleeves; a silk collar encompasses a white kerchief and the latter is held in the front with an enamel brooch. Her hair is parted in the centre and drawn backwards and upwards into a bun. Prominent earrings are draped from exposed ears. The young face, unconscious of her pending fate, stares out softly from the image. The eyes of Bartholomew look inquisitively at the camera. First colour photos didn't appear until the early twentieth century but the colours are gleaned from an oil painting of mother and child created by Charles Russell from the photo.

Russell was the son of a Scottish painter. He worked in Dublin for Chancellor of Sackville Street, which was located near James' business premises. My great-grandfather commissioned him to create the painting. In Russell's image we have an unambiguous signal that James was reaping the rewards of success and aspired to participate in a sophisticated cosmopolitan culture, totally at variance with the poverty associated with the main urban and rural Irish Catholic cultures of the late nineteenth century.

Portrait painting has been a sign of wealth and sophistication for centuries and merchants worldwide have used this medium as a sign of refinement. For example, from 1500 onwards, growing welfare in the young city of Amsterdam led to an increased demand for family paintings. At the end of the nineteenth century a similar movement seems to have been afoot amongst Gaelic business families in Dublin. In another work entitled: *Portrait of Mrs Jane O'Connor and Her Son John Martin O'Connor*, Russell created an image of the wife and child of John J. O'Connor, managing director of Clerys department store.

Unfortunately, the tide of good fortune suddenly changed against James and his family. Their second child—George McGuinness Keogh—caught whooping cough. The baby died at only nine months in the presence of his mother. He didn't live long enough to see his second Christmas. James and Mary Jane celebrated the nativity of 1878 in the shadow of their dead child. There was another shadow over the table. In late summer of the same year, James received tragic news from Washington that his sister-in-law, Alice, had died aged only thirty-four. James' brother John M. lived in the US at the time.

In early December 1879 James' young wife, whose gentle image still stares out from Russell's canvas, contracted chronic pneumonia. Nothing could be done for her. At the height of his success his world imploded as he watched her pass away. It was the second time in two years that he was forced to Glasnevin Cemetery to attend the funeral of one of his own. He had lost his entire family save his son Bartholomew. In his understandable dejection he made a bold move. He decided to go to America. Oral history suggests that he took the opportunity to collect money for the Jesuits or the Land League. The best explanation for a fund-raising tour is found in the history of the League rather than the Jesuits. Parnell's visit to America appears to have been the opportunity James exploited to escape the awful tragedies that befell him. The concurrence between personal and contemporary history is particularly well demonstrated here.

In December that year, Parnell set sail for the US aboard the steamer *Scythia*. He landed in New York in January 1880 then toured throughout the States and Canada until March. Pleas for large donations were made to the American urban working-class for support of the League. *Parnell's wildly successful tour of America in 1880 established him as the greatest political leader of nationalist Ireland since O'Connell.*[48] In all he travelled 16,000 miles, spoke in over sixty cities and raised over £70,000.[49] On the eve of his return to Ireland he launched the American Land League to keep up the flow of funds.

In Irish political terms, the years after Parnell's tour were hectic. Land agitation, associated with the Land League, and opposition to coercive legislation, eventually led to his arrest and imprisonment. At this time an agreement was reached that is commonly called *The Kilmainham Treaty*, after which Parnell was released. He then changed course and pushed exclusively for Home Rule instead of trying to settle the land question.

Unfortunately, a serious potential problem hovered in the background. Ever since 1880 Parnell had begun an affair with Katharine O'Shea, the wife of the Catholic MP of his own party. This led to the filing of a petition by Captain O'Shea for divorce from his wife, citing Parnell as the co-respondent. A crisis erupted the following year, which divided the Irish Party and the nation and produced inexorable strain on Parnell's health, leading to his untimely death in October 1891.

When James Keogh return from America in 1882, he went back to work at Sackville Street. Two years later he remarried. His new bride was eighteen-year-old Mary Walsh of Cullenswood, Dublin, daughter of Joseph Walsh, who—as we have seen—owned property around Ranelagh. The couple went on to have a large family whose lifestyle was at variance with the typical rural or urban Gaelic Catholic identity of the late nineteenth century.

When growing up I knew that my great-grandfather was a businessman. The two families into which he married—the Delaneys and the Walshes—were merchants and traders. It was apparent to me that these families were part of a cultural anomaly, because there was little or no reference to it in the version of Irish history I had been taught. Ireland has long been portrayed as a country of rural Catholic peasants dominated by a class of rich Protestant landlords. I had only to think of a play like John B. Keane's *The Field* to understand the stereotyping of Irish rural society. Books and novels also portray the Irish in a similar perspective, such as Somerville and Ross' *Some Experiences of an Irish R.M.*

---

48   Foster, 1989; p. 405.
49   Lyons, 2005; p. 101.

Most films have the same impact, such as *Ryan's Daughter* or *The Quiet Man* and many others. Even urban Catholic Ireland is mostly portrayed from the point of view of abject poverty—as in Frank McCourt's *Angela's Ashes* or Seán O'Casey's *The Plough and the Stars*. The identity of the social stratum to which James Keogh belonged was completely at odds with the stereotype and underlined the fact that this society has been, to a large extent, airbrushed out of Irish history.

Cultural Shock

For many years I made little progress in uncovering anything more about James Keogh or his Gaelic forefathers. In that time I grew into early adulthood and went through several life-changing experiences that resulted in the foundations of my career. I went abroad and, in this manner, opened myself to foreign cultures which gave me an appreciation of the meaning of cultural identity in a way that would have been impossible had I stayed at home. Unbeknown to me, I was setting the scene for a fundamental change in my understanding of what is meant by "identity".

In the early 1970s, after I graduated as a forester from University College Dublin, I began to work in the Irish Civil Service and commuted each day into the city from Blackrock train station. The research division to which I was attached was located in town rather than in the country. I observed the waiting passengers on the platform. There were young school goers bedecked in uniforms that failed to sedate their playful irresponsibility. Their true nature burst through in cheeky pulses of energy. The older college students embraced a wildness of a different type; their talk was of weekend nights. Men in suits, postgraduate types, carried the aura of promise of great conquests. The somewhat tired middle-aged men were greying, balding and growing fat; and the old ones, set like concrete in their ways, their potential having collapsed, had reluctantly accepted their lot. Yet they held sway, with what was left of their dignity, in adopted poises of importance before any topic on the daily commuter agenda.

The ghosts of times-past and times-future were present on the platform. Was this to be my destiny? I felt trapped and planned my escape. Perhaps I should have studied archaeology or history. These disciplines would have given me the time and the means to grapple with the incessant desire I had to clarify my identity. But I had chosen an unrelated career in forestry and found myself dissatisfied with a job in the Irish Civil Service.

My wish to become a forester was ignited, at least in part, by my love of the Irish countryside, which captivated me. Each year during the 1950s and '60s our family went on holiday to Courtown Harbour in County Wexford. As I grew towards my teenage years I began long walks round the village and lived out my imagination through these exertions. I discovered endless idyllic landscapes along the shore and in the woodlands and fields further inland. There was always a new adventure to savour in these treks; always fresh surprises at each level of experience.

I happened to come across the biography of Colonel P. H. Fawcett in a small shop in this seaside village. Fawcett was an Englishman who, in 1886, received a commission in the Royal Artillery. In 1904 he was stationed at Spike Island in County Cork where, two years later, he was offered boundary-delimitation work in Bolivia. The rubber boom was at its height and it was important for Bolivia, Peru and Brazil to know precisely where their jungle borders ran if these countries were to avoid conflict. A neutral party was to undertake the work and Fawcett was accepted for the position. He left for South America in 1906 and from that moment his infatuation with the subcontinent began.[50] His theories were often unorthodox and his observations sometimes bizarre but his accounts

---

50   Fawcett, 1968; pp. 37, ff.

were always exciting. He carried out eight expeditions between his first arrival in South America and 1925; but he disappeared on his last journey when searching for a lost city and civilisation.

I read many similar books that dealt with exploration of the tropical forests. These narratives, often consumed in the afterglow of Christmas dinners in a cold northern climate, exacerbated the mental contrast between cold and heat and made the equatorial latitudes appear doubly attractive. My boyhood dream became a craving to undertake an expedition into the jungles of South America.

Years later, as a commuter on the platform of Blackrock train station, a desire to inject adventure into my life germinated. I wrote to several developmental organisations with the intention of working in a tropical environment, the real aim of which was to satisfy the long-standing yearning to experience the reality of the rainforest at first hand. I received an offer with the United Nations in the Yemen through the Irish organisation Gorta, despite a statement in the application about my preference to gain experience of the natural forests of Latin America. But, shortly before I was to travel to the Yemen, a telegram arrived from the UN, which stated that I was being offered a post as a volunteer in Project ELS/73/004 instead of the Middle East. Did *ELS* mean El Salvador? I went to the local library to read up on the country. The outstanding features of El Salvador that surfaced were its exceptional aesthetic attractiveness and its regular seismic activity; the beauty and the beast.

I had interpreted the acronym correctly—I was going to El Salvador in Central America. My overseas career had begun. The experience would prove to be superior to any academic study I could have undertaken in archaeology or history. It gave me first-hand experience of a foreign culture from the inside, which would help me in the long run to clarify the meaning of identity in a deeply personal manner.

On my first weekend in San Salvador, the capital, I found myself in *Parque Cuscatlán*. I felt completely isolated and lonely as I sat on a bench in the park, but I was not let brood for long. Two poor young girls and a little boy, who were selling sweets on wooden trays, came up and asked me if I would buy something. I refused. They insisted and went through each item on the trays asking me if I would purchase this or that item. I continued to refuse. Then the young boy pulled out of his mouth the lollypop he was sucking and said, teasingly: *'Do you want this?'*

'Yes', I said. *'I want that one.'* The three little figures were taken aback; then left me alone. They had finally got the message. To my surprise, they came back with an identical lollipop to the one the boy had, still in its paper wrapping and gave it to me. To my greater surprise, they refused to accept money for it. My first cultural exchange in the country was a mild shock.

Real cultural shock is hard to define; does it even exist? What is certain is that people suffer in different ways from a variety of difficulties when living in cultures that are not their own. It can be a simple problem of realising that you cannot buy toothpaste at night because the shops are not open at the hour you are accustomed to. At the other extreme it can be a feeling of total alienation against the collective character that defines the people amongst whom you live. To me, cultural tensions expressed themselves in several guises and in different ways at different times. Of course, tensions can be felt on both sides of a social divide. I was walking through the central plaza of a town in Guatemala where there were many indigenous people in traditional tribal dress. One of these ladies saw me coming towards her. She immediately covered her baby for fear I would cast the evil eye on her child.

Before understanding cultural shock it is necessary to understand the very concept of culture, which is often equated with artefacts uncovered by the archaeologist's trowel, or with dress, music, dance, sculpture, painting, language, literature, religion and race. The reality is; culture expresses itself through all of these traits. The mental divisions between cultures are probably as great, if not greater, than the visual. Culture can be thought of as a collective agreement of a people about outlook and behaviour.

Those with fragile cultural affinities are more easily induced to move from their home and seek attachments in other societies. I tended to put myself into this category because of the low sense of cultural attachment I had toward Irish society. I felt this way, despite a fascination for her past.

Cultural outliers reap certain advantages in foreign countries. Those who appear different in their own societies and act differently become a potential threat to the norm and are greeted with suspicion or are rejected outright. Outliers who move into new cultures find it relatively easy to accept being an oddity abroad because they have long felt at odds with their own. There is a greater freedom for the oddity beyond his frontiers, because a foreigner is always regarded as being strange and his idiosyncrasies are tolerated as being the way things are done in his land, providing his behaviour is not too outlandish. This endows the stranger with great freedom. Often the outsider is accepted after a trial period, and this acceptance can become generous when it is realised that, in essence, he shares their basic traits as a human being.

Children, who have not quite grasped the collective outlook of their tribe, are the easiest bridges on which to cross into a new culture. Likewise are the outliers and misfits. But the ones who are rigidly embedded in their preconceptions find it difficult to cross the divide and, in extreme cases, are xenophobic.

When we place ourselves—alone—at the stark interface between cultures our differences are exacerbated and we are forced to define and redefine ourselves. An avalanche of new incidents and experiences jolt the analytical segments of our minds into a perpetual internal dialogue. We continually compare our given set of norms with the new ones we have to come to terms with. In this way, new insights about ourselves, and the people amongst whom we live, are derived.

I found attitudes sometimes surprising or even shocking in my new world. Before going to El Salvador I spent one month in Antigua, Guatemala, learning Spanish. I talked to an old Indian woman who was working in the kitchen of a house I was staying in. She was a gentle creature, dressed in traditional colourful weaves. Later I was advised not to be so friendly: *'Don't talk to them - they are animals.'*

On another occasion—it was my third day in El Salvador—I saw an injured shoeshine boy lying on the road as people stood looking on. A car had struck him but no one went to his aid. When I expressed shock I was warned that it was not advisable to go to help anyone in this situation; doing so indicates guilt. To reinforce the point, I was told the story of a foreign doctor who went to help an accident victim; he was cut down and killed by a bystander with a machete, even though he was not responsible for causing the crash.

In my case, cultural impacts were not confined to interactions with local people. In San Salvador I was invited to the British Club and well remember the stark contrast between the attitudes of the British towards me compared to Americans from the US whose mind-set was one of firm empathy for things Irish. Although animosity has lessened considerably amongst younger generations, the Irish and British carry a heavy weight of historical baggage that can produce tensions at each encounter. If there was fault I cannot exonerate myself, but I wanted to be rid of such stress. I thought I had cast aside Irish/British tensions when I left Ireland and I felt irritated that they appeared in a land that offered so many alternative attitudes to choose from.

Many external observers cannot distinguish the cultural differences between Ireland and Britain. We both drink tea; celebrate Christmas with turkey, plum-pudding and fruit cake; we share a parallel architecture; speak English and so forth. But basic attitudes are very different. We have many common traits, yet remain mentally apart and resist any hint of belonging to each other.

Cultural complexity in Ireland has parallels in Latin America, but the contrasts between entities are more obvious in the New World. The demons of cultural contradiction are present here and are closer to the surface. Similar tensions between belonging and isolation, or inclusion and separation, have given rise to an identity crisis in Latin countries. The *criollo* or Spanish descendant on the subcontinent is a dominant though weakening stratum. The *mestizo* is not a single identifiable entity, rather a spectrum of mixes with many shades between the *criollo* and Indian. The Indian is often rejected and falls back on a silent dignity. As each culture—*criollo, mestizo* and Indian—tries to define itself against a common background, confusion arises. According to Bernal Herrera the *mestizo* feels neglected by his or her rich ancestors, the Spanish, but, in turn, neglects his or her poor ancestors, the Indians.[51] A major problem that most Latin Americans have with their identity is that they have both these streams in their blood. The bias in favour of one side of their identity produces tension and out of this tension an inferiority complex arises.

The Latin American subcontinent stretches from Tierra del Fuego—the tip of South America—to the Mexican/US border and from Guatemala to the Antilles. The 600 million people that constitute Latin America are at once distinct and at once united. There are many races, including a peppering of black populations from Africa. Latin American culture is complex and invites a never-ending analysis and reanalysis in order to come up with something approaching a satisfactory identity.

Its history is tainted by what Herrera calls the *black legend*. This is the classical history of savage brutality that the Spanish colonisers inflicted on the indigenous peoples when

51 Herrera, 2006; p. 19.

bringing the subcontinent under their domination. The followers of the legend may not be convinced that there are any grounds for discussion about its reality. They may not accept that the pleas of Friar Bartolomé de las Casas on behalf of the Indians are any more than a remote exception; they may not accept that the major cause of widespread death was of indirect natural causes rather than deliberate genocide. A more realistic and mature reflection recognises the brutality against the Indians and cases of deliberate genocide, but also recognises that other factors, like disease, have had a major role to play.

Herrera puts the Latin American conquest into the wider context of the colonisation of the whole American continent. He compares the domination of North America by the Anglo-Saxons with that of the Caribbean and Latin America by the Spanish, and though he warns us that it would be unwise to say which of the aboriginal people suffered less under their respective colonisers, the northern occupation is characterised by apartheid, while that of the south is one of cultural intermingling resulting in the *mestizo* race.[52] He makes the point that, despite all ills, the intermingling of the races was a better option than apartheid. I tended to agree; but, did this spring from an ingrained anti-English bias?

---

52   *Ibid;* pp. 14, 15.

Foreign Bride

German forester Henning Flachsenberg and I participated in the same UN project in El Salvador. He shared my sense of adventure and curiosity. Henning and I began to travel together in Central America and, one Easter, we visited Péten in Guatemala where we sought to find the elusive pristine forest and come in contact with a tribe that lived in harmony with its environment. I concluded that firsthand experience of a primeval tribe would provide a clear view of what life was like for humans freed of all subsequent contamination and modernisation. There was something of the *noble savage* in this notion; something of the perfect fit between humans and their natural surroundings; something of the ultimate definition of identity.

We drove to Tikal, the site of the Mayan archaeological ruins. As we neared the ancient remains, the natural forest came into sight, but it had been cut away in a wide swath of several kilometres on both sides of the road. Scattered palms, stumps and isolated trees remained. We crossed the Rio Dulce at a place called Castillo de San Felipe and comforted ourselves that the road would enter the forest at any moment. However, nature kept its distance. We drove into the town of Flores, which I expected would be a village in the middle of the jungle. It turned out to be a town built on an island that had brick and adobe houses, plenty of cars, an airport, hotels, hippy tourists, and swimming pools. Tikal itself was also full of tourists and prompted us to leave it quickly and drive to another more northerly and isolated Mayan site called Uaxactún.

As we drove north the forest closed in on the road for the first time. At last we were on a rough car-track going through the jungle, though I wondered how pristine it was. It had a modest canopy in terms of height, and its tree diameters were relatively small. This suggested regeneration after removal of an older forest. Nonetheless, it was a natural ecosystem and contained a large variety of tree and palm species and interesting animals, including a form of wild turkey. We encountered no one as we drove along the track. At one point we stopped the car to observe an unusually steep incline under the trees and realised that it was an artificial structure. It was a Mayan pyramid covered in twisted roots. It is speculated that the Mayan civilisation succumbed to an ecological disaster of its own making and their ruins are a collective and stark reminder of the eventual fate that awaits all people who do not live sustainably with their environment.

We continued driving north but felt that we had taken the wrong road. A deserted hut came into view and there were signs of humanity in the form of paths through the forest. But, just as we made up our minds to turn back, we met an Indian lady and her children; she said that Uaxactún was just up the road. We entered the small town, which was really a group of dwellings close to an airstrip. The hotel was under construction, though this didn't prevent me from stringing up a hammock under one of its shelters. Henning slept on a couple of boards. It was a beautifully-still moonlit night and singing voices at a religious service in the local church wafted over the forest.

Next day, after a rapid inspection of the ruins of Uaxactún, we journeyed north of the village. A boy called Carlos became our guide. If we wanted to encounter local Indians, he suggested that we could make our way to Chibal, a nearby village in the *selva*. We decided we would try to reach this place. When the track became impassable we abandoned the car and walked into the forest. The track turned into a path and it was fortunate that Carlos had accompanied us, because it would have been difficult to find the village if we were on our own. After walking for some time we came to two clusters of huts in a clearing in the forest; this was Chibal. The Indians, mostly women and children, were shy or frightened of us. Only the oldest lady could speak Spanish.

It was clear that the villagers of Chibal lived by the slash-and-burn system of agriculture that is practised widely throughout the tropical forests of the globe. The villagers open a clearing by cutting the trees and burning the debris; they then sow their crops, build their huts and stay in the clearing until the harvest-production decreases. After a number of seasons of cultivation they leave the patch to recuperate and move on to another segment of forest. In time, the fertility of the first area recovers after natural vegetation reinvades. Eventually they return to it and begin the cycle again. In addition to cultivation in this manner, their diet is supplemented by hunting, fishing and gathering of fruits in the surrounding forest. These Indians live mid-way between sedentary agriculturists and hunter-gatherer communities. They could be considered to live in harmony with nature but their lifestyle necessitates a certain destructive element of the natural environment. Where the population numbers increase, the cycle of felling and cultivation is reduced and pressure on the forest and soil becomes highly destructive.

Unfortunately, time was against us and we had to turn back. However, the trip that Henning and I had made to Chibal led, inevitably, to an urge to undertake a more ambitious journey. This would be the expedition that I dreamed of since boyhood: to observe, at first hand, the pristine forest, the primeval tribe and the natural wonders of the South American subcontinent. I leave the details of this journey until later in order to place them in a more meaningful context with my developing views on human identity.

On my return to El Salvador, I planned to buy a motorbike. My mother's outlook and teachings, which had a strong Catholic ethos, prevented any feelings in me of fundamental barriers between races of humans and I took full advantage of this attitude. I allowed myself to be attracted by the feminine beauty that Latin America had to offer a young single man. I was undeterred by the dangers that existed of bringing down the wrath of jealous *Latinos* who didn't want to see their women stolen by a *gringo* or, in my case, a *vikingo*. I was about to create the foundation for the most intimate state of preparedness possible in order to understand cultural differences; and this would, in time, influence my own sense of the real meaning of identity.

I went to the Suzuki dealer in San Salvador. At the time the salesman was absent. The accountant had to attend to me. She was a young lady: small, dark-haired and interesting. We talked about many things, including learning English. I suggested that the best way to learn a language was to make acquaintance with someone who spoke it fluently. Before we parted I invited her out to learn English. Maria agreed.

In the 1970s it was expected that one would approach the girl's parents to get their approval even to form a casual and innocent relationship. But Maria and I were dating each other for some time before trouble began. Her parents lived in the countryside and the role of looking after her while she was in the city fell to her older brother. She had to be in her brother's house before eight each night. I was used to getting home at ten or eleven and objected to returning to my *pension* early in the evenings. Maria was caught between my irritation and the anger of her brother. He didn't approve of her risking her reputation with some *gringo* who would behave unbecomingly and leave her to her own consequences. Her family warned that there were many foreigners who acted like that.

Eventually I felt it was necessary to visit her parents at their home in La Paz, about a one-hour drive from San Salvador. The appointed day arrived. I drove Maria and her brother into the country and we came to the village at mid-day. It was hot and sunny. I was brought into the *patio* of the adobe house and introduced to her father and mother. Everyone left. It seemed to me that the villagers abandoned the main street—the only street of the *pueblo*—and I was alone with Maria's parents under the shadow of the tiled roof, out of the direct glare of the mid-day sun.

'So what's this I hear about you and my daughter?' Came the direct question. What had he heard? I went into a clumsy discourse in poor Spanish about how we had met; and were seeing each other; and got on well; and sometimes went to the Spanish Club, of which I was a member. Maria's father, Don Tadeo, looked at me seriously and unmoved. He was a small weather-beaten rugged *campesino* and his sharp eyes were fixed on me. He was not in awe of the *gringo* as can be the case for many in the countryside. His wife sat to my left but said nothing. I could not read her thoughts. I knew I was making no impression on Don Tadeo and I suddenly changed the course of the conversation. *'If you think that I am going to get your daughter into trouble and leave her, you are mistaken.'*

As soon as I had uttered the last word of the sentence an energetic emotion burst through the lively eyes and weather-beaten features of Don Tadeo. *'That's exactly what I want to talk about.'*

The ice broke and the whole tone of the discussion changed. He agreed to let me date his daughter. From that moment, both Don Tadeo and I developed a respect and a friendship for each other. After our meeting, Maria and her brother returned gingerly to the house. She was relieved by the developments. Other brothers and sisters appeared and people were, once more, in the street. Visitors came into the patio as if on a particular errand, but really to see the *gringo*. Life returned to the village.

A short time later I was back in La Paz to ask Don Tadeo for his daughter's hand in marriage. After our wedding we returned often. I had time to sit and listen to her father and mother, brothers and sisters and other people of the village. I began to understand the wisdom of the *campesino*. Don Tadeo, like other countrymen, knew things about the influence of the phases of the moon on plant life. The *menguante* is its waning phase. Country people only plant seed during this period, though the practice was ridiculed by scientists at the time. Now many of the ways of country-folk are beginning to be respected and fathomed by scientists.

Don Tadeo knew how to convert yellow and green bamboo to green-only plants by cutting a bud from a point directly above a green streak on the stem. There were many other things he knew. There were many things of which I was totally ignorant, despite my college education and scientific background. I was part of a forestry project that was bringing knowledge of trees to simple country-folk. But, the picture of a UN expert, paternalistically providing words of wisdom to the peasantry under blue tropical skies, melted into a question mark about my real role in the development sphere.

I have grown up in many ways since I first went to El Salvador. Amongst the many lessons I learnt was to avoid the risk of making judgements about others. When walking round the Mayan pyramid near Chalchuapa, one of El Salvador's ancient monuments, a barefoot ill-kempt boy followed me and asked me, in English, for money. He did so in a variety of ways: he could show me the ruins; he had jade treasures to sell; the list was endless.

I had many ways to keep this annoying beggar in his place. I came out with a phrase in French—one of the few I had—in the hope that he would realise I was from a strange European land and would leave me alone. To my utter surprise, he broke into fluent French. My Spanish was not good enough at the time to keep up a conversation. I relented and we spoke in English. When he produced a jade sculpture I examined it as if I knew about these things. Then I said with disdain: '*This is not an original.*'

'*Who said it's original?*' he retorted. There was no winning with this intelligent young vagabond from Chalchuapa.

*

Cultural shock is normally associated with someone who experiences difficulties when entering a new country after leaving home. What is not often realised is that, on returning, a similar re-entry shock can take hold. Many people have this experience. When I returned to Ireland after half a decade in Latin America I descended into a long dark period of mental gloom. The fragile cultural ties I had to my homeland resurfaced. Gone were the heady daily experiences of the new, the surprising and the foreign that gave life a continual lift. In my dejection I began to write a novel on Saint Patrick.[53] By choosing this subject I was responding to a latent passion which had been ignited many years previously when I was touched by Celtic romanticism. I had no idea that this exercise would, in time, help me to understand the nature of Gaelic society from which my cultural base was partly derived.

I still pined after an overseas career and managed to work outside Ireland on short contracts. Then, after about fifteen years employed mostly at home, I gained a longer stint as a training coordinator in a World Bank project in Kenya. Shortly before I left for Kenya I received unpleasant news about my mother. The hopeful outcome of the operation was not to be. Words like "benign" evolved into "malignant". I then hoped for a sufficient recovery to communicate with her before the end. Finally I prayed for her release.

As she faded, the inner person never faded. As her body was consumed from within till she was skin, organs and bone, the inner self glowed bright. Even when she was beyond talking, she put her arms about me and I put my head against hers in a final embrace. I know she knew me; it was her last goodbye. Next morning I was beside her as she departed. Within my sight her ancestral memory snapped and the "knowing" of former times expired. In her last and forceful breath she reluctantly constructed the ultimate barrier that separates one generation from the next.

---

53 Keogh, 1995.

When we came to place the coffin in the earth, I felt her very close. She was lowered into the same grave with her mother. It was a motionless, quiet and sunny September morning in a corner of the cemetery garden. The difference between natural light and celestial light drew thin and a bird celebrated in the branches of a tree. A forest of stone sculptures formed the backdrop and from these shapes the past could be perceived with little prompting. A vision of the two women, who had often shared tea and cigarettes in the kitchen of our home when I was young, came forcefully to mind. Their humour against life's ills was pushed to the fore and they gave me the near uncontrollable desire to laugh aloud. Though I had cried bitterly, she—who tried all her life to keep her children from distress—had me laughing at her end.

I later dreamt a strange but highly realistic dream. I was entering the dining room of my parent's house in Blackrock, a redbrick structure that dates from the beginning of the twentieth century. I looked out through the tall window that gave view to the back garden. Then I saw her. My mother had come back and stretched up to knock on the windowpane to get my attention. She was smiling. I was elated and rushed from the entrance of the room towards the window to greet her. As I did she retreated back from the dividing glass into the garden and, at the same time, transformed into the emaciated figure she had become in hospital; then disappeared. It was as if she returned to reassure me all was well.

My mother died just before we left for Africa and my father didn't last two years after. As a couple they were inseparable. His passing was extraordinary and he did not resist his final demise. He approached his end in the same organised manner as he approached everything he did in life. He was blunt about his own condition and began to sign away his petty cash in order *to help with the arrangements*—meaning the funeral. Though of advanced years, he was totally lucid and without a hint of mental instability. My brother-in-law visited him in hospital and promised that he would return at the weekend. My father said he would not be there. On the following Thursday he made it known that he would die next day. He did.

I was returning to Ireland from Kenya to attend his funeral. The in-flight film, called *Shadowlands*, was an emotionally-charged drama based upon the real-life romance—during the 1950s—of the British writer C.S. Lewis and his American fiancée Joy Gresham. Lewis was an Oxford don; he married Joy. The film was partly set in the English countryside and the vehicle that brought the couple through the exquisite scenery was a Morris Minor. She developed cancer and Lewis tried to cope as best he could with her death.

The parallels between the narrative and the situation my father had to face, before my mother died, were stark. The evocation of images of the 1950s brought me back to the days he drove us through the Irish landscape when I looked from the moving windows upon the changing panorama. It was a most inopportune film for me at the time, steeped in pathos and heartbreak. I cleared my eyes repeatedly in silence as I watched; there seemed to be no end to my tears.

Death of a loved-one forces us to assess our own progress, like a rambler-of-old reflecting beside a milestone. Moving onwards divides—in a singular manner—all that comes before, from that which comes after. The division intensifies the mysterious separation between who we were and who we become as we move forward in time. This partition of self is identical, in fractal form, to the separation between what a generation or a nation is and what it becomes when shaped by the slow and apparently unobtrusive but relentless accumulation of deaths of the members of a family or those of an entire society.

Kate's Curiosity

When I returned to family research after a long absence, I quickly realised that dissolving the barriers that separated the generations which came before James Keogh—my great-grandfather—from those that came later, was going to be a great deal harder than I had anticipated. I was still obsessed with the possibility that I could find a connection between my Gaelic forefathers and their former property in Wexford, which would link me, authentically and finally, to the tribes of Leinster. The first impasse I encountered was finding James Keogh's father, who remained nameless. Snippets of information hinted at something sinister behind the dark veil of censorship that enveloped this man. His history had been concealed for well over a century and it was impossible to divide fact from fiction.

It appeared impossible for me to trace James' father using the data I had already gathered. However, James had a brother—John M.—who appeared to offer a bundle of untapped sources of new information. My instinct was correct and I eventually made the breakthrough I desired. But I achieved a positive result in a most roundabout manner. The experience underlines the frequent need to scrutinise a much wider scope of material than depend exclusively on births, marriages and deaths, which are normally employed by the family researcher to enable key breakthroughs to be made in determining our ancestors. Far from being a waste of time, the detours into the background of John M. provided me with a better understanding of the family's collective cultural identity.

John M. had crossed the Atlantic sometime before the Civil War and enlisted on the Yankee side, at Yonkers, in June 1861. I was bound for Yonkers and hoped to learn something more about his period in the army. In the normal course of events Americans come to Ireland to trace their ancestors. I turned to the US in search of mine. Whenever I was there on business, I took the opportunity of free time to follow his story.

My train from New York stopped on the banks of the Hudson and I alighted. I walked up to Philipse Manor House, which was built in the seventeenth century and now overlooks the road that runs from the station directly into the middle of Yonkers. It would have been one of the first sites seen by John M. as he entered the town. What brought him here in the first place? Why did he emigrate from Ireland? How long was he in America before he joined the army? What prompted him to enlist—money or adventure? Did he see action?

The best way I had to follow his story and answer some of the many questions posed was to investigate the history of his unit during the time he was part of it. I didn't expect John M.'s career to answer detailed family questions. Nonetheless, I would leave no stone unturned in my quest to know more about him and his people.

It soon became clear to me that contemporary history and the lives of ordinary men become united in a very special way in the army. If we know the story of a man's regiment we automatically identify times and places associated with a segment of his life; we can often reduce place to less than ten miles across on one part of a front line; and we can sometimes reduce events to the day, if not the hour.

John M. was born in 1839. At the time of enlisting he was only twenty-two years old, a little over five feet tall, of dark complexion, grey eyes and brown hair. These details come from his pension file which contains a wealth of information about him. There was, unfortunately, no reference to his father; at least no direct reference. When John M. enlisted in E Company, 40th New York Infantry Volunteers, the Civil War was in its second month. E Company was part of the *Mozart* Regiment so called because it had been raised by the Mozart Hall faction of the Democratic Party. Between 14th June and 1st July 1861 the regiment was mustered into the service of the United States for three years.

Civil War newspaper clippings provide a detailed picture of John M.'s regiment and record that: *In addition to a full equipment of Enfield rifles, an artillery company of twenty men and two twelve-pound rifled cannon have been provided. Twenty-four baggage wagons have been made for the regiment, and an ample supply of powder, shot and shell will be taken with it to the seat of war. The uniforms are handsome and substantial, being of dark blue cloth, with red facings and trimmings, and large gilt buttons; the coat, pants and caps are of the same material, and all trimmed with the same color.[54]*

Certainly, money would have been a factor in John M.'s decision to join the army. Enticements for new recruits were readily available. For example, the 135th Regiment, New York State Volunteers, which was also in Yonkers for a time, provided new recruits with two dollars on enlistment, thirteen dollars or one month's pay in advance and fifty dollars on mustering into service. A tent belonging to a recruitment officer was pitched conveniently near the little green plot in Getty Square to attract recruits.[55]

In his *History of Yonkers*, Charles Elmer Allison states that The 40th Mozart Regiment ... *encamped on the hill at the then extreme upper end of Palisade Avenue, where their white tents were pitched to the number of two hundred.[56]* I walked through Getty Square and up the hill to where the Mozart unit had camped. From this time John M. is likely to have become very familiar with the smell of tarpaulin. To me there is something strangely stirring about the notion of a Yankee army encampment. It embodies the idea of imminent transfer into a vast and varied countryside of changing landscapes, of forests, swamplands and prairies. It conjures up the fragility of the building-bricks of history. It was through such frail components that the story of the United States, and that of the modern industrialised world, was built. We become aware of the reality of human development by linking ourselves to the basic experiences of the people who lived at that time. Indeed, overarching human history is richly illuminated from below through personal narratives. But we become intimately connected when these people are of our own flesh and blood.

No major engagements were fought in the Civil War until July 1861, one month after John M. joined up. Then, Federal forces under General Irvin McDowell clashed with a Confederate army commanded by General Pierre de Beauregard at Bull Run, Virginia.

---

54 *40th Infantry Regiment, New York Volunteers Civil War Newspaper Clippings. The Encampment at Yonkers.* New York State Division of Military and Naval Affairs: Military History. < http://www.dmna.state.ny.us/historic/reghist/civil/infantry/40thInf/40thInfCWN.htm > (August, 2015)
55 Allison, 1896; p. 202.
56 *Ibid*; p. 201.

The battle resulted in a rout of the Northerners. After this, General George McClellan was placed in command of all Northern forces in Virginia and Washington, and they collectively became known as the *Army of the Potomac*. The 40th New York Infantry Volunteers joined the general manoeuvres that followed.[57] On 4th July the Mozart Regiment, now over 1,000 strong embarked on steamers for Elizabethport and proceeded thence by rail to Washington, D.C. They crossed into Virginia by the Long Bridge and were stationed at Alexandria to garrison the town and protect the railroad. The regiment became engaged in building several fortified defences and also in road making. John M.'s movements coincide. In September he went to Bennetts establishment located in King Street and had his photograph taken. He sent the image home to Ireland.

In spring 1862 cautious George McClellan made an effort to capture Richmond, the Confederacy capital. The Mozart unit became part of General Kearny's First Division of the Third Army Corps and remained in the vicinity of Alexandria until Saint Patrick's Day. It then sailed for the peninsula between the York and James Rivers before advancing towards Richmond, reaching Yorktown on 4th April. One month later John M's regiment saw action and was ordered to charge and seize several enemy fortifications. In this advance it received its first casualties. After a difficult march through heavy rains that created sticky muddy conditions underfoot the unit arrived before Williamsburg on 5th May and here encountered its first real experience of battlefield conditions. The North was victorious on this occasion.

Sergeant Fred Floyd, who was in Company H, kept a diary and wrote a history of the regiment. He remarks that, after Williamsburg, they moved towards Richmond. By 15th May they were about twenty-five miles from their destination. However, it took another ten days before they crossed the Chickahominy River about ten miles from the southern capital. Advancement was slow and even afforded time for levity. Sergeant Floyd observed that: *Our progress up the peninsula was marked by genuine enjoyment. Our steps were punctuated by singing, and as one regiment finished, another in front or rear took up the refrain, and so we were constantly moving in a musical sphere. "John Brown's Body" was the most famous song, and everybody could sing it.*[58]

Levity ceased around the Chickahominy, where they met some light resistance. The Mozarters camped a mile beyond the river on Sunday 25th but it was not until the following weekend that the real battle of Fair Oaks began. A strong rainstorm broke during the evening of Friday 30th May which made conditions difficult for the troops. The boom of a rebel cannon at noon the next day was followed by stiff rifle fire. The Mozarters spread themselves out at right angles to the Williamsburg Road that ran into Richmond and their line extended to a railroad on their right flank. It was near here in woodland that some of the hardest fighting took place. Sergeant Floyd quotes from the field report of Lieut. Col. Egan, which refers to happenings on Saturday 31st May:

About eight o'clock in the morning, sharp firing commenced in the woods on our right, when I wheeled the battalion to the right in order to face the enemy, and under a galling fire charged over the fence into the woods, our men at the same time delivering a vigorous fire

---

57 Information about John M.'s regiment is sourced from: Murphy, 1902; his personal details are based on: his army pension file; his military service record; family archives and Carnahan, 1899.
58 Floyd, 1908; 151.

upon the rebels. The enemy advanced upon us and I then ordered my men to charge bayonets. In an instant they were advancing at double-quick, which the enemy perceiving, and not relishing the idea of cold steel, turned and fled. We continued driving them to the front, and when near the edge of the woods we received a heavy fire from the front and left. Here many of our men fell, notwithstanding which, not one faltered, but with tremendous cheers continued to advance, driving the enemy entirely from the woods and scattering them in all directions, notwithstanding they made a desperate resistance. The victory was complete.[59]

Next day John M. was promoted to Sergeant for gallant services on the battlefield.[60] The regiment itself was complimented for its valour by General Birney, who commanded the Brigade to which it belonged. General Kearny, commander of the Division and General Heintzelman, commander of the Army Corps, were equally complimentary. Many skirmishes, reconnaissance trips and battles followed and the 40th gained a considerable reputation in the Army of the Potomac.

The Yankees were later repulsed and withdrew to their old lines around Washington. It was during the retreat from Richmond that John M. received sunstroke; this occurred somewhere between Savage Station and Charles City Cross Roads, where he was cared for in an ambulance.

More action followed for the Mozarters. In an accompanying series of skirmishes, known as Second Bull Run, John M.'s unit was depleted by 147 men who were killed, wounded or missing. Being reduced in numbers, it was ordered to Alexandria where two weeks were devoted to the double purpose of resting and re-equipping. Shortly afterwards Lee crossed the Potomac River and, for the first time during the war, invaded Northern territory. He was pushed back by McClellan after a fourteen-hour battle on the banks of Antietam Creek on 17th September in which over 20,000 men were killed or wounded. Thereafter there was a lull in the fighting until December 1862. On 31st August John M. was detailed at Division HQ as orderly. It was during this period that he wrote a letter from his post at Fairfax Seminary, Virginia. It reads:

Fairfax Seminary

Nr Alexandria Va.   *Oct. 13th 1862*

> *My dear Uncle*

I received yesterday a regular batch of letters from home, one from you arranged amongst them, under date of Sept 18th. I am also in reach of yours of Augt 30. As I am now in the enjoyment of an unwanted spell of idleness I think I cannot employ my time better than by answering you and mother, at least.

On the 11th our Division moved up to join Genl Stoneman at Poolesville, where he already had one of the Brigades. Gene Birney, who commanded by virtue of seniority in Genl Stoneman's absence, remaining here to attend a c't martial now in session in Washington, ordered me to stay here too. Here therefore I am and whether I shall ever return to the Division

---

59 *Ibid*; 154.
60 Source: family records: document (serial number 16375) signed by J. W. Carnahan U.S. Army and Navy Historical Association.

is problematical. From various significant circumstances I am inclined to think that Genl Birney will shortly get a new command (a Division very likely) in which case I should not be at all surprised to get an order to accompany him: in fact as much has been intimated to me. This should it transpire would I think be a very good opening for me, and would I am pretty sure eventually lead to a commission. A young fellow named Cannon, who was Genl Kearney's Chief clerk, and who for a short time acted in the same capacity for Birney, has now got his commission as 2nd Lieut (Ensign) in the 40th N. Y. Vols., with the promise of a staff appointment soon. In any case, the position of Chief Clerk at the Head quarters of a Genl of Division, is a great deal more comfortable, if less remunerative than a commission in the line. And if I do not get this position with Genl Birney, I am sure of it with Genl Stoneman. This is my exact position now, and whatever better it may be, I calculate it certainly will not be worse. Under existing orders from the War Department Genl Birney may find some difficulty in having me detached from my Division; he cannot in fact take me away without a special order of the Department. He has however influence sufficient for this. I merely mention it to show that there may be some obstacle to carrying out above programme.

I am sorry I cannot grant that 'particular favour' you so urgently press for, 'tis the least I may do to pay the postage upon my letters when I am able. You know or rather you don't know, I am now in receipt of extra pay at the rate of 25 cents per day $ 7.5 pr month, which helps me along considerably, and I would always have paid the postage but at one time we were kept so long without our pay, that I thought it better to write anyhow, than defer it Sine die. We got paid a short time since, when I laid in a regular stock of stamps, I have got to use them, so you must forgo the pleasure of paying for my letters for a while at least, perhaps you'll have to redeem them yet. I may lie somewhere that I can get neither money or stamps.

I cannot agree with your opinion that the States will never again be 'United'- They must be, let the cost be what it may, in blood and treasure. As for the interference of foreign powers, it is all bosh. What right have they to interfere pray? Did we ever meddle in European politics, and will we submit to be cozened or cajoled or frightened into a disgraceful peace, and the disruption of the Union founded by Washington, by England and France? What are their interests to ours, they are inconvenienced by a derth of cotton, and because they are, we must be good boys and let a parcel of traitors sever the Union, and spill the blood of our best and bravest for what; that the United States may be the laughing stock of the World? Never. This struggle is now merging into slavery or no slavery the South has chosen to put the issue upon this and the North has accepted it. Slavery & Union are incompatible, when the South is brought back to her senses & the Union she must come back free. Then will forever be erased that blot upon Escutcheon. Ours will then indeed be the 'Land of the Free!' I speak as an American & I feel as one. My countrymen have had a good deal to do with the making of this country and they are doing a great deal to preserve it and I am proud of it. I am proud that I am a countryman of such men as Meagher and Corcoran, & Shields, & Mulligan, & Casey. Why this army is full of Irishmen and from the private in the ranks to the General of Division Ireland may be justly proud of such sons.

By Jove I must not forget to satisfy Kate's curiosity. In the first place then, I have slept regularly every night for the past month, in a feather bed!!! Every time I think of marching orders I shiver. We have splendid quarters here in the late residence of Bishop Johns of Virginia (Episcopal) and luxuriate in hair bottom chairs, lounges and such like vanities. It may be sinful but I have a great fancy for vanities. And then as for eating & drinking Uncle Sam supplies us well, and we have a man detailed from one of the Regiments to cook for us, Mon's Pratini an Italian & professor de Cuisine, who gets up the most marvellous dishes from the most unpromising materials. Pratini is a treasure, and I assure you we value him highly. We get fresh meat twice every five days, and coffee & tea as much as we can use. We draw pork or salt beef for two days. You understand that we draw five days rations at a time, this includes tea, coffee, rice, sugar, syrup, vegetables, dried apples etc. in fact our commissary department is well attended to, and we are supplied when in camp regularly and well. Of course it sometimes happens when in the field, that it is impossible to supply as regularly as in camp but generally, we are well supplied. Give my love to Kate and _her_ Jack and _your_ Molly. She must be a regular little fairy. She will be a pretty big fairy by the time I see her I am afraid. Kiss her for me and tell her I send it all the way over the ocean. Remember me to Mr. McArdle James and all friends, give my love to Nannie James Jane & Alice. I was rejoiced to hear of James's return. I will write him soon perhaps by this mail.

In future you had better direct to me thus -

Mr. John M Keogh
Care General D. B. Birney
US Vols.
Via Washington D.C
US

Your affectionate nephew

John M. Keogh

The letter is a fascinating historical document in its own right and provides a valuable insight into John M.'s Irish relations in the 1860s. Though I didn't know it at this stage of the inquiry, his _Dear uncle_ was his mother's brother, George; and Kate was George's wife. He was prepared to pay for stamps without reserve and, therefore, was not without money. In fact, he was a Dublin businessman and made a living in various trades, including cabinet making and warehousing; in time he became the manager of Brooks Tyrrell, the high-class furriers of Grafton Street. A regular two-way communication was taking place between these men. John M. was kept aware of what was going on at home and the family was conscious of his progress in the army.

The letter conveys no feeling of threat from the Confederates. Rather, it exudes an air of confidence that the South will be brought back to her senses. John M.'s uncle differs in his opinion about the outcome of the war and is, obviously, not optimistic for the future of the Union. Slavery was abolished in the District of Colombia during April 1862. In September Lincoln announced that, with effect from January 1863, it would be abolished within all states. Slavery, then, was a hot issue when John M. wrote home and explains the emphasis he puts on the subject. Once more, the harmony between personal and contemporary history is demonstrated in these examples.

John M. is ambitious for a commission. However, it was not realised. According to his Military Service Record, from the time he wrote the letter he was on almost continual detached service in the capacity of clerk at Division HQ, the Adjutant General's Office or in the War Department.

A woman's curiosity divides John M's letter sharply into two. In response to Kate's questions, he provides a wealth of intimate details about himself, his quarters, rations and other snippets about the family in Ireland. I got the definite impression that his father was dead. I came to this conclusion based on a complete lack of reference to him in his letter and the fact that he says: *I think I cannot employ my time better than by answering you and mother, at least.* His sisters Nannie, Jane and Alice and his brother James—my great-grandfather—are also mentioned: not his father.

Through his writings, John M. unequivocally demonstrates that he is literate and articulate, and he has an elegant calligraphy. His uncle is educated, is a businessman and holds views on international affairs. The inconsistency that I observed earlier, between the Keoghs and the stereotypic Gaelic Irish Catholic of the late nineteenth century, is reconfirmed here. His family was firmly rooted in an urban, rather than a rural environment, was educated and gave the impression that they were not poor—though that is not to say they were rich.

John M. was honourably discharged on 14th June 1864. The war had almost one year to run but his three-year contract was complete and he was free to leave. I wrote to the Library of Congress to find out more about his movements after his involvement in the war. I received the following reply from Lloyd Dunlap, a specialist in the Civil War and Reconstruction Manuscript Division: *In the Washington city directories your great grand uncle, Mr. John M. Keogh, is listed as a clerk in either the War Department or the Adjutant General's Office, a branch of that department. No mention was found of his service in the White House, but it was not uncommon for clerks in other agencies to be detailed there for prolonged periods.* This note provides confirmation that he continued as a civilian in the same position that he held as a soldier.

I could not answer all the questions posed earlier about John M. I followed his movements from Yonkers to Alexandria, where he had been stationed, and then I went to Washington where he resided after the war. He met and fell in love with an Irish girl, Alice Flynn. It appears that they were married in 1866. However, tragedy struck when she was only thirty-four, barely twelve years after their union. They now had four children. John M. married for a second time to another Irish girl, Anna Cleary, in January 1880. I found his last residence in Washington, where he died in 1904 six years before his brother James passed away.

John M. had spent forty years in the capital. I visited his grave at Arlington Cemetery that bears his name and the words *40th NY Vol.* In the quiet graveyard close to a large oak tree and beside a simple slab, amongst many other simple veteran tombs, I read the letter he had sent home all those years ago. As I read his words in silence, I felt for a brief moment the mood of a generation that had passed away. His was a world divided from homeland by an ocean, united by letters carried to and fro in steam and sailing ships. Though divided from him by an ocean of time, I realised that a residual flavour of his life was present like a ghost in my grandfather's house at Beechwood Road where I had sensed its flavour; now I had found its source.

I visited Saint Peter's church where John M. and Anna Cleary were married; it is several blocks from the Capitol Building in Washington. I had written to the church to obtain the marriage certificate. Monsignor William Awalt, Saint Peter's Rectory, sent me a copy of the document with some additional information. He wrote: ... *the man was a widower from Washington, D. C., the son of Thomas Keogh* ... Here, at last, was the information I coveted for so long. James Keogh's father, my great-great-grandfather was Thomas or Thomas J. Keogh to be precise.

Family Secret

Breda Ryan of the Archives Section of Saint Patrick's Hospital was not at her desk when I called. I would wait for about one hour then call her again. In the meantime I drove into the Phoenix Park and stopped my car near the Papal Cross that overlooks the city of Dublin.

I wanted to uncover the true story of Thomas J. Keogh by lifting the unyielding cover over a well-guarded century-old family secret. I wanted to solve the mystery of my great-great-grandfather once and for all. If I was hampered in this step I feared that I would never be able to follow the family back in time and determine where, precisely, they came from. I would never be able to link them definitely and finally to their tribal roots.

The Civil War letter of John M. sent to his uncle from America gives, as I said, the definite impression that his father was dead. Later, I was surprised to discover—in a marriage certificate—that Thomas J. was still alive in 1883, twenty-one years after the letter was written. The mystery of this man was as persistent as ever and was not resolved by finding his name alone.

I had spent several fruitless years trying to obtain more information about Thomas J. The fact that he was alive after 1864 provided the first real hope for a successful outcome, because all deaths in Ireland have been registered since that date. I turned to the national archives and started by examining registered deaths from 1882—when he was still alive—to 1892. If unsuccessful, I vowed to search the records for each month of the following decade until I found his certificate.

I joined the morning researchers trawling through the large leather-bound books in the General Register Office in Lombard Street. I obtained the indices of deaths; these showed me that some seventy persons, bearing the name Thomas Keogh, or Kehoe, passed away in the decade beginning in 1882. One third of these came from Dublin. I assumed that Thomas was about thirty when his son John M. was born in 1839. This ruled out all but the most elderly man on the list.

It transpired that this Thomas, originally from Drumcondra, died in 1888 and—of great significance—the record stated that he was a draper, the same profession as my great-grandfather, James. The Keogh family had a long association with the clothing industry in Dublin. However, my uncle had told me that Thomas J., though he didn't know his name at the time, had something to do with *customs*.

I could not draw a final conclusion too soon. The Thomas I had found was not necessarily my great-great-grandfather. I had no definitive proof. I pursued the matter further and went to Glasnevin Cemetery to find his grave. The plot is divided into two, one part of which is associated with the Keogh family and the other with McGuinness. The link with McGuinness was promising. A George McGuinness was interred there. You will recall that Bartholomew, my grandfather, had a younger brother called George McGuinness who died in early childhood. Many more clues confirmed that I had indeed found the grave of my great-great-grandfather, the man who—for so long—had had no name.

The Glasnevin grave gave me information about the parent's generation of Thomas J. Revealed was the date of death of an old man, also called Thomas Keogh, who lived at the family home in Prussia Street in Dublin. He died there in December 1846. This Thomas was, I assume, the father of Thomas J. He was born in 1766. For convenience I distinguish the two Thomases—both of whom lived in Prussia Street—as: Thomas *the Elder* and Thomas J. What the *J.* stood for is unknown; I use it as a convenient acronym for *Junior*.

Was I about to make another breakthrough? I would soon know. A light drizzle fell over the Phoenix Park as I reflected on the many years I had pursued the obscure life of Thomas J. After finding his grave I managed to gather enough information in the Dublin records to piece together an outline of his young adult life. In 1837 Thomas J. was an accountant and ran a circulating library, which he housed at High Street. Two years later he appeared at Rose Grove, Harold's Cross. The motto of his business was: *Disarranged accounts adjusted upon moderate terms.* He married Margaret McGuinness in the late 1830s and the couple then moved to Prussia Street. It appears that Thomas J.'s change of address coincided with his exit from private practice, for he is described as a *public accountant* in the Dublin directories at this time.

Prussia Street lies close to the Phoenix Park. In the 1840s it was in a developing sector of the city with its own peculiar history. The road outside the family front door was said to have been one of the principle arteries of Ireland that ran north from the Liffey to the ancient Gaelic centre of Tara.[61] The road passes through the village of Stoneybatter and immediately becomes Prussia Street. Around the 1760s the so-called "primitive" nature of the area began to hold great appeal to Dubliners coping with an increasingly hectic pace of life in the crowded city. Its simplicity and homeliness were enticing and Prussia Street became a desirable and fashionable retreat amidst old woodlands and spreading apple orchards.

A corn and frieze market was held on the village green of Stoneybatter and farm-folk converged there for trade and shopping. By 1800 nearby Smithfield had grown into a large market for cattle and hay, and most of the city's dairies were concentrated there. Country people were ever present in the neighbourhood with their animals and carts loaded with a variety of farm produce according to the season of the year. The Irish language was widely spoken because local traders and shopkeepers were obliged to understand and speak Gaelic in order to carry out transactions with farmers and their families from the nearby Meath *Gaeltacht*.

In the early decades of the twentieth century an artisan's dwelling project put an end to the open fields and orchards around Stoneybatter. But, when Thomas J. and Margaret came to live there, Prussia Street was part of a semi-rural landscape. It was mid-way in development between its elegant past and its post-famine artisan future, totally suitable for a man aspiring to middle rank.

A rush of excitement provoked a response in me. I would soon call Breda Ryan but not directly. I turned on the car engine, left the scene of the Papal Cross and drove out of the Phoenix Park to the vicinity of Prussia Street. I parked the car and walked to what had

---

61   Kearns, 1996; p. 23. (Note: information about Prussia Street and environs depends mainly on this reference.)

been the house of Thomas J. It was a two-story, redbrick, grey-slated terrace dwelling with a gable structure over an entrance to a yard adjacent to the hall door. I strained to see what was behind the large wine-painted double doors of this side entrance. Through the cracks there appeared to be an ample enclosure and it was full of boards and steel poles leaning against walls and against each other as in a builder's yard. These doors and the enclosure behind were likely used in former years to confine horses and there was room enough for a coach.

Thomas J. and Margaret celebrated half a dozen Christmases here. Before Thomas the Elder died, the oral memory of the family and the flavour of fireside and table conversation surfaced from a period before the 1798 rebellion. Thomas the Elder repeated fading anecdotes from the era of his grandfather, when the city of Dublin was extending beyond its medieval confines to become the Georgian venture that graced the growing metropolis with grand architecture; when the Irish Parliament houses on College Green were under construction; when the exploits of King William of Orange were recent and important events; when the Penal Code was still operative and when the Protestant Ascendancy was reaching the height of its domination.

The house in Prussia Street held family memories of a decade of changing seasons when friends and relations like Thomas Tighe, Margaret Mooney, Catherine O'Neill and Edward Duffy visited—a lost society that are now only names on official certificates. These acquaintances came to mourn the deceased or celebrate new life. At least three children were born in the house. The family tasted death when baby Thomas passed away aged only one year, and again when Thomas the Elder died. One can imagine something of the spirit of a Charles Dickens' novel here; indeed this was the era of Dickens. He published *A Christmas Carol* round the time that Thomas J. and Margaret moved into Prussia Street.

The children developed their concept of the world in the hallway, kitchen, rooms and inner yard of this house. April rains against windows; smell of apple-blossom in spring; doors habitually closed—opened during the heat of summer; voices of children playing in the yard heard by the one who was sick and confined indoors in bed; fires against the cold of winter; warnings to avoid animals and carts in the busy street outside. These were the memories the children bore with them in the ensuing years; it was what John M. carried into the battle of Fair Oaks and what James remembered when he buried his wife in Glasnevin.

I looked at the upper windows of the house. They had no curtains. The place appeared to be uninhabited. Below, at street level, a lace curtain was draped across the window and dust had gathered on it. I found myself walking across the street under a strange compulsion. I went to the door and knocked twice. The sounds exploded into the hall and reverberated. Then stillness. I had hoped someone could give me information about the house or let me see the yard. But no one was there. I left and went to a nearby restaurant where I ordered coffee.

I have witnessed long stretches of progress, development and decline of four generations, including the autumnal and winter years of my grandparents at Beechwood Road. I have observed the family cycle of one of my uncles and his wife from the time of their marriage in the 1950s to the birth and growth of their children and to their passing away in recent years. I have lived through the summer and winter years of my parents. I have created my own family and have watched over its development into adulthood. I have lived to see the birth of my grandson. For these reasons I understand the dynamic of change from generation to generation. Water in a fountain is an appropriate metaphor; the shape of the family stays in rough form but is continually refreshed by new elements. The same process happened in Prussia Street for the family of Thomas J. and Margaret in the mid-nineteenth century.

In 1849, two years after the Great Famine, they left Prussia Street with their children and went to Richmond Drumcondra. This move was fully in line with the custom of the time. The middle-class was escaping from the centre of Dublin as a fever-prone flood of famine refugees entered the city.[62] Joseph Brady states that: *In the Dublin of the period there was certainly plenty of incentive to move out ... By moving to healthier surroundings the middle classes also avoided the financial costs of the city's workhouses, hospitals and police. The increasing demand for suburban housing was also a reflection of the expanding middle class population.*[63]

After he left Prussia Street, Thomas J.'s career becomes bewildering. In the first marriage certificate of his son—James—dated 1875, he is listed as having no profession. But, in 1883, his trade is identified as *customs*. Finally, on his death in 1888 he is classified as a draper. Significantly, there appears to be no record of him as an accountant from the date he leaves Prussia Street. However, Thom's Dublin Directory mentions a Thomas Esq. Board of Works between 1852 and 1855 but, most unusually, carries no home address, though it does mention *customs house*.

I finished my coffee and left the restaurant to search for a public phone. I called Breda Ryan again. One hour had well passed. She was at her desk and was willing to meet me. I would be able to inspect the records immediately. I hurried to Saint Patrick's Hospital.

---

62 Prunty, 2002; p. 190.
63 Brady, 2002; p. 265.

Trevelyan's Claque

Breda Ryan had painstakingly gone through the records of Patrick's Hospital and said that she had found something of interest for me. She brought me into the old segment of the building where the wards and cubicles of the patients had been. A painting of Swift hangs here. This genius, whose legacy to literature is *Gullivers Travels,* bequeathed his estate to build this home … *for idiots and lunatics.* Much has been discussed over his reason for establishing such a place: Was it a bizarre joke against the Irish? This is doubtful, because the hospital catered mainly for the descendants of English Protestants.[64]

Breda and I walked across the old stone flags and descended to the basement where the records are stored. The door opened into a room where the atmosphere was regulated. The Register of Patients was in a glass case before me. The book was open at page thirty-three made ready for my inspection. The record showed, under patient Number 580:

> Name: *Thomas Keogh*
> Age: *Forty-two*
> Date of admission: *April 1852*
> Occupation: *Clerk*
> Former resident of: *Drumcondra*
> Probable cause of illness: *Over anxiety to business*
> Length of illness before admission: *Six months*
> By whom recommended: *Margaret Keogh*

I thanked Breda and left the buildings. The awful truth had broken through the veil of censorship that the family had so doggedly constructed. Thomas J. had spent thirty-six years in this mental asylum. The news stung me. It is not pleasant to encounter a revelation of this sort in one's family and is one of the risks we face when tracing our ancestors.

I had two concerns: firstly, could the demise of Thomas J. have had a hereditary base and secondly, would knowledge of it damage the family? Some people are too willing to use such facts to cast aspersions on one's immediate relations. For a time I agonised over the dark revelation I had uncovered. I wondered should I eliminate it from my narrative. Should I block this knowledge from my family? But, on reflection, in the interests of truth I should hide nothing. I was now making a commitment to truth as the only virtue needed to overcome all barriers to uncovering my identity, wherever this would lead. A concoction of the truth would not be helpful. I could do nothing but accept the situation, despite my discomfort. In hindsight, it was fortunate that I took this approach.

Many things became clear after unearthing the real story of Thomas J. The tragedy explained John M.'s reference to his mother in his Civil War letter from America in which he omits any mention of his father, even though he was alive at the time. It also explained the confusion about Thomas J.'s profession after 1849. Earlier I mentioned that vague snippets had come through the well-constructed veil of censorship dividing the generations previous to my great-grandfather, James. These hazy notions sprang from the underground whisperings of a boy culture, which make sense in light of my findings. My uncle and his half-uncle spoke

---

64 Malcolm, 1989; p. 99.

of these things but tended to focus on the melodramatic that could not be substantiated. They talked of a man roaring through the streets of Dublin who *died with his boots on*. Thomas didn't die in such a manner. On the other hand, rumours of him roaming the city in a delusion of madness are now credible. But, was there something sinister going on, as my uncle suggested; something to do with a court case and a whisky tax?

To find out, I tried to answer the question: Why did Thomas J. suddenly become sick—a man in his early forties and father of six living children, the youngest of whom was born the year before his confinement? If his sickness had a hereditary base, why did it not appear earlier in his life? If it was a genetic weakness, then it would surely have appeared somewhere amongst the six subsequent generations of his descendents. Yet no mental illness is recorded. No. His infirmity was—almost certainly—provoked by his environment.

Perhaps his demise was caused by a physical accident? I think it very unlikely, otherwise it would have been inscribed in the hospital records and the family would have had a legitimate excuse for his condition and no reason to hide his illness.

Perhaps he had a contagious disease like syphilis. Certainly there were places around Prussia Street where one could fall into licentious abandon. From 1704, when the Royal Barracks were built to the west of Stoneybatter, a military influence radiated over the surrounds and attracted prostitution. Dramatic change also came to the area with the opening of North Circular Road in 1768. Nearby Benburb Street became a magnet for traders, shops, infirmaries, workhouses, hotels and singing halls, and developed into one of the busiest streets on the north side of Dublin. It was a raucous district with a reputation for shameless behaviour, quite at odds with the rest of "respectable" Stoneybatter.

However, death from syphilis was described in Saint Patrick's in terms of *general paralysis* or *dementia paralytica* and not "anxiety". Some ten or twenty years after the initial infection, serious degeneration of the nerve fibres in the frontal lobes of the brain occurs. This degeneration often produced bizarre, violent and demented behaviour and sufferers were normally confined in mental hospitals. Death usually resulted within a short time of admission or the patients were sent to other asylums outside Saint Patrick's. However, Thomas J. died in old age and his death was recorded as *apoplexy* accompanied by a coma, which was similar to that of his son John M., who died in Washington in 1904 aged sixty-four after a cerebral haemorrhage and coma. This appears to rule out syphilis.

The cause of his demise might have been alcohol. There were plenty of opportunities for drinking in the vicinity of Prussia Street in the mid-nineteenth century. Popular eating-houses sprang up to cater to the early-rising market crowd and many local pubs had a license to open at seven in the morning. Patients with a drink-related sickness differed from the rest of the males admitted to Saint Patrick's in that they were generally married and over forty years of age, with occupations ranging from shopkeepers, to doctors, to church ministers. Thomas was clearly in this category but his diagnosis does not mention alcohol.

Was Thomas J. confined wrongfully? According to Elizabeth Malcolm, psychiatry was sometimes used as a powerful weapon to control and silence dissenters.[65] Was Thomas a non-conformist? If so, to what did he not conform and who would have wanted him put away?

Could he have been poisoned? The mid-nineteenth century was a time when the issue of poisoning gripped the public imagination. Toxicology emerged as a leading speciality of forensic medicine and drew public attention through several high-profile murder cases. But what motive would anyone have had to poison Thomas J., a public accountant or clerk?

There are too many unanswered questions here. They might be cleared up by an examination of Thomas J.'s remains. If his sickness was caused by poisoning or by an infection it might be possible to trace evidence in his bones. For example, for the skull of a syphilitic to become riddled with lesions the person must stay alive long enough for this to happen. Clearly Thomas J. survived many years after the first appearance of his illness and this would allow such a test to be carried out—if the bones are in an acceptable state. Also, some toxins can stay in the skeleton indefinitely, making such a test worthwhile.

To check if it were possible to exhume the body, I contacted the State Pathologist at the time, Dr. Harbison, but he informed me that this would be difficult. The state owns the remains of a person once burial has taken place and permission to undertake an examination has to be requested. If the objective is to uncover wrongdoing, there would have to be the chance of apprehending the criminal, clearly not possible in Thomas J.'s case.

The more I delved into his illness, the more I was perplexed. His stay in the asylum is strange on several counts. He was a Catholic. There was a tendency to favour Protestant patients. Besides, he is classed as being *free of payment*. There were severe restrictions against free patients. Why, then, was he exempt?

I faced a dilemma. Should I now leave aside investigating the life of Thomas J. as a futile exercise or should I follow all leads to their finality? Was I wasting time searching for elusive answers, or would I stumble across a nugget of information that would produce final clarity? My objective was to uncover the true story of my forefathers and try to identify their rural property in order to establish an authentic link with Gaelic Leinster. Pursuing nebulous leads could distract from my central aim. Alternatively, extraneous information might produce serendipitous leads that would shorten the path to my ultimate goal. I mentioned that the direct path in ancestral research is not necessarily the most fruitful. On balance, I felt that time spent searching for every scrap of existing information would not be, in principle, a waste of time. At worst it would provide a greater understanding of the family, its rank and status. At best, it could provide the ultimate answers I was seeking.

I explored several avenues for enlightenment. In the back of my mind I pondered on my uncle's comment about Thomas J.'s association with a whisky tax. Had he been provided drink to assist someone in the industry avoid paying taxes? Did the guilty conscience of the culprit suffer after Thomas' demise, to the extent that indirect support was provided to the hospital on his behalf? I grew increasingly inquisitive about the possibility of third-party involvement. I surmised that if anyone had any reason to feel guilty about the fall

---

65   *Ibid*; ix.

of Thomas J. and wanted to compensate him, he would have provided donations at the precise date, or very close to his date of admission. It was inevitable that, in time, I would return to Saint Patrick's Hospital in search of the phantom patron.

I called Breda Ryan again. She informed me that a professional archivist, Mr Andrew Whiteside, had just been appointed and it was best if I wrote to him directly. In response to my letter I received a telephone call from Mr Whiteside who told me that he had discovered a total of eight items of correspondence, three of which were written by Thomas' wife Margaret. *'When could I see them?'* I asked.

Within a few days I was in the office of Mr Whiteside. He carefully placed a number of old documents on the table and, with gloved hands, began to go through them one by one. Incredibly, two of Thomas J.'s letters exist from the time he became a patient. His first letter is addressed to *Mr James Cummins Esq., Governor Saint Patrick's Lunatic Asylum* and dated April 1852. It opens with the statement: *I am now a prisoner in this house for nearly a week and I am sorry to perceive that the power of the Trevelyan claque to whom the fact can be traced to have originated has followed me into it. For perhaps 2 years that claque has caused me to be drugged to weaken my mind and affect my head and I am sorry to be obliged to say that the like pranks have been practiced and … (?) in this house. I have been (?) unjustly drugged here too.*[66]

The letters give the impression of a troubled mind made worse through the forced intake of drugs. Thomas J.'s letters also indicate that he was suffering delusions of grandeur. He was certain that God was revealing truths to him and says: *He has warned me in my sleep every night since I became an inmate.* There is no reference to his Gaelic origins. In fact he aspired to be raised to the rank of Duke, fulfil the office of Lord Lieutenant of Ireland and be rewarded with matching estates and a handsome fortune. He breaks off suddenly with the statement: *I am summoned to breakfast and must defer what else I intend to say on the subject of a second epistle.*

The only facts that can be drawn from his overall account is that he had two brothers and two brothers-in-law; recalled visiting Dr. Cusack and Dr. Croker with one of these men and mentioned walking … *on Saturday in the garden during the hours of recreation.* He was convinced that at least one faulty investigation was held in reference to him before the Board of Works. His association with the Board was indisputable; he was a chief clerk in the organisation.

The source of Thomas J.'s perceived problems revolved around what he called *the Trevelyan claque*. In January 1840 Sir Charles Trevelyan began duties of Assistant Secretary to the Treasury in London. He discharged the functions of that office for nineteen years up to 1859. He administered the Irish famine-relief works of 1845-7 through the Board of Works, when upwards of 734,000 men were employed by the government. Trevelyan is often blamed for making the famine worse by adhering to Britain's controversial policy of minimal intervention. He saw the disaster as an act of God's providence to keep the Irish in check. Today his name is heard whenever *The Fields of Athenry* are sung. The poignant lyrics relate to Michael, who *stole Trevelyan's corn* to keep his family alive and was deported to Australia for his effort.

66 Letters of Saint Patrick's Hospital relating to Thomas, transcribed from oral recordings (author's records)

I was beginning to dismiss any suspicion about a conspiracy against Thomas as a delusion on his part. However, as mentioned at the end of the last chapter, Thom's Dublin Directory lists, under merchants and traders between 1852 and 1855, a Thomas Esq., Board of Works but carries no private address. I am now certain that this is a reference to Thomas J. himself. He was confined from 1852 and no reference could be made to the Board in public without permission of that institution. Therefore, it is highly probable that the Board arranged for the record to be placed in the directory. As such, it appears that they were attempting to conceal his demise from the public by ensuring that his name didn't disappear abruptly from the Dublin directories. Was the Board trying to help the family conceal their embarrassment? Surely a benevolent act of this type would have been at odds with normal practice on the part of a mid-nineteenth-century government body?

Did the Board itself entice Saint Patrick's to accept Thomas J. in the capacity of a patient, free of payment? I consulted Elizabeth Malcolm's history of the hospital to find out if there had been any specific arrangements between the Board of Works and the hospital that would explain this. I scanned the index and found two references. The most pertinent one states that the governors: ... *followed some of the advice given to them in 1849-50 by their agent, J. J. Verschoyle: in 1851, for instance, they applied to the Board of Works for a loan of over £1,100 in order to drain nearly 10 per cent of the Saggart estate* ... which they owned.[67] Under these circumstances, if the Board—the lender—wished to place Thomas J. in Saint Patrick's, the hospital would have, understandably, acquiesced to their request.

But why would the Board go to the trouble of concealing his fate or place him in Saint Patricks? It occurred to me that stressful events like the famine produced mental problems. Could it be that Thomas J. was working on famine relief and witnessed situations that turned his mind? As a result the Board felt that he merited compensation and did what it could for him? Instinctively I think this conclusion unlikely, though not impossible.

I surmised that the final answers to Thomas' demise, if they did exist, must lie within the Board of Works itself and so I began a new search. I found the location of the Board's records in the National Archives in Dublin. The minute-books expose the painful details of his case. However, the benevolence of the Board and Treasury towards him is clear from these records.

In November 1851 the accountant made a formal complaint against Thomas J. for irregular attendance and lack of attention to his duties. The complaint was so serious that it was forwarded to Treasury in London by the Chairman of the Board who, after a full review of the case ... *considers it his duty to recommend Mr Keogh's removal from the Board's Service.* Surprisingly, the return letter in December, which was from Sir Charles Trevelyan himself, requested that, instead of being dismissed immediately and because of ... *his former good conduct which led to his being selected for the appointment held by him* ... Thomas J. be given a trial period of three months.

Unfortunately, the situation didn't improve and in early January of the following year he was ordered to attend a meeting of the Board. Was this the enquiry that Thomas J. mentioned in his correspondence? *The Chairman remonstrated with Mr Keogh upon his continued unsatisfactory conduct notwithstanding the decision of the Treasury already*

---

67   Malcolm, 1989; p. 125.

communicated to him. Despite Thomas J.'s promises to be more punctual, a month later another letter was sent to Treasury ... *expressing the hopelessness of expecting any amendment on the part of Mr Keogh* ... and he was suspended pending a fresh decision from Treasury. He was finally dismissed in February 1852.

The minutes are punctuated by a letter from Margaret Keogh at the end of February, on Thomas J.'s behalf, requesting that her husband be reinstated *when his health shall be restored.* Twelve days later the Board ordered that the essence of Margaret's letter be made known to Treasury and recommended that ... *as his length of service would not entitle him to a pension, they would recommend that a gratuity of one year's salary be allowed to him under the painful circumstances of his case.* Treasury responded positively and authorised the payment which was to be issued in trust to the Chairman, to be disbursed as he saw fit.[68]

The Board and Treasury did all in their power to help my great-great-grandfather. There may have been some substance in Thomas' suspicions—and the suspicions within the family—about a conspiracy, though the true nature of the matter is hard to decipher behind carefully-worded official correspondence. Without further proof there is no way of reaching an adequate conclusion. However, there is plenty of room for speculation.

After the initial shock of Thomas J.'s fate washed over me, my courage grew bolder. There would be no gain in ignoring the darkness that I could not remove. Neither would it be wise to remain perpetually fixed on the gloom. Therefore, I cast off my reluctance to submit to the reality of what I had discovered. I then penetrated more deeply into the demise of Thomas J. in an effort to pass beyond it—or break through to another level.

I turned to Elizabeth Malcolm's book and used it as off-duty reading during consultancy work in Cameroon that began shortly after my visit to Saint Patrick's. I paged through Malcolm's work in an attempt to unveil the life that Thomas J. must have led in his confinement. Several lasting thoughts stayed with me as I became more familiar with the history of the hospital. There was no return from this mental leper colony. It was not pleasant for patients or employees. It was not a good place to live in during the latter half of the nineteenth century, where the staff were little more than semi-slaves to judge by today's standards; where the quality of life deteriorated after 1850; where disease was rife; where smallpox broke out occasionally; where resources were so poor that closure of the institution was contemplated; where no case-studies were undertaken; where the doctors had little way of knowing how to treat the maladies that tortured their patients behind the thin layers of cranium that presented an immense gulf to them. Under these conditions care concentrated more on survival and the attempted cure of physical rather than mental disease.

Thomas J. could have visited the library that existed for well-educated patients or attend church. Both activities helped the inmates and reflected Swift's own desire to assist the mentally ill. A daily routine was also helpful to an extent. After being awoken and after having breakfast Thomas J. may have been allowed into the exercise yard or may have gone into the grounds where internees could work in the gardens. It was noted that the growing of vegetables helped patients, though this may have been beneath the dignity of a chief clerk. On the opposite slopes of the Liffey was the Phoenix Park; further downriver at a small

---

68   Quotes from: National Archives Ireland Board of Works; OPW 1/1/1 Vol. 17: 30.10.1851 – 20.4.1854.

remove but on the same side as the Park was Prussia Street, the former family home that was beyond Thomas J.'s reach forever. From his perspective he was a prisoner, unjustly confined and silenced.

A single thought emerged most prominently as I read Malcolm's book. One of the worst aspects of the hospital, I felt, was the suffering Thomas J. experienced because of winter cold. Heating was totally inadequate until the 1880s. This reaction was stimulated by my thorough dislike of the cold and my contemplation of his condition in the luxurious heat of tropical Cameroon.

Despite the lack of a final conclusion about Thomas J., my investigation was far from a waste of time. It was about to take a more productive turn that would not have been possible had I abandoned the search for the finer details of his life. Many times during my quest I learnt the same lesson: our investigative pathways are seldom straight.

I could not avoid noticing the persistent involvement of my great-great-grandmother— Margaret—Thomas J.'s wife, and her doggedness in requesting help for him. She exhibited a heroic stubbornness in his favour. The part she played in rearing her children, without a male breadwinner and as her social standing and financial circumstances collapsed, provides a revealing perspective on the sufferings of nineteenth-century women under such conditions and also serves to reveal a lot more about the social history and status of the middle-class family to which she and Thomas J. belonged.

Decline and Recovery

Without doubt, the facts that I uncovered about Thomas J. omit the profound suffering that is implied for Margaret, his wife. The analogy with a Charles Dickens' novel takes on a macabre reality. What black thoughts were in her mind as she sat in front of the clerk who copied, with quill in hand, the cold statistics and morbid information into the Register of Patients of Saint Patrick's Hospital in April 1852? She suffered before bringing herself to this point. She must have known that it was exceptional for a wife to commit her husband to an asylum. But her suffering drove her to it after months of desperation, watching him disintegrate and realising that his condition was beyond recuperation. And what of her love for and her memories of Thomas now; were marvellous expectations and fond emotions reduced to cold indifference, regrets, bitterness or relief?

And what of her family? Unrelenting tension is likely to have driven Margaret's mother—Jane—to her death in November 1851, three months before Thomas was finally committed to hospital. The older siblings understood that something fundamental was wrong with their father. Under these circumstances, Margaret and her children lived a period of dreadful uncertainty in the months leading up to his confinement.

To make matters worse, the suburban area into which the family had moved, prior to Thomas J.'s hospitalisation, was known for a degree of snobbishness. It was the normal practice in Richmond Drumcondra to provide the townland address without adding the street or house number, as if it were taken for granted that each family was so unique and well-known that the provision of mere details were troublesome and unnecessary. However, this attitude was more pretentious than real. The northern side of the city never developed middle-class enclaves to the same extent as the south. Joseph Brady reveals that: ... *the aspiring suburbanite had to pass through insalubrious areas before reaching Drumcondra.*[69] Notwithstanding, it was probably the best that Thomas J. could afford in his position. Though the disgrace that Margaret had to endure in front of judgemental and scandalised neighbours may have been of a slightly lesser degree than it would have been in Rathmines or Rathgar, this provided slight comfort against Margaret's deep mortification.

Undoubtedly, the family, especially Margaret, lived a nightmare. The joy she felt when they moved out of Prussia Street was now reversed. She had to find accommodation in areas of the city that she could afford and, as time went on, she could afford less. She didn't seem to benefit in any way through the *gratuity of one year's salary* granted by Treasure to Thomas J. It was a period of quiet desperation for her as she tried to shelter her children as best she could while her social standing crumbled. She had to cope with her six young children alone. The eldest was only about thirteen years old; the youngest was taking her first steps. The letters from Margaret, which are conserved in Saint Patrick's Hospital, show a steady decline in the family's conditions once Thomas J. is diagnosed insane. The first, written round April 1852, reads:

---

69   Brady, 2002; p. 272.

To the Governors of Saint Patrick's Hospital

The humble petition of Margaret Keogh wife of Thomas Keogh late one of the senior clerks Board of Works Ireland.

Humbly showeth that he was dismissed from said office in February last in consequence of irregularity of attendance caused by insanity.

That Petitioner has a large and helpless family of whom he has been the sole support and that she has no means whatever to pay for him in an hospital.

That Petitioner understands that in certain cases patients are admitted on the 20 £ list as free patients, and Petitioner being quite destitute of all means and most anxious at the same time to place him with his equals, humbly implores the Board will kindly admit him on this class of patients, and hopes by the will of God, he will be in a short time restored to perfect health and enabled again to provide for herself and family.

And Petitioner will pray.

Shortly after writing this letter the family fled from Richmond Drumcondra. Domestic help had to be forfeited at this stage despite the burden of six children, and accumulated valuables sold off. The family returned to the rough life of the city; first to Bolton Street where, in July Margaret again wrote to the governors of Saint Patrick's thanking them that Thomas J. had been accepted as an inmate in April as a gratuitous patient on the twenty-pound list for a period of three months. As that period had now expired, she requested that he be kept for a further three months. She added that: *My means still continuing to be very limited with a helpless family of six children.* A note on the outside of the letter states: *This request to be granted.* It was signed by the Chairman, Mr Shaw. Three months later, in October of the same year, she again requested an extension of his stay, this time mentioning that: *I have to respectfully inform you that my circumstances are in a much lower condition than when he first became an inmate as I am still struggling to maintain my children, 6 in number and helpless.* Once more the Board of the hospital responded positively to Margaret, and Thomas J. was kept permanently as an inmate.[70]

Margaret moved house again, this time to Nixon Street near the North Wall, to an enclave of low-value cottages on an infill site close to the Royal Canal, not far from the sea. Jacinta Prunty reminds us that many cottages could be better described as shelters, which in some cases were scarcely more than nine or ten feet wide. *Separate closet accommodation was non-existent, but there was usually a closet and a single tap located in the general vicinity of the housing for use by all and sundry.*[71] It was under these foul conditions that Margaret's youngest baby girl succumbed to the strain and died in May 1853 aged two-and-a-half years.

---

70   Letters of Saint Patrick's Hospital relating to Thomas transcribed from oral recordings (author's records)
71   Prunty, 2002; p. 189.

Margaret's adjustment to the squalor of Nixon Street was all the more difficult considering the degree of comfort she had enjoyed during her life. She also had to contend with a society which would have regarded her as an outsider and a *snob*. Hopes for her husband's recovery were not realised. Thomas J.'s pleas to be released fell on deaf ears. Things got worse. A report written by the Medical Officer in December 1854 contains the following scary statement: *We certify that Mr Keogh still continues diseased in mind. He is subject to paroxysms of excitement at which times it is unsafe to approach him.*[72]

I have no window into the details of the dark years of Margaret's life that followed her move to Nixon Street. Undoubtedly, it was a full-time job to ensure the survival of her family. To understand something of the settings they were living in, I scrutinised James Mahony's view of Dublin, which hangs in the National Gallery.[73] The large painting was created in 1854 from the spire of Saint George's Church and shows the environs of Dublin at that time. The family cottage lay between the Royal Canal and the railway terminus at Amiens Street. There was plenty of open space close to Nixon Street in a growing industrialised area surrounding the canal; the seashore was close by. Visions came to me of five little figures running about Margaret, picking up driftwood along the windswept shore in Dublin Bay to keep themselves warm during the winter months around a hearth where she schooled them as best she could.

There is reason to believe that Thomas J. began to accept his fate. In time his general conduct was described as *systematic and correct*. He continued writing and a note from Dr. Croker in September 1862 mentions that: *The letter Mr Keogh has written to the Board is the only sensible one I have seen. I have no doubt that he still labours under mental disease and is not a fit case for removal.*[74] Thomas J. had to spend another twenty-six years in the hospital before his release through death.

Margaret survived the passing of her youngest daughter by almost two decades. At this time—and to her great credit—she had reared her remaining children. It was more difficult to heal the deep wounds of a dysfunctional family. Even in this she had much success. However, she appears to have remained in a very low state. The location of her death, in October 1872, is recorded as: North Union Workhouse. In Irish lore the workhouse was shunned by every self-respecting person: it was the leper colony of the destitute.

It is likely that the family got some help from George McGuinness, one of her brothers. He was the uncle to whom John M. wrote home during the Civil War in 1862. The fact that James Keogh named one of his children after him confirms gratitude. Unfortunately, there were limits to what George could do, as he had to cater for his own family.

It seems that Margaret's children also obtained what indirect help they could from the wider family which allowed her son James to steadily gain a foothold within the business community and regain the family's middle-class credentials. He entered Bergin and Keogh's business in Sackville Street. A Joseph Keogh participated in the new company and may have been responsible for introducing James to the tailoring trade. This is a good

---

72 Note from Board Minutes Saint Patrick's Hospital; 1854.
73 *Dublin from the Spire of Saint George's Church*: Watercolour by James Mahony; 1854.
74 Notes from the Board Minutes Saint Patrick's Hospital; 1859 and 1862.

example of how a family with a particular social standing and rank recovered its position in society despite the lack of social insurance, after their world temporarily collapsed.

James, as we have seen, emerged extraordinarily successful, at least in financial terms, through the family enterprise. The three-storey detached house in Dartmouth Road where he lived in the late 1870s provided a stark contrast to life at Nixon Street. He probably chose this south-Dublin residence to distance himself once and for all from his frightful boyhood memories. His charitable demeanour undoubtedly owed its origins to his bleak experiences. But it must have appeared to him that he was destined for continual setbacks when his happiness was dashed by the death of his first wife Mary Jane and his son. Nonetheless, his fortunes improved once more after he met Mary Walsh.

Margaret's son John M. left Ireland as a young man. His American descendants claim that his family was in the boot-making business and was deported for subversive activities. If so, he is unlikely to have been sent directly to the US because, from the British point of view, it was a foreign country. His life in America could be described as a success; he came through the American Civil War relatively unscathed and survived to marry Alice Flynn with whom he begot his own family.

The girls never married and seem to have been side-tracked by society. If their plight was a result of the stigma of a diseased father and a destitute mother, then this was a double tragedy. A man could be more discrete because he dealt with the paperwork, including all records and could, therefore, hold a secret from his fiancé or let her know only what he felt was necessary. James' sister Alice passed away in 1910. Another sister, Jane, died at Beechwood Road in 1917. My father had a fleeting memory of her—when he was five—tying up his protective boot-leggings. This was the closest memory he had of the family of Thomas J. and Margaret.

The house at Beechwood Road is my nearest link to my great-great-grandparents. It was here that I looked back from the rear seats of our Morris Minor and waved to my grandfather for the last time as he peered down from the window of his sick-room. How much did he know of these things? Though I had little inkling of the dark secret that the house contained when I began my quest, I sensed deep mystery within the magical aura it exuded. This sensing provoked me to begin a search that lasted decades. But what did I achieve for all my effort? I made little progress towards my goal of tracing my ancestors to their tribal homeland or original farmland in Leinster. Yet, I did break through the ring of censorship and wall of isolation surrounding my great-great-grandparents. Perhaps, in a strange way, my obsession to uncover the history of the family was driven in response to a muffled cry seeping through the silence and the unsaid from generation to generation. Of one thing I am certain: because of my intervention, prompted by the residual ancestral forces I sensed in Beechwood Road, their story and their voices are now heard after more than one-and-a-half centuries of forced silence.

II. A Forgotten Society

Anthropology of an Urban Tribe

I had a surprising breakthrough in clarifying the identity of my father's people when a good friend of mine persuaded me to read James Joyce's *The Dead*.[75] I found it conveyed an uncanny familiarity. I related immediately and intimately to the Christmas-time party scene. The parties that were held in my grandfather's house at Beechwood Road may have been less dramatic affairs, but the sensations evoked by Joyce captured the feelings generated at these gatherings. I was so taken by the experience that I read the entire *Dubliners*. Here, at last, was a portrayal of Irish culture which I knew and was part of.

As a young man Bartholomew Keogh created a business which was located in Nassau Street in Dublin. However, it failed. Details are sketchy, but during this unsettled period he went to London and was also involved as a commercial traveller, journeying the length and breadth of Ireland. In time he joined Brown Thomas' Department store in Grafton Street. Our narrative now enters the precise period of Joyce's *Dubliners*. In fact, Bartholomew and Joyce were of a similar vintage, Joyce being some six years his junior.

It is stated that Joyce's writings accurately portray life in Dublin at the turn of the nineteenth and twentieth centuries. Indeed, it is said that they personify the city itself. The writer published the first story of *Dubliners* in 1904 and completed the last, *The Dead*, in 1907. He dedicated one of the pieces—*Ivy Day in the Committee Room*—to the political fallout after the defeat and death of Charles Stewart Parnell. The story marked the anniversary of his passing on 6th October 1891. Parnell continued to incite controversy long after his death, partly because support for him involved the question of the morality of divorce. The Catholic Church stood firmly against him—thus Joyce's reference to *fawning priests* in his accompanying poem. Nonetheless, not all Catholics agreed that Parnell the politician should be ostracised for what he had done in his personal life. I had a strong feeling that the Keogh family generally took this view, though certainty is ruled out. As illustrated in another of Joyce's short stories called *The Sisters*, Dubliners could be very circumspect about topics in their conversation, particularly when they referred to controversial issues, and our family was no exception. In the piece in question old Cotter left his adult listeners to extract the underlying meaning from his unfinished oblique sentences.

Joyce recognised that there were deep hierarchical rifts dividing the urban classes. This comes through in *An Encounter* in *Dubliners* when Father Butler catches clumsy Leo Dillon with a copy of *The Halfpenny Marvel*, a Wild West comic, in class. *'I'm surprised'* said Father Butler, *'at boys like you, educated, reading such stuff. I could understand it if you were ... National School boys.'* State schools catered for children of the working-classes. The parents of the children who went to the paid Catholic colleges like Clongowes and Belvedere were the better-off. Joyce attended both. On an intermediate level were the Christian Brother establishments which mixed the classes. Joyce had to go to one of these schools on North Richmond Street when the family fortunes slipped away because of his father's drinking habits.

75　Quotes from *Dubliners* originate from: Johnson, 2000.

In the short story *A Mother*, Mr Kearney—on special Sundays—went with his family to the Pro-cathedral. After Mass, a little crowd of people, many of whom were nationalist musical friends, would assemble at the corner of Cathedral Street. The references to religion by way of their attendance at Mass and the nationalistic flavour of their politics illustrate much about the social stratum that was central to Joyce's writings. The musical dimension of the life of at least some Dubliners, which finds echoes throughout his work, provides further insights into this class.

In the society that Joyce was describing we see repeated signs of aspirations to be part of a sophisticated cosmopolitan culture. These aspirations are clear in their attitudes towards the Irish language. When James Keogh, my great-grandfather, was in America to collect money—ostensibly for Parnell—his son Bartholomew, then four years old, remained in Ireland. He stayed with minders in a large house in the country village of Santry outside Dublin. A lasting memory of this experience was a particular woman who looked after him and talked Irish. She used the expression *suigh síos*, which means *sit down*, though Bartholomew thought she was saying *shi-shi*. My grandfather mentioned his encounter with this Irish-speaker as a curiosity and the comment highlights the fact that Dubliners might have been from a nationalistic background but not necessarily Irish-speaking.

The linguistic distance between many Dubliners and live Irish comes through in James Joyce's *A Mother*, when Mrs Kearney purchased a blush-pink charmeuse in prestigious Brown Thomas' for her daughter's singing event. She also brought a teacher to her house to give her lessons in the Irish and did so more to elevate her in a society that had adopted an Irish revival, rather than out of a love for the language.

In Joyce's *The Dead*, Miss Ivors asks Gabriel: '... *haven't you your own language to keep in touch with ...?*' '*Well ...*' he answers: '... *if it comes to that, you know, Irish is not my language.*' Gabriel is more interested in his literary column, books, travel and speech-making in English. Miss Ivors subsequently accuses him of being a *West Briton*. Later she uses the Irish phrase '*Beannacht libh*' to bid adieu to Gabriel's wife before exiting from the party. She would not stay for supper. Miss Ivors, who dressed conservatively, carried a large Irish emblem in the form of a brooch. She represented the class of Dubliner that would be insulted by any demeaning of Irish, a touchiness that pervaded segments of society at the time Joyce wrote, and still does today.

It was recorded in an exhibition in Saint Enda's—Patrick Pearse's school—that James Joyce, three years younger than Patrick ... *attended Pearse's Irish classes at University College. He left after a few lessons, deploring Pearse's attempts to elevate the Irish language by running down English.* Eoin MacNeill, Irish historian and patriot, also took issue with Pearse over the language: *I cannot at all agree with you ...* he stated ... *that any course of instruction at school will produce really Irish-speaking children, unless there is a domestic foundation, or its equivalent, to build upon. I fear you have in your mind some imaginary state of things which does not exist. Nothing but life can teach a whole live language ... You cannot live life in a day-school. You cannot have passions, emotions, cares and endearments ... Your school-taught language will never be more than a simulacrum of the living thing. The contrary notion is a fatal delusion ...* [76]

---

76   Dudley Edwards, 1990; p. 114.

Such admissions were unacceptable to the more extremist visionaries of the new state; they were unacceptable to Eamon de Valera and his ilk, who were determining what they considered to constitute the genuine definition of Irishness. Gearóid Ó Tuathaigh in his contribution to *de Valera's Irelands*, states that the Irish leaders saw the revival of the Irish language as imperative. Its loss was equated with ... *part of the shame of being conquered, of experiencing defeat, dispossession, humiliation and general impoverishment.*[77] The Irish language revival became the cornerstone of de Valera's project of cultural decolonisation. However, in this respect, the reality was far removed from the dream.

Ireland was placed geographically along the Anglo-American highway of communications and entertainment, increasingly the main artery of a global technology-grid whose dominant language was English. *Ó Tuathaigh*, who made these observations, goes on to suggest that by the turn of the nineteenth and twentieth centuries the majority of the Irish were speaking English and many were content with ... *nothing too burdensome, nothing beyond a symbolic recognition of the ancestral language and a care to ensure its presence in the ceremony and ritual of occasions of state ...*[78] English was also the language of the vast majority of the Irish diaspora and of the countries in which most emigrants settled.

The Irish urban-classes had adopted and used English for their own practical purposes and to their own way of thinking, even if it meant discarding the rulebook. Joyce was conscious of this reality and made a unique contribution to English literature; indeed he changed the English language to suit a way of thinking that was aligned to the Dublin Gael, who daily debased its strict form of usage and wielded it irreverently as a plastic instrument of expression. He articulated, in literature, the essence of the idiom of a people in Ireland whose native language had been discarded under foreign pressure and domination. Declan Kiberd reminds us that ... *Irish was for him* [Joyce] *no longer a feasible literary medium, but a means whereby his people had managed to reshape English, to a point where their artists could know the exhilaration of feeling estranged from all official languages.*[79] By *his people* is normally understood to mean the people of Ireland; but in Joyce's view it is his Dublin community.

The most forthright recognition of the Catholic business and professional class is found in the retreat scene in *Grace* in *Dubliners*. Joyce tells us: *The transept of the Jesuit Church in Gardiner Street was almost full; and still at every moment gentlemen entered from the side-door and, directed by the lay-brother, walked on tiptoe along the aisles until they found seating accommodation.* During his homily, Father Purdon delivered a special sermon - *It was a text for business men and professional men.* In this one phrase Joyce identifies a class of people not often recognised in Ireland; the fact that there were sufficient men to fill Gardiner Street Church is a statement about the strength of this social group at the beginning of the twentieth century.

When reading *Dubliners* it is clear that the city's middle-class Catholic identity was large and included a substantial Gaelic element. The outstanding marks of the class were found in the main activities carried out by its working male population. These activities

---

77   *Ó Tuathaigh*, 2003; p. 170.
78   *Ibid*; p. 175.
79   Kiberd, 1996; p. 331.

were strongly related to business undertakings and the professions. In *Dubliners* Joyce refers to drapers, commercial travellers, journalists, tea merchants, agents, pawnbrokers, councillors, corn factors, moneylenders, men of civil and municipal services and many others. Not all, of course, were successful. The shopkeeper was a type of safety net amongst the lowest ranks of the class. In Joyce's *Grace*, Mr Fogarty was a modest grocer on Glasnevin Road but had failed in business.

James Joyce himself exhibited the memes of the Catholic middle-class or petty bourgeois society in Dublin. In fact the urban background on every side of his family insulated him, almost totally, from the rural experience in Ireland, with which he had no empathy. This was not to go unchallenged in his psyche. It is not hard to see that Gabriel in *The Dead* in *Dubliners* was Joyce in disguise and Gabriel's wife Gretta displays an almost perfect parallel with Joyce's wife, Nora Barnacle, who came from Galway city. Gabriel consciously or half-consciously begins to accept rural Ireland, which he has hitherto scorned because of its associations with ignorance and backwardness. Towards the end of the story the country dimension is presented in a different light and Richard Ellmann in his biography *James Joyce* summarises it thus: ... *Gabriel is conceding and relinquishing a good deal... He is surrendering, for an agonising moment ... his sense of the importance of civilized thinking, of continental tastes, of all those tepid but nice distinctions on which he has prided himself. The bubble of his self-possession is pricked; he no longer possesses himself, and not to possess oneself is in a way a kind of death.*[80]

But the examples Joyce uses to illustrate rural life are inappropriate. Nora Barnacle had a previous sweetheart, Michael Bodkin. Michael died young and was buried in Galway city, Nora's birthplace. In *The Dead* Gretta's previous boyfriend was Michael Furey who died for love of her and was buried in the country village of Oughterard in County Galway. Joyce used Nora—or Gretta—as representatives of rural authenticity, but in doing so had missed the reality: his wife was not a country lass; she was city-born and her father was a baker. She belonged to the equivalent class in Galway as he did in Dublin. This social stratum was invisible, even to Joyce who belonged to it and married into it. His Dublin-based attitude of superiority blinded him to the subtleties of the urban reality of smaller cities in Ireland. His myopia confirmed that I was not alone in being confused about the true extent and nature of the identity to which I belonged.

It is without question that Joyce expressed the mind of the native Catholic business and professional class of Dublin, which he understood, for he was a part of it and was its primary representative in terms of written artistic expression. All his observations about the city—rich or poor—or about Ireland are from this perspective. Joyce is the great legacy that the native urban middle-class has left to the world, yet it has never occurred to them. Joyce has been usurped, yet his own are totally unaware. The reason is now outstandingly clear and can be traced back to a lack of acknowledged identity which the class suffered from; in the early twentieth century it appeared to be a non-culture.

Joyce was unable to accept the artificial definition of Irishness being created at this time because it was not inclusive. It excluded him. In the charged emotional atmosphere of the embryonic state, awash under a tsunami of Celtic verbiage from Pearse and Yeats

---

80   Ellmann, 1983; p. 249.

and Gregory and other so-called patriotic Irish writers, there was no chance for Joyce. Besides, social architects like Eamonn de Valera were having a field-day. Joyce refused to join the growing movement. He stepped beyond the boundaries laid down by those who were trying to define Ireland in the lead-up to and in the aftermath of independence. Unlike de Valera, he avoided nursing regressive dreams in the past. He left behind a narrow nationalistic definition of identity to embrace a universal one, yet he expressed his revelation in the familiar terms of the ordinary middle-class Dubliner.

I began to understand an aspect of Joyce's life that seems to have escaped other writers, his critics and even Joyce himself. The fundamental cause of his self-imposed sadistic exile was his inability to see—at least when he was in Dublin—that he was part of a real identity. He sensed, in extreme form, the emptiness resulting from a lack of belonging. He took his search to its logical conclusion. Without possessing a clearly defined base, he decided to extract himself from his surrounds and immerse himself in a distinct culture where he could best pursue the self-understanding that his own people had lost. He lived out his frustration through an extraordinary lifestyle in which he struggled to make sense of his cultural isolation through his unique and original writings.

In England, the historic British versus Irish antipathy remained and would cloud his analysis. He attempted, therefore, to make a clean break from all cultural attributes associated with Ireland. Declan Kiberd remarks that Joyce cut himself adrift in continental Europe and became a nomad writer, tangential to the cultural life of both Ireland and England.[81] He rejected, with varying success, Irish nationalism, the Irish language, the Irish literary movement, Catholicism, home politics, English officialdom, Irish rural roots and even Irish friendship. In reality he was not as much rejecting as distancing himself from most of these influences to bring them constantly into sharp focus and clarify them. He possessed a homeless mind, yet didn't seek comfort in his quest. Perhaps he went too far. Jeri Johnson admits that in some ways he is unduly naturalistic and in her introduction to *Dubliners* quotes the text of an unsigned review: ... *the power of genius is in every line, but it is a genius that, blind to the blue of the heavens, seeks inspiration in the hell of despair.*[82] Alternatively, his exile can be described in terms of a metaphor: a musician tensing violin strings to make melodious sounds; for without tension there is no music. Were it not for his pain of loss, there may have been no triumph of his universal art.

Others, and I include myself here, have felt cultural remoteness from Ireland because my particular identity was not given recognition. Unfortunately, historians have been woefully negligent in their treatment of the indigenous urban middle-class. It seems as if the academic world has accepted it as being a non-culture or a social grouping that does not merit historical analysis or anthropological study.

The indigenous middle-class Dubliners stood uncomfortably between the would-be *true Irish-Irelanders* on one side, who saw them as *West Britons,* and a British public on the other, who saw them as a bog trotters. Their class was isolated from other classes. Edith Somerville observed that it had ... *practically no normal points of contact with any*

---

81 Kiberd, 1996; p. 327.
82 Johnson, 2000; p. ix.

other class, either above or below it.[83] Being unsure of who they were, they just got on with making a living. Meanwhile, the sculptors of the new Irish State ignored them as a unique identity because, in their view, representatives of *real* Ireland were restricted to rural entities, especially Irish speakers in the West of Ireland.[84] This attitude, held by many Irish Renaissance followers and young republicans, blinded them to the actuality of life in all towns and cities in Ireland. In response, Gaelic urbanites who were heavily involved in the national revival and revolutionary movements acquiesced to a handful of loud voices, lived in denial of who they really were and embraced the fiction that was in vogue. If the indigenous urbanites had to be considered in the new vision of Ireland, then, the rural authenticity that was being lauded would be weakened and, by implication, many other entities would have to be accommodated. This was inconvenient to the nationalist leadership because it would change, fundamentally, the social ideal that was being nurtured.

As a direct consequence, those who were inventing the new state identity tried desperately to make themselves part of it, even though they existed outside their own fiction. Eamonn de Valera was an example *par excellence* of this attitude. He had become part of the urban middle-class himself but lauded the virtues of the simple peasant life, yet didn't live in a cottage with country-folk. He went to Blackrock College, which mimicked much of the English Public Schools' system. He lived in an urban setting and, towards the end of his life, chose as his abode a large mansion near Blackrock—one that the English upper middle-class in Ireland would have been comfortable with. Patrick Pearse was similar. His school at Saint Enda's enjoyed the facilities of the *Big House* and the luxurious surrounds of an estate that was created by the British in Ireland. I do not begrudge de Valera his abode or suggest that Pearse should have created a hedge school. However, they were fabricating a myth that they didn't live by. How, then, could de Valera expect that the urban middle-class would be inclined to follow him or share his wider vision?

De Valera's vision for Ireland conjured up a society with a sturdy rural ethos; it desired industrialisation without urbanisation; it lauded "authentic" living in the frugal comfort of cosy homesteads close to nature, especially relevant in Ireland with an emotive history of land dispossession. As such, de Valera and his cohorts failed to recognise or give recognition to Irish social complexities in the formative years of the state. They chose to ignore the indigenous urban reality at the beginning of Irish independence.

83   Kiberd, 1996; p. 71.
84   O'Sullivan, 2008; p. 175.

Radically Inclusive

It was becoming ever-clearer to me why, when I was young, I didn't feel that I was fully Irish. I had difficulties with the particular concept of "Irishness" that was being promoted. In the mid-twentieth century, Irishness was associated with speaking Gaelic, or at least lauding its virtues. My immediate family never spoke Irish; to us it was as foreign a language as Latin. In the eyes of some, this is heresy. We may have used the odd word here and there and participated in compulsory classes in school, but the full weight of officialdom could do little or nothing to change the basic reality: Gaelic was not a living language in my family on any side and, as far as I can tell by the records, we didn't use it as a means of communication for generations.

Irishness, in the 1950s, was closely linked with the land, even though the bond may have been through tenant-leasing or poor holdings. We owned no land and had little or no association with it, except through peat-cutting lots in the Dublin Mountains during the Second World War.

Irishness, in the '50s, was associated with participation in GAA games. I had never attended a match in Croke Park. I played rugby, followed rugby internationals, played almost no football and, when I was in early secondary school, some cricket. These were regarded as foreign sports. The GAA's ban on its members playing such games built an enormous divide within society. I was on the wrong side of the partition, which implied disloyalty. All this accentuated the differences between us and country people; our accent exacerbated these differences. Yet I knew that it was unjust to equate us as *traitors to the cause*.

Cultural definitions of Irishness in the young state may have been attempts to right the wrongs of the past. An alternative excuse is that the development of an Irish myth was a necessary evil for cohesion within the embryonic state. However, the fundamental principle of truth was violated and truth can never be compromised without backfiring. Irish culture, in the lead-up to and at the beginning of independence, was being defined by the few in power. It was being forged by men and women who were not seeking the truth. Unfortunately, falsehood exacerbated internal and external cultural tensions, as exemplified in the nationalist versus unionist divide.

There is a stark lesson here, to be learnt by leaders and social architects everywhere who are trying to define cultural attributes of their people. If a segment of society is not recognised, its identity may become invisible but, sooner or later this will lead to underlying tensions that will disrupt the artificial social order: at least, the overarching cultural fiction will not last. Leaders, therefore, are well advised to take cognisance of the travesties created by former social designers. Had a ruthlessly honest approach been taken by politicians of the young state, much suffering and pain might have been prevented and much bloodshed avoided, particularly in Northern Ireland.

To be authentic, the national culture must embrace all its disparate parts, including foreign ones. In his attempt to be honest James Joyce took the view that the people clearly needed to be radically inclusive. No single segment in Ireland had a prerogative on Irishness. He recognised the complexity of divisions contained in the Dublin urban reality at the beginning of the twentieth century just before the birth of the Irish State and knew that all these component parts had to be accepted on an equal footing. Quoting from Joyce, Declan Kiberd elucidates: ... *to exclude from the present nation all who are descended from foreign families would be impossible.* [End quote] Furthermore ... *a unitary racial nationality could never be more than "a convenient fiction", and that fiction would only be convenient if it could evolve a form hospitable to the many strands that made up Irish experience.*[85]

I have learnt a lot from the work of Kiberd and admire much of what he has written. However, in his complex review of how independent Ireland was *invented* I find a major blind-spot when he deals with the indigenous middle-class. His stance is not unique and has played a part in sidelining the urban Gael as a social group. The lack of historical analysis by the academic world has allowed Kiberd to treat the class as a caricature. A hostile attitude bubbles to the surface every time the indigenous urbanites appear in his work. Linked phrases like *middle-class vulgarity*; *petty gradations of snobbery*; *shabby-genteel city life*; *hard-nosed bourgeois materialism*; *pretentions to respectability*; *the new comprador middle-class*; *this philistine group* ... are never far off.

What seems to bug him is the audacity of pretentious and ignorant country people who flood the city in the lead-up to independence and then become the elite of the new state. He claims that members of the nationalist movement for Irish political and cultural freedom ... *were to a man the urbanized descendants of country people* ...[86] It is true that all urban people can trace themselves back to the country at some stage. But the urban elites who seized the positions of power, according to Kiberd ... *tended to be dominated by first- or second-generation immigrants from rural areas.* He goes on to demean the native middle-class of Ireland which, he claims ... *had not yet fully emerged as a social formation* ....[87] This is incorrect. The class developed much earlier as I have already shown: Thomas J. Keogh was part of this class as far back as the 1830s. Although until recently there was uncertainty about the real point in time at which it began to emerge, this happened long before the eve of independence. Without doubt, the class was augmented through a continual influx of country people through time, right down to the present day. But to assume that a particular influx of country people produced a disproportionate influence on the class itself on the eve of independence is highly questionable.

Kiberd suggests that at the beginning of the twentieth century, Dublin was a periphery-dominated-centre. In other words, the capital was overrun by a pushy, snobby, philistine and barbaric would-be *bourgeoisie* who had not yet washed the stains of turf from their hands. In their attempts to trot after nobility they claimed to be descendants of the Gaelic aristocracy. *They falsely vilify the rhythms of a city life which they have never entirely mastered, and correspondingly sentimentalize the rhythms of a country life which they have not yet, in their minds, completely abandoned.*[88] To press home his point, Kiberd provides verbal illustrations of a flock of sheep being herded across Carlisle Bridge into Sackville Street and thistledown blowing along the fashionable arcade of Grafton Street to show that the city is never far from the dung heap. Those who carried manure into its streets on their brogues didn't dream of a free Ireland but wanted to don collars and ties

---

85   Kiberd, 1996; p. 337.
86   *Ibid*; p. 481.
87   *Ibid*; pp. 484, 491.
88   *Ibid*; p. 485.

... replace their former British overlords and take over their privileges.[89] Besides ... *the vast majority of them never learnt how to produce, only how to consume.* Even when they did attempt to *do* something Kiberd puts them down as *shoddy native manufacturers* who worked behind protective tariff barriers.[90]

In his overall generalisations he is including my father, who came from a family of native manufacturers whose roots in the industry sprouted well before independence and ended well after the tariff barriers were gone. In other words, they survived and produced a quality of goods that didn't depend on protection alone. They produced shirts for a Victorian society and ties and bibs for generations of Dubliners who were willing to buy them, whether or not they were exposed to competition from textiles coming from the UK or the Far East.

The nationalist middle-class was far more complex than Kiberd makes out. Besides, all those who took part in the Rising and subsequent independence movement, were not all first- or second-generation immigrants from the country. The Keoghs of Ranelagh serve to underpin the fact. Another example is the family of youthful Patrick Pearse who belonged to this class. His father, James, inhabited a low rung on the ladder. James Pearse's background serves to illustrate how varied and dynamic the class identity really was. He was not even Irish; he was born into an artisan family in Bloomsbury in 1839. In the second half of the nineteenth century, a new church-building boom accompanied the accelerating prosperity of Catholics in Irish cities. This gave rise to a need for craftsmanship in marble, stone, wood and wrought iron. Ireland offered exciting possibilities for men with skills in such crafts, even for many beyond her shores. These possibilities came to the notice of James Pearse and stimulated him to emigrate from England.

Largely self-educated, James succeeded as a renowned stone-carver in Ireland, winning a first-class award for his work in the 1882 Dublin Exhibition. James, who had an interest in religion but an ambivalent faith, converted to Catholicism about 1870. After the death of his first wife he met and married Margaret Brady, a girl who was much younger than he and whose family had originated in County Meath. Several of her ancestors were killed during the 1798 rising and her grandfather, who could speak only Irish, was forced to move to Dublin in 1848 during the famine.

Margaret was a staunch Catholic and, up to the time of her marriage, lived with her father, a *coal factor*, in one of three of his small cottages off the North Strand. After their marriage the couple lived *over the shop* in James' premises at Great Brunswick Street, present day Pearse Street. He was part of an English community of craftsmen that grew up in the area. The couple had four children, including Margaret, Patrick, Willie and Mary Brigid.[91] The boys were sent to the Christian Brothers' in nearby Westland Row. Because they mixed the classes, these establishments were useful gateways through which a small number of youths, like the Pearses, could move up the social ladder and enter college to become doctors, engineers, secondary teachers and the like.

---

89   *Ibid*; p. 517.
90   *Ibid*; pp. 551, 552.
91   Dudley Edwards, 1990; pp. 2, ff.

Patrick's formative years were spent in this lower middle-class area near Dublin docks, at one remove from the poverty of the dark inner city tenements. His parents were from very different backgrounds, though both of their families had experienced poverty. It cannot be denied that Patrick's mother had aspirations to gentility, which were realised when James' business became so successful that the family was able to move to a comfortable house in Newbridge Avenue, Sandymount. Though social aspirations may have been more a characteristic of the female members of the Pearse household than the male, Patrick himself *was not innocent of all snobbery*.[92] He developed expensive tastes, a desire for gracious living and after his father's death moved the family to better and better houses with domestic servants, ending up in Sallymount Avenue. All this is a far remove from the caricature of the new elites as clodhoppers from the country.

The complexity of the middle-class is further illustrated through the life of James Joyce. Though not participants in the independence movement, his family story is the reverse of the Pearses. John Joyce, father of the writer, moved downmarket around the city because of the weakness he had for drink. Joyce's ancestors, as far back as his great-great-grandfather, came from the equivalent strata of society in Cork city where they had property. They were yet another middle-class family, in another major Irish city, that could trace their urban origins to the beginning of the nineteenth century, if not earlier. The Joyces—who came from the completely Hibernicised *tribes of Galway*—were business people, if somewhat unsuccessful. The writer's grandfather married into the O'Connells, a prosperous Gaelic Catholic draper and tailor family in the city. As a result he was able to maintain his wife and child in the fashionable suburb of Sunday's Well. But, they moved to Dublin about 1875 when the mother of John Joyce decided to take her son away from what she considered dangerous Fenian influences and used family connections to find him work in his adopted city. John participated, for a time, in a joint venture in the Dublin and Chapelizod Distilling Company; later he became a Collector of Rates. He married into the Murrays of Rathgar, who were agents for wines and spirits and hailed from Longford.

The Joyces, the O'Connells, the Keoghs of Ranelagh, the McGuinnesses, were all native middle-class families who could trace their city roots back to a time before the great famine. The families into which they married like the Murrays, the Walshes and the Delaneys had tenacious urban backgrounds. The McDowells and Morans of Belfast were of the same identity. The McDowells and the Pearses were hybrids with English and Gaelic roots. These families represented the tip of the iceberg. By now I was certain that the indigenous urban middle-class was a large and long-established identity, dispersed across the cities and towns of Ireland and occupying an assortment of niches in business and the professions.

Young men like Patrick Pearse and Gerald Keogh, who were at least third-generation urbanites, gave their lives to the nationalist cause in 1916. They may have acquiesced to the notion that the western seaboard was the authentic centre of Irish culture, because they had been persuaded to recognise it as the location where the inhabitants were closest to the pure descendents of the Celtic people of their dreams and visions. Besides, when it came to demanding their rights, as I already mentioned, the Dublin communities were more likely to achieve the reforms they wanted through agitation at the national level using rural

---

92 *Ibid*; pp. 112, 113.

grievances, than through direct pleas for limited urban improvements. Their reverence for things rural had nothing to do with the interval between their family's exodus from the country and their emergence in the city. But their support for rural issues did contribute to dimming the visibility of their real identity.

However, it must also be acknowledged that Kiberd is correct when he indicates that many rebellious Irishmen were born in the country. Men like Thomas MacDonagh and Michael Collins came into the city and, finding there a well developed infrastructure of friends and allies, joined them and were welcomed by them. But these recent migrants were not the mainstay of the indigenous middle-class.

Why were the native urbanites so vilified and maligned? There are several reasons. Part of the answer lies in the widely-held concept of an emerging gombeen middle-class in the twentieth century. Such a view developed amongst writers like Somerville and Ross, who represented the dying stars of the Protestant land-ascendency period, and W. B. Yeats, a representative of a minor landowning class and also a Protestant. Kiberd points out that Yeats ... *liked to think of himself as the scourge of this philistine group.*[93]

It needs little analysis to show that in the lead-up to independence, the New English were not happy with a situation in which they were descending, to a social level that the nationalists were rising towards. The indigenous Irish had established themselves in numbers alongside middle-class Protestants. In short, the old war between the Protestant Ascendency and the Gael had developed an urban front. The unthinkable was now in sight; the Gael had successfully infiltrated the urban realm and began to resist their enemies on an equal footing. It was inevitable that sooner or later, they would sit next to the New English in the driving seat or worse, might take hold of the steering wheel itself. All manner of schemes were thrown up by the Anglo-Irish to frustrate these ever-more-powerful Gaelic elements and included the denigration of character; ridicule on the basis of their social manners; corralling the better positions against them; coercion; and, finally, when all these methods were shown to be inadequate, they attempted to usurp the Irish Renaissance in order to dominate and mould the natives to their own way of thinking and in their own interests. In the long-run they were unsuccessful.

In addition to the likes of Somerville, Ross and Yeats—Brendan Behan and Sean O'Casey at the opposite ends of the social spectrum, as might be expected, despised the middle-income factions, but for very different reasons. There are other critics—the intelligentsia—who consider themselves too enlightened to be classed amongst the *bourgeoisie*, but who have little to distinguish them from the social group they criticise, except their criticisms. James Joyce, too, could appear to rank amongst those that inherently denigrated the middle-class within Dublin. But he was not so much demeaning the social order to which he belonged: he was a keen observer who made no attempt to hide its faults and hypocrisies and reveal uncomfortable truths, because he wanted to understand its real identity. It is relatively easy to extract quotes that portray his views as an outright onslaught on the class, rather than a highly critical scrutiny.

---

93 Kiberd, 1996; pp. 101, 483.

The native urban *bourgeoisie* has been demeaned by most social groups around it and has been undefended by its own. This provides an understandable—but not excusable—reason for a type of group-think which accepts widely expressed views as facts. A logical follow-on is to believe that, as the class is so bereft of virtue; so shallow; so full of pretentiousness, it does not merit further analysis. Reluctance to give due recognition to the native urban middle-class allows it to be portrayed as a social caricature and not to be taken seriously. But the victim is not so much the class, as Irish history itself; as we shall see.

The Merchant and the King

I had made much progress in understanding the society to which the Keoghs of Ranelagh and their ancestors belonged. But uncovering the details of the family's route out of the past in the years prior to Thomas J. and Thomas the Elder was like searching for old footprints on a sandy beach. Without a series of miraculous finds, I would never succeed in joining my ancestors, in an unbroken chain of forefathers, back to their Gaelic homeland.

On the other hand, there were tantalising possibilities of discovering associations between similar first-names in the sources that might help me forge links with previous generations. For example, the Bartholomew Keogh, who lived in Park Street in 1845, might have been a relative of my grandfather who had the same name. Also, the Thomas Keogh, who resided at Holles Street and disappeared at the time that Thomas J. first appeared in the directories, might be Thomas the Elder himself. But, this approach required proof of relationship and demanded a genealogical study of several families at the same time.

In future, it might be possible to undertake a comprehensive survey of a particular surname using all existing records like births, baptisms, marriages, deaths, grave records, wills, newspaper notices, correspondences and many other sources, and begin to establish links between different families and sequential generations. It may also be possible to determine associations of given first-names with certain time-periods, particular families and identifiable locations. Unfortunately, converting a vision of this sort into reality is only possible on a very limited scale today.

I had no evidence that any individual mentioned in the archives was associated with our family and little expectation of obtaining proof, unless I was very lucky. I was wasting time speculating. But, inevitably, I would return to the records, focus on someone who captured my attention and stubbornly waste more time trying to forge connections. My hope was akin to that of a compulsive gambler. When I finally acknowledged the uselessness of these exercises I relinquished the expectation of ever being able to re-create a detailed family tree of the generations before Thomas the Elder.

But I refused to abandon my main quest to—somehow—link my family to its Gaelic roots. I then found myself repeatedly facing the same question: When did the Gaelic middle-class first arise in Dublin? Knowing when native urbanisation was initiated and how the class grew might help me pinpoint when the ancestors of the Keoghs of Ranelagh came into the city. And knowing when they urbanised might also provide indications about the circumstances surrounding their rural homeland exodus if this took place at the same time.

I mentioned that in the short story *Grace,* in *Dubliners,* James Joyce observes that the Jesuit Church in Gardiner Street was almost full of gentlemen who were about to attend a retreat. In this single phrase he tells us something valuable concerning the city's Catholic middle-class during the early twentieth century. They were *not* newcomers. They were a long-established social group and must have taken time to grow and develop into the positions they held in the early 1900s. These men represented a mixture of Gaelic and Old English entities.

Christopher Morash in *A History of the Irish Theatre* noted that in the lead-up to emancipation in 1829, the *first wave* of newly confident Catholic elites, which was increasingly detaching itself from Gaelic culture, began moving steadily into areas that were the exclusive preserve of Protestant gentlemen.[94] But, Morash has not traced the indigenous middle-class to its beginnings. Most observers also fail to define the point at which the Gaels first joined this class in the city. It was exceedingly difficult to come up with hard data on which to answer the question. Unfortunately, the majority of academic studies that deal with the history of urban populations in Ireland tend to lump Catholics into a single category rather than examine the Gaelic or Old English segments separately.

In the absence of adequate quantitative data to pin down the beginning of Gaelic urbanisation, I began extracting information from the Dublin directories. I counted the numbers of recorded merchants and traders with native surnames for selected years between the second quarter of the eighteenth century—when these records began—and the early decades of the twentieth century. But I faced a number of challenges. It was not as simple as I had assumed to determine who in the lists were actually Gaelic. Surnames on their own have limitations in indicating ethnicity. Nonetheless, through the use of sampling techniques, I was eventually able to construct a table showing the relative growth of the native merchants and traders in Dublin, based on principal native surnames for selected years.[95] The results are presented below:

Year	Percentage, by principal Gaelic surnames, of all merchants & traders in Dublin
1738	7.4
1800	10.8
1850	11.4
1911	11.6

The table shows clearly that, even a century-and-a-half before Joyce wrote *Dubliners*, there was a small but significant native middle-class stratum in the city, indicating that it must have originated sometime in the early eighteenth century, if not before.

What surprised me, as I dug deeper into the subject, was that Dublin's Catholic middle-class had an enormous influence on political life and economic development well before 1800, not only in the city but throughout Ireland. Even more fascinating was the fact that the man who was pivotal in extending its influence was a namesake: John Keogh.

It turns out that, as early as the mid-point of the eighteenth century, urban Catholic merchants, both indigenous and Old English were growing confident of their influence. A major concern of these merchants was liberty to practice their religion, and in 1756 a formal public identity was established when they came together and formed the Catholic Association.[96] It was a significant and radical body. When they obtained sufficient

---

94 Morash, 2004; p. 84.
95 Keogh, 2015; p. 157.
96 Gwynn, 1928; p. 16.

resources and achieved an adequate level of strength, they began to agitate for reforms of the Penal Laws. The clergy were—on the whole—reluctant to participate.

The Old English aristocrats soon posed a threat; they became outraged as native merchants stepped into leadership roles. The Old English felt that the Gaels were usurping their traditional position; after all, the original Anglo-Irish had represented the interests of the monarchy in Ireland up to Tudor times and still felt they were the only ones who had the right and capability to express the interests of all Catholics in Ireland. It may be argued that the tensions that existed in the Catholic Association represented rivalry between aristocrats and commercial interests rather than between Gaelic and Old English elements. However, this is an understandable misreading of the situation. The non-aristocratic Old English would have regarded the aristocrats as their natural leaders and would have been reluctant to oppose them; the native Irish didn't harbour such reverence for their old enemies and led the opposition. In the urban environment of the eighteenth century the rules were changing and an open power-struggle was beginning. Both groups split, echoing tensions that had always existed between them and caused the Catholic Association to dissolve from 1763. The division serves to demonstrate that the Old English and Gaelic Catholics were not indistinguishable.

However, continued Ascendancy opposition against full Catholic Emancipation maintained the need for an association of some sort. A new organisation came into being a decade later in 1773, called the Catholic Committee, in which Lord Kenmare, an Old English aristocrat, was the most prominent figure. But it was not long before tensions between the factions resurfaced and came to a head because of the temerity with which Kenmare was dealing with the Dublin Government.

John Keogh, who opposed Kenmare, was anxious to see progress achieved. He defeated Kenmare in a vote in 1791 and was now the undisputed leader of the Committee. This victory was significant. It represents the emergence—almost unique in modern history—of the Gael in a formal leadership position over the Old English. From then on the Gaelic identity would act on equal terms, no longer subservient to their old enemies.

At this time, radical changes were afoot, bringing England and Catholic Ireland into a closer working relationship. After King James was defeated at the battle of the Boyne in 1690, his Stuart descendants continued to fight from the Continent to retrieve the Crown of England. But, the Jacobite rebellion of 1745 under Charles Edward (*Bonny Prince Charlie*) failed in Scotland. Irish Catholics, including Gaels and the Old English, began to see that hopes for a Stuart return were no longer realistic. Their support waned further through their disillusionment with the defeated Charles, who became an alcoholic and whose life was considered a scandal. As a result, Irish Catholics finally shook off their loyalty to the Stuarts in the 1760s and 1770s. They were now prepared to conform to the Protestant Hanoverian King George. Some Protestants even mourned the political demise of Jacobitism, *which they believed caused the Hanoverians to prematurely repeal the Penal Laws.*[97]

---

97 Ó Ciardha, 2004; p. 367.

John Keogh stepped up to become one of the principal and most successful agitators for Catholic reform in the late eighteenth century. Through his considerable energy and influence he obtained the support of Protestants like Wolfe Tone and Edmund Burke. They provided vital links between the Committee and other sympathetic Protestants in Ireland and England. In effect, these prominent figures became agents for the Catholics and increased the influence of the Committee substantially. The connection with Burke, who was outspoken against the French Revolution, sent out a signal from the merchants that they were not necessarily in favour of the direction in which France was moving.

The merchants confronted the law using legal arguments expressed through legal representatives while, at the same time, professing loyalty to the king. They organised throughout Dublin. They lobbied the Irish Parliament in College Green, petitioned the Irish Government in Dublin Castle and addressed the Government and King of England through requests signed by hundreds of their members. Though not numerically dominant—constituting about one third of the merchants of Dublin in 1780—they employed their wealth and a deliberate clannishness to maximise their influence against discrimination. Though the Catholic clergy stood aloof, at first, later on some of their number became active participants in the Committee.

Catholics had to function outside full participation in trading and manufacturing guilds. They had to make a contribution called *quarterage*—a statutory anti-Catholic tax—but they were beginning to resist paying it. As early as 1763 Protestants introduced a Bill in the Irish Parliament to establish its legality. The opposing merchants were in a position to hire lawyers to contest the legislation. The lord lieutenant, after hearing their case, was convinced in their favour and quashed the Bill. The merchants had gained their first real taste of constitutional victory. Later they were influential in bringing into being the Relief Acts of 1778 and 1782 that established limited property-rights for Catholics.

A fresh petition for rights was presented by the Committee to Parliament in Dublin in 1792 but was denounced by the Commons and, in an unprecedented action, was removed from the table of the House. The move backfired. It gave the English Prime Minister, Pitt, a weapon in his growing determination to abolish the independent Irish Parliament altogether. A factor of utmost importance in favour of the Catholics in the second half of the eighteenth century was the dual problem that England was facing vis-à-vis the independence movement in the American colonies and the threat to European monarchies presented by the French Revolution. England was concerned about the attitude and position of the Irish Catholics and knew that they would appease them or drive them to hostilities. Pitt was engrossed in preparations for a war with France and could not afford to have the Catholics of Ireland join with the enemy. The English Government was thus conciliatory to the point that it was growing increasingly impatient with opposition from the Protestant Ascendancy Parliament in Ireland.

The removal of the petition by the House spurred the merchants to redouble their efforts under the guidance of John Keogh. The Catholic Committee was confined to Dublin. Initially they experienced difficulties in incorporating countrywide elements but they devoted themselves to finding solutions to this impasse when they realised that, if they didn't include the whole country they could not speak on behalf of the Catholics of Ireland. A scheme was then developed in which supporters in other towns nominated representatives in Dublin. This strategy prepared the way for the organization of a nationwide Convention in 1792 at which delegates from all over the country attended.

A new petition for reform was to be made to the Dublin Parliament. In a mood of exhilaration, the Committee decided to seek complete Catholic Emancipation and to request the elective franchise for members of their religion. The moves alarmed the Dublin Government, particularly because the methods of organization employed by the merchants were similar to those of the French revolutionary forces.

Undeterred, the 1792 Convention engendered great hope and enthusiasm amongst the delegates and in their excitement they resolved to compile a list of their grievances and petition the king himself for total Catholic Emancipation. The Dublin Government, in an attempt to retain control of the dramatically changing situation, agreed to dispatch the petition to the king if it were handed first to the lord lieutenant. The merchants were suspicious and decided that they could not trust the Dublin Government. Instead, they elected five members to approach the king in person. Instructions were given to the representatives in the following terms: *In whatever conference you may hold with His Majesty's Ministers ... you are fully to apprise them that it is the expectation, as well as the wish, of the Catholics of Ireland that the penal and restrictive laws, still affecting them, be totally removed ; and that nothing short of such total removal will satisfy the doubts and anxieties which at present agitate the public mind in this country, or carry into effect His Majesty's gracious wish for the union of all his subjects in sentiment, interest and affection.*[98]

The elected members, the most prominent of which was their Gaelic leader John Keogh, now had instructions to go to London and bypass the Dublin Government. A ship was not available at that moment, so they went by way of Belfast. In a curious footnote to Irish history, particularly in light of happenings in Northern Ireland in the twentieth century, the Protestant Dissenters of Belfast were supportive of the representatives. Wolf Tone recorded that: *... they were met by a number of the most active and intelligent inhabitants, who had distinguished themselves in the abolition of prejudice, and the conciliation of the public mind in Ulster to the claims of the Catholics.*[99] As they departed the city, their horses were removed from their coach and, to demonstrate support and good wishes for their mission, the people of Belfast drew them along to the precincts of the town.

When in London they met the Home Secretary, who offered to present their petition to the king. However, the representatives insisted on a personal interview with the monarch. With the threat of war still looming, they sensed their strength. Besides, they were aware that many behind-the-scenes activities had taken place before the meeting in London. When the Catholic Convention had been in full swing in Dublin the Home Secretary had written to the Viceroy to encourage him *... not to lose the assistance of the Catholics in support of the established Constitution.*[100] Also, Dublin Protestants who had helped the Catholic cause, such as Grattan and Lord Donoughmore, hurried to London because, in their view, the delegates were totally unused to undertaking such a mission. This gave them a heightened feeling of strength.

The representatives had several meetings with the Prime Minister and the Home Secretary

98   Gwynn, 1928; p. 86.
99   *Ibid*; p. 86.
100 *Ibid*; p. 89.

at which they continued to press for an audience with the king. Finally, on 2nd January 1793, John Keogh and his colleagues achieved their objective and met King George at Saint James' Palace where they presented their petition. Wolf Tone, who was also in London for the occasion, records that: *Their appearance, was splendid, and they met with what is called in the language of Courts, a most gracious reception ; that is His Majesty was pleased to say a few words to each of the delegates in his turn. In these colloquies the matter is generally of little interest, the manner is all ; and with the manner of the Sovereign the delegates had every reason to be content.*[101]

The king's speech of January 1793 revealed their triumph, which was followed by the Relief Act of the same year. As a result the Catholics of Ireland gained greater liberties than their co-religious in England. Property was discharged from the restraints and limitations of the Penal Laws, and the professions were now opened to them. They could enter the army, the navy and public office. They could obtain university degrees. The Catholic merchants of Dublin had reached the pinnacle of their political success. Though their victory was short of total emancipation and though they could still not be elected to parliament, Catholics obtained the franchise.

Despite these advances, the Protestant Ascendancy stoutly resisted the application of the law in practice. Prime Minister Pitt continued to support the Catholics and in January 1795 sent over to Ireland a new Viceroy—Fitzwilliam—who acted quickly. He dismissed several men who held key positions in Dublin Castle and then went on to present an outline for total Catholic Emancipation, which he intended to achieve. The hopes of the Catholics were elevated and the fears of Protestants were exacerbated. Fitzwilliam's lack of finesse in dealing with ultra-sensitive issues in Ireland caused Pitt to recall him after only seven weeks.

Later Grattan introduced a Bill for emancipation in the Irish Parliament, but it was defeated in May 1795. The recall of Fitzwilliam and the defeat of the Bill were followed by an almost complete polarization of Catholics and Ascendancy Protestants in Ireland. The United Irishmen, rather than the Committee, now emerged as the stronger force. It attracted activists and began to agitate on more radical lines. Within a few years the political situation in Ireland deteriorated remarkably, leading to open rebellion in 1798.

The Irish Catholics realized that they had little hope of emancipation under an Irish Protestant Parliament. Furthermore, Prime Minister Pitt continued to woo them with promises of full emancipation if they would support his government in creating a complete union between England and Ireland. The Irish Parliament would be dissolved; furthermore, no clause would be inserted in the Act of Union that might preclude the admission of Catholics to parliament.

The Irish Catholics thus supported Pitt. Unfortunately for them, the situation changed utterly after the Act of Union was passed. Denis Gwynn states that: *They were no longer an overwhelming majority, able to exert an always increasing pressure in all manner of ways upon a Parliament of Irish landlords sitting in Dublin. They were now no more than*

a despised fraction *of the electorate of the United Kingdom, and neither professions of*
101 *Ibid*; p. 87.

loyalty nor the actual proof of loyalty by years of military or naval service during the long war with France were of any avail whatever in supporting their claims to justice.[102]

John Keogh, who led the Catholic Committed throughout its finest political moments, died in 1817. The life of this city merchant personified how a native Catholic freed himself from the grips of the Protestant Ascendency and gained a position of considerable wealth and power in the second half of the eighteenth century. In Keogh we have not only an example of a successful entrepreneur but a mover who helped the Gaelic middle-class to surface as a strong political entity and gain equality in leadership with its rival—the Old English aristocracy.

But, perhaps the most outstanding legacy of the work of John Keogh and his Committee was the development of a constitutional process that was subsequently built upon. They had designed the blueprint for lawful agitation for their rights that would be followed in later years. The approach used by Keogh's Gaelic rival and successor, Daniel O'Connell, was a replica of the patterns that had been established by the Catholic Committee in the sense that O'Connell's followers depended on a national organisational framework, pressed for reforms using fully legal and constitutional means and employed eminent lawyers in achieving their aims. In fact O'Connell himself was an outstanding lawyer. His goal was to achieve total religious emancipation, but it took almost three decades before this was granted after a torturous route, accompanied by further agitation. O'Connell's triumph allowed Catholics to become members of parliament and paved the way for a firm representation of their business and professional communities in Parnell's Irish Party during the final decades of the nineteenth century.

But the path to freedom was not a smooth one. When progress towards a specific objective based on constitutional methods was hindered, violence erupted. Unfortunately, British resistance to Irish aspirations was unrelenting and led to constant unrest, beginning in 1798 and erupting periodically during the whole period up to the formation of the Free State.

Although the emerged indigenous middle-class of Dublin led the way in creating the structures for constitutional agitation in the country that continued for more than a century after the Act of Union was passed, they forgot their achievements and their history. They forgot who they were.

---

102 *Ibid*; p. 141.

Beginnings of Native Urbanisation

In the last chapter we saw that the Gaelic component of Dublin's merchants and traders—as represented by principal indigenous surnames—was more than seven percent in 1738.[103] Therefore, native urbanisation must have begun at some stage before this date; but how long before? The best way to answer the question about "when" the process might have started is to identify the earliest point at which it "could" have happened.

It is clear that a marked division has to be recognised between modern Gaelic town-dwelling, which is of concern here, and that of the medieval period. Medieval Irish cities had two familiar features: the defensive wall and the associated *Irishtown* that lay outside the urban centre but was—essentially—urbanite in nature. The close proximity of this native enclave, separated from contact with the city itself, may be read as a metaphor for apartheid or a sign of the fear with which the foreigner held the Gael. In fact, both images are correct. The leaders of the cities, who were mainly of English stock, ruled over the Irishtown outside the wall, used it for their own benefits but kept it under strict vigilance at a safe distance. At times of stress, when the natives grew restless and dangerous, the wall took on its role as a defensive mechanism rather than a vehicle for apartheid. But the Irishtown has little or nothing to do with post-medieval indigenous middle-class urbanisation.

The Gaelic inhabitants of medieval cities mainly occupied inferior positions.[104] But they were not the only native presence. A small number of Irish merchants, like the Dermotts, had been in Dublin perhaps as early as the sixteenth century.[105] Likewise, several Gaelic mercantile families inhabited other cities; like the Ronaynes of Cork; and the Kirwans and Dorseys of Galway.[106] Families such as these played a role in the development of the modern native middle-class, but they were a minor component. The main contributors to the class were former owners of native property and their descendants, whose lands were confiscated during the seventeenth century.

The period between 1600 and 1700 was the most disruptive phase for native landowners in the entire history of the country. In 1600, the Gaels held on to their traditional territories which they possessed since pre-history or since their displacement by the Normans. This area amounted to about sixty per cent of the land of Ireland. At the same time they maintained their tribal structures; spoke their own language and behaved according to their own laws. Then followed a century of relentless foreign colonisation; a century in which native culture underwent a major transformation. By 1700 all had changed; they had lost most of their lands. Here is how it happened.

After the battle of Kinsale in 1601 and the *Flight of the Earls* in 1607, key Gaelic areas were left leaderless and the disintegration of the Irish overlord system began. Fresh English and Scottish plantations soon started, particularly in Ulster, the most Gaelicised segment of the country. This region was to the invaders what inner-Africa was to medieval

---

103 Keogh, 2015.
104 Ní Mhurchadha, 2008; p. 12.
105 MacDermotRoe, (nd).
106 Nicholls, 2005; 146.

explorers; the poverty of information on sixteenth-century maps demonstrates ... *how little the administration in London and Dublin knew of the geography of Ulster.*[107] But three decades later the island of Ireland was divided roughly into equal parts between the Gaels, the Old English and the new Protestant invaders[108] and, by this time, significant inroads had been made into native areas in the northern segment of the country.

In reaction against the loss of native property and in retaliation to poor treatment, a vicious rebellion broke out in 1641 in Ulster. Tensions came to a sudden violent head in the province. An attack was launched on new Protestant colonisers of the North by their Gaelic neighbours; reprisals against the native Irish added to the death toll. Unrest spread south. Roy Foster acknowledges that: *What people thought happened in that bloody autumn conditioned events and attitudes in Ireland for generations to come.*[109]

The Gaels and the Old English, who maintained their fidelity to Catholicism, then joined together in a loose coalition of convenience against the invaders and the government. The coalition became known as the *Confederation of Kilkenny*. This was an outstanding example of cooperation between old enemies when it was in their mutual interest, though these cooperative ventures did not tend to last, showing unequivocally that the two cultures remained totally separate entities.

Political events in England opposed the interests of the confederates. Charles I was enmeshed in a tug-of-war with a growing fundamentalist Protestant Parliament that had puritan and Calvinist leanings. The parliamentarians disliked Charles' marriage to a devout French Catholic princess. Unrest between monarch and Parliament culminated in a civil war, which began in 1642 and lasted three years, after which Charles surrendered to his enemies. This led to his execution in January 1649.

The English Civil War was followed by the staunchly Protestant Cromwellian conquest of Ireland, which represented the most devastating wave of onslaught of all against native society. Cromwell arrived at Dublin in August 1649 in his position as lord lieutenant and commander of the army of the English Commonwealth. According to Berresford Ellis, *he bore a typical English racial contempt for the Irish.*[110] He had several aims in his undertaking, amongst which a high priority was to suppress the remnants of the Confederation of Kilkenny. He was also determined to exact revenge for the 1641 Rebellion and associated atrocities, and began with the defeat of Drogheda followed by a massacre of its civilian population.

The subjugation of Ireland by Cromwell was more thorough than any previous English conquest. Methods included open warfare; the burning of crops; slaughter of cattle herds; annihilation of the fishing industry and the destruction of Irish shipping. Retaliations from the Irish side, whose strategy changed from direct confrontation to guerrilla tactics, brought further havoc to agriculture. When the military campaign finally exhausted large-scale Gaelic and Old English resistance, the administrative suppression began.

---

107 Bardon, 2012; p. 112.
108 Clarke, 2009; p. 169.
109 Foster, 1989; p. 85.
110 Berresford Ellis, 2000; p. 20.

Those responsible for the 1641 Rebellion were to be brought to trial and executed, deported to the West Indies or sent to a reservation in Connaught. Further confiscation of Irish property followed. An ambitious reconstruction of the entire pattern of ownership was to take place in which fifty per cent of the land of Ireland was earmarked to change hands. The beginning of the largest social upheaval of Irish history followed Cromwell's conquest of the 1650s and involved the demise of all Catholic entities that had participated in the rebellion. Under Cromwell, Catholic land-ownership decreased from about two thirds to about nine per cent of the country.

After the return of the monarchy under Charles II in 1660—known as the *Restoration*— the hopes of the Catholics were elevated; but they were to be disappointed again. Those who suffered under Cromwell were not compensated as they had anticipated. The existing Cromwellian grip on the land, parliament, the towns and trade of the country was not relinquished. *Too much had changed.*[111]

However, when Charles died, King James II ascended to the throne. He maintained a stubborn adherence to Catholicism and so the situation radically reversed for Catholics and Protestants. Protestants became concerned about the increasing favour towards Catholics on the part of the new monarch. The Gael and Old English now hoped to regain substantial power. These hopes were reinforced over the following years when King James removed the Lord Lieutenant of Ireland and put Richard Talbot, a colourful character of an Old English family, in his place. Richard became Lord Tyrconnell and set about strengthening pro-Catholic policies. Protestants became further alarmed when several regiments of horse and foot were raised by Tyrconnell for the service of the king. They felt that a repeat of the atrocities of 1641 was imminent. In this charged atmosphere sectarian suspicions and divisions were rife.

Protestant fear, both in Ireland and England, provoked a search for an alternative leader and one was found in forty-year-old Dutch Prince William of Orange. He opposed James on behalf of the Protestants and was crowned King William III of England. King James was ousted from the throne by William in a *glorious revolution* so called because there was no fighting involved. But, conflict was delayed rather than avoided. After spending some time in France, James came to Ireland. William followed him and all was set for a major showdown between the two rival kings on Irish soil. In May and June 1690 the entire Irish Jacobite army—under King James—was assembled at Dundalk. King William moved south. James withdrew to the River Boyne.

In early July 1690 the two kings faced each other on opposites sides of the river; William on the north and James on the south. James had about 25,000 troops and William opposed him with some 36,000. William won the battle and James fled Ireland before the end of the campaign. Conflict continued but William ultimately gained victory and the war came to an end in Limerick after which both sides signed the *Treaty of Limerick*.

As far as King William was concerned he tried to administer the treaty fairly. However, the all-Protestant Irish Parliament took a completely different line and embarked on a series of Penal Laws against Catholics. In the aftermath of King William, Catholics were to be a

---

111 Dickson, 2008; p. 4.

non-people; but, as they outnumbered Protestants, the Ascendancy was paranoid about the possibility of losing power once again, despite having gained the ownership of most of the land. Catholic ownership recovered a little after the Restoration, but eventually fell back to five per cent of the country.[112] Some of the decrease represents conversions in religious allegiance rather than loss of property. But by 1700 the native Irish, as we have seen, had been relieved of most of their lands.

Surprisingly, the overall number of displaced indigenous owners was not exceedingly large. In the process of redistribution, the Gaelic landless labourers, who made up the bulk— perhaps three-quarters—of the native segment of the population, were scarcely affected at all by dispossessions. The reason being: they were a valuable asset for the invaders who required them to work their estates.[113] In traditional native society there was a hierarchy of different classes above the landless, which included the ruling elites and those with specialist clan roles. In other words, the upper echelons of Gaelic society were displaced when the tribal system broke down and some of these went on to create the modern middle-class of the towns and cities of Ireland.

Based on a native ownership pattern of fifty to sixty per cent of the land in 1600 and assuming historical carrying capacities, the Gaelic segment of the population that was still living within their traditional territories at that time, would have been in the order of 250,000. The ruling families and professional classes constituted a little over 60,000, or twenty-five per cent of that population.[114] However, not all left their land; the plantations forced many to lose proportions of their properties or to be downgraded to the status of tenants on land they once owned.

Some native urbanisation may have taken place after 1600 and before the end of the Cromwellian Period but is likely to have experienced reversals. It was observed that: *Poor immigrants to* [Dublin] *tended to cluster in the suburbs in the early decades of the seventeenth century, erecting flimsy shanties of timber, mud and straw, which were rather grandiosely called 'cottages'.*[115] A portion of these were probably dispossessed native landowners. Later in 1647, a note from Nicholas Plunkett to Thomas Preston shows the extent of overcrowding in Kilkenny at this time. The inhabitants of Saint John's Street, for example, were seeking relief of the Confederation as a *... considerable part of the said street is inhabited by gentlemen who lost their estates by the distempers of these times ...*[116] However, we don't know if these examples represent permanent urbanisation. Expulsion of Catholics from the cities in the aftermath of the defeat of the Irish under Cromwell complicates our understanding of the process. Cromwellian proclamations ordered the towns to be cleared of papists, though these were ineffective in the long-run.[117] Nonetheless, up to the beginning of the reign of Charles II in 1660, cities like Dublin were in no position or humour to accept a large influx of Gaelic Catholic proto-traders, traders, merchants or professionals on a permanent basis.

---

112 Foster, 1989; p. 155.
113 Corish, 2009 (b); p. 374.
114 Keogh, 2015; p. 152.
115 Lennon, 2008; p. 1.
116 Ó Siochrú, 2008; p. 130.
117 Corish, 2009 (b); p. 374.

Roy Foster states that: *Up to the 1660s Capuchins and Franciscans led an underground life: petitions to Rome show such friars doubling as gardeners and coal-porters in Waterford ...*[118] It is likely that their secular counterparts were equally adept at adopting such guises. As early as 1678, edicts appeared that opposed *... further Catholic migration into the major towns.*[119] This indicates that Catholic urbanisation was increasing after the Restoration and it is almost certain that little could be done to prevent Gaelic participation. However, it was a mainly invisible process. Wealth was not a necessary prerequisite for membership of the middle-class during its early stages of growth; the embryonic identity, at this time, was defined more by skill-levels and potential for development.

Despite suffering disadvantages because of the Penal Laws, the Gaelic presence in Dublin started to become visible to mainstream society at the end of the seventeenth century. For instance, in 1696 the Protestant coal-porters of the city complained to Parliament that: ... *one Darby Ryan, a catholic coal-dealer, employed coal-porters of his own persuasion, to the great injury of the protestant interest ...*[120]

By the first decades of the eighteenth century, the modern Catholic trader of the city was a recognised economic force. Patrick Fagan points out that as early as 1707 Dublin Corporation made reference to the fact that ... *great numbers of Irish papists of late repaired to this city and follow several trades therein.*[121] By 1714, the impression given by Protestants was that Catholics were crowding in on Dublin, causing loyalists to flee from the city amid heightened fears of a Jacobite revolution.[122] A similar pattern of growth seems to have occurred in other cities of Ireland, too. As early as 1708, Catholic men of commerce were making an impression in Cork city which had doubled in size since the 1680s.[123]

In resume: a native middle-class could not have begun to develop in earnest until the economic climate of the main urban centres improved and this happened after the Restoration. As such, 1660 marks the beginning of a permanent and visible Gaelic middle-class in Dublin.

---

118 Foster, 1989; p. 119.
119 Dickson, 2008; p. 19.
120 Hansard, 1812; p. 716.
121 Fagan, 1991; p. 133.
122 Ó Ciardha, 2004; p. 144.
123 Foster, 1989; p. 205 and Cullen, 2009; p. 391.

Roads to Wealth

According to the last chapter, between 1600 and 1660, native urbanisation was extremely restricted. However, this was the period of greatest displacement of Gaelic owners, in which only a relatively low number of the evicted could have entered and remained in the cities and towns of Ireland, particularly in view of administrative antagonism, as well as the lack of opportunities due to economic difficulties. In the majority of cases, therefore, the time of urbanised would not provide indications about the circumstances surrounding their rural homeland exodus. A major question surfaced from these conclusions: How did the bulk of the dispossessed live and how did they eke out a living after losing their land before the Restoration? A follow-on question is: What economic activities sustained them after 1660 when they became a visible and growing force in the urban environment?

As I began to seek answers to these questions I suspected that the outcome would, at best, provide little information about the ancestors of the Keoghs of Ranelagh. Yet, I hoped that I would stumble on something interesting or find a new and fruitful direction of inquiry, which would enlighten me about the family. The actual outcome was unexpected. In hindsight, I have learnt that gaining knowledge around a subject of interest absorbs a lot of time but is almost never wasteful; it can provide surprising answers to our most obstinate puzzles. The appropriate phrase is: never give up.

We have seen that a little over 60,000 Gaelic owners-plus-family-members would have been affected by changes in land ownership in the seventeenth century. Those who maintained sufficient estates on which to survive, or who had been forced to become tenant farmers, would not have moved to the cities, at least not directly. But, as production shifted from subsistence farming to farming-for-the-market in the eighteenth century,[124] the native Irish who had remained on the land became more familiar with urban centres when engaging in selling their produce. In this way a number of them would have been attracted by better opportunities in alternative occupations and, so, turned their backs on the land. In such cases, the impact of colonisation on urbanisation would have been protracted and indirect. And the first appearance of these families in the city may have been extended to the sons or grandsons of those who were inconvenienced by the plantations, rather than the original landowners.

Another point to consider is that dispossessions spiked at the height of each plantation and caused communal rather than individual disruptions. Not all of the evicted were deported, or sent to Connaught. A relatively small number probably existed as rural middle-men, trading agricultural produce. Others became teachers, scholars, clerics, smugglers or rapparees. It is becoming increasingly clear that an important number spent time beyond Ireland's shores. Communications between Ireland and the Continent were strong at this time. A complex system of Irish colleges developed on the mainland and became the centres for the education of Catholic clergy. Some families involved themselves in business and trade overseas. Many young men joined the armies of Spain and France. Recruitment to foreign armies was a lucrative business in its own right. We know that an extensive land-based and seaborne communication network began to develop. It functioned openly amongst dispossessed Catholics in friendly or neutral territories like

---

124 Cullen, 1990; p. 67.

France, Spain, the Netherlands and Sweden, or underground in the hostile environments of Ireland and surrounding seas. Within this network established agents ferried potential exiles and returnees to and from the Continent.[125]

Clandestine correspondence travelled back and forth carrying information about the movements of English troops and rumours of prospective invasions. Individual contacts were maintained through priests, soldiers, rapparees, fishermen, ship-owners and merchants at home and abroad. The risk of being intercepted ensured that many Catholic writers didn't dare put their true sentiments on paper[126] and often wrote in codes. The reluctance to keep detailed written records goes a long way to explaining why the former landowning Irish seemed to vanish from history in the seventeenth century and suddenly appear as a formidable political force in the urban environment during the middle of the eighteenth century. What happened in the intervening years is largely guesswork. It is difficult, for example, to determine the precise influences that the continental Irish Jacobite world exerted on the process of native urbanisation. Nevertheless, a strong external influence has to be assumed.

After the Restoration, indigenous elements came into the urban environment through an array of connections in Ireland and overseas. A proportion of the diaspora returned home. Meanwhile, in Ireland, many who had been forced to move to Connaught under Cromwell remained there until opportunities arose in the cities. A number probably spent time within several alternative occupations and geographical areas in Ireland and overseas and would have benefited through the development of new skills, particularly in language and commerce.

Whatever option they chose—to go abroad or stay at home—all the dispossessed natives had to undertake a major transformation of their lifestyles before they or their offspring emerged amongst the urban middle-class. Two factors helped in this process: education and links to trade. Education gave them the means to retrain and survive. Families with specialist clan roles in defence, law, medicine, education, genealogy and other professions within the tribal system coped by adapting their indigenous knowhow to deal with the changing social and economic order.

Numerous individuals from the educated ranks became teachers in an underground system known as the "hedge schools", which later became pay schools. Hedge schools emerged from a long tradition of patronage to learning under Gaelic chieftains. After the defeat of native leadership, this form of support dried up but was replaced by contributions from the parents of the pupils. In this way a very old tradition continued in another form and the schoolmasters, who were proudly aware of this age-old connection, reminded their pupils of their Gaelic past. They told them they were the *children of kings, the sons of Milesius*.[127]

According to Antonia McManus, hedge schools had their true nascent period during Cromwellian times, though they only really took root at the beginning of the eighteenth century despite restrictions of the Penal Laws, which forced Catholic teachers to work underground. Despite widespread poverty in the country and the outlawing of Catholic

---

125 Ó Ciardha, 2004; pp. 114, ff.
126 *Ibid*; p.125.
127 McManus, 2006; p. 74.

education, the numbers of pay schools grew to over 500 in 1731 and mushroomed to over 9,000 by 1824, catering for about 400,000 children in town and country. This network eventually was overtaken by the national school system of Ireland.[128]

During the Penal Laws, school was held in ditches, hovels and mud cabins and this explains why they were called *hedge* schools. Later they improved. For example, in 1824 an establishment in County Dublin was run by one Hugh M'Guinness in ... *a house, two stories high*.[129] Incredibly, a wide array of subjects was offered to hedge school pupils amongst which were: arithmetic, bookkeeping, history, science, surveying, land measuring, astronomy, geography, religion, Latin, Greek, Hebrew, English and Irish.[130] Particular emphasis was placed on mathematics and related subjects, which were meeting the demands of the market place.

Without doubt these schools assisted enormously in providing individuals with the means to elevate themselves from a rural background that was no longer providing a livelihood, into a range of entrepreneurial and professional pursuits in Ireland and overseas. However, before 1793, most of the professions at home, except medicine, were closed to Catholics by law.

The second factor that helped native owners to survive after becoming dispossessed was trade. Indigenous involvement in commerce had deep historic roots. For example, Emmett O'Byrne indicates that: *Trade was ... common between the Wicklow élites and the English, particularly in wine, timber, butter, weapons and corn. The depth of this commerce was captured in Gerald O'Byrne's 1392 offer of a barge to Esmond Berle, a Dublin merchant, as payment for debts. In 1395 Phelim O'Toole also attested to trade's importance, exclaiming 'for without buying and selling I can in no way live'...* [131] Gaelic families who had long experience of commerce would have been a vital catalytic force in the process of modern urbanisation by introducing displaced elements to related activities.

The one chink in the Protestant Ascendency armour, which permitted segments of Gaelic society to move into the commercial sphere, came about because the new Protestant landowners held trade in contempt. This explains why making money through business was ... *the only road to wealth that was not blocked up against them by law*.[132] The ruling classes reluctantly acquiesced to Catholics becoming involved in related pursuits after the Restoration. As a result, they were unable to prevent the development of native links to rapidly-growing commercial activities in the towns and cities as it was in their own interests to ensure that daily commerce and the wealth of the country continued to improve.

Fresh insights into the impacts of Catholic traders have led to several surprising conclusions. Writing in 1718, Archbishop King observed that ... *the papists being made incapable to purchase lands, have turned themselves to trade, and already engrossed almost all the trade of the kingdom*.[133] As early as 1739 an anonymous pamphleteer

---

128 *Ibid*; pp. 15, 19, 31, 242, 243.
129 Commissioners, 1826; p. 590.
130 McManus, 2006; p. 118.
131 O'Byrne, 2005; p. 19.
132 Bartlett, 1998; p. 287.
133 Wall, 1989 (a); p. 76.

declared, in relation to Irish Catholics, that: ... *they had captured most of the commerce and current coin of the Kingdom.*[134] Regarding those who made money in eighteenth-century Ireland, Roy Foster says: ... *here one encounters that important, if unexpected, element, the middle-class Catholics of the towns. From about 1750 their economic power becomes a prime preoccupation in political calculations.*[135] When the Bank of Ireland was set up in 1783 Catholic commercial and financial interests contributed ten per cent of the total capital. This is an extraordinary statistic considering that they were still subject to anti-Catholic restrictions. But, bank assets probably represented a fraction of the wealth of these merchants and traders. By the final quarter of the eighteenth century, the wealth and power of the Catholic middle-class blossomed. Wolfe Tone notes that, at this time, Catholics ... *constituted a considerable portion of the mercantile interest.*[136] As they were debarred from owning property in Ireland, they began to discover the possibility of investing overseas. To counteract this trend and assist new Protestant landowners who had squandered their assets, a Bill had to be introduced as early as 1763 to enable Catholics to lend them money.[137]

Prospects for native self-liberation came by way of increasingly diverse economic activities that were becoming available from 1660 and throughout most of the eighteenth century. The period was one of radical change when a relatively backward agricultural system diversified and internal and external trade played increasingly important roles. At first, the scale of Irish industry was miniscule, but expanding in tandem with a rising population. The economy accelerated rapidly from the mid-1740s when Anglo-Irish trade in textiles and agricultural produce entered a quarter-century of boom. Towards the end of the eighteenth century, the English industrial revolution worked to complement rather than hinder the economy, though the majority of Ireland was not touched by the revolution itself. The opportunities that presented themselves directly and indirectly to native Catholics over the period in question included:

- The provisioning trade to the armed forces;
- Increasing imports, especially coal;
- Increasing exports, particularly oats and barley;
- Brewing and glass-making, which made the important transition to large-scale production;
- The development of textiles in the form of widely-distributed cotton and linen industries;
- Sugar-refining and flower-milling;
- A spreading communications infrastructure; and
- A building boom.[138]

All these growing economic activities required service industries like communications and transportation. There was increased mobility with new roads, canals and stagecoach routes radiating from the main cities like Dublin. Urban and rural buildings were created,

---

134 Gwynn, 1928; p.15.
135 Foster, 1989; p. 205.
136 Bartlett, 1998; p. 41.
137 Gwynn, 1928; p.14.
138 Foster, 1989; pp. 195, ff.

which became the very symbols of Protestant Ascendancy culture and gave the particular stamp of identity to the landscape and cityscapes of Ireland for generations to come. Dublin continued to spread out from her medieval core, which resulted in it becoming an important metropolis to which thousands gravitated for employment. Georgian Dublin was thus created. It was under these circumstances that former dispossessed Gaelic Catholics and their descendants continued to ferret out opportunities in the urban environment.

It is logical to assume that transformation from tribal to urban existence occurred along the route of least resistance or most advantage. The initial process of urbanisation was driven by a desire to gain any permanent or semi-permanent employment. Once the first steps were secured, the breadwinner would have used every available means at his disposal to elevate himself into the best positions open to him. A labourer or artisan lifestyle may have been a brief transition for those who were upwardly mobile. Particular working niches had to be discovered through stealth and experimentation but, once found, were exploited to the full. The dispossessed Gaels became petty dealers, handicraft-men and shopkeepers of every kind. A deliberate clannishness was employed to good effect amongst groups and individuals as a means of mutual support. Men with the most energy and ambition or who had possessed greater advantages in the tribal system lifted themselves beyond the lower ranks and became involved at a mercantile level in international trade and commerce. Depending on abilities, skills, initial wealth and luck, they achieved various levels of fortune.

Urban-Rural Links

Gaelic urbanisation involved the uprooting of individuals from their rural homelands—or other intermediate abodes—followed by their subsequent transfer into cities and towns throughout Ireland. What was it like to have lived through this process? Documented evidence, from the perspective of a small number of native writers who underwent these disruptions, can be found for the late seventeenth century onwards. Their observations cast light on the inconveniences that my forefathers probably suffered after making their final decision to move permanently to Dublin.

The earliest evidence for the existence of my ancestors in the city is found in the life of Thomas J., who resided at High Street in 1837. But oral history may point to a prior point-of-entry. An instruction appended to one of Margaret Keogh's letters to Saint Patrick's Hospital in 1852 states that any communication ... *will please be forwarded to Mrs Keogh at her brother-in-law's residence Mr John Keogh 8 Portland Place*. The fact that Thomas J. was not the only relative in Dublin at the time, lends weight to a possible longer-term presence in the city. Furthermore, Finola Keogh alleged that her ancestors had a connection to the United Irishmen movement, which was originally an urban phenomenon that lasted from 1791 to 1803. The likely association of Thomas the Elder—or his father—with a mainly urban-based organisation, hints that they may have resided in the city during this period, or earlier.

The notion—also derived from oral history—that the family stayed in the West of Ireland, before coming to Dublin, but without any reference to Cromwell, suggests that their removal to Connaught happened at some stage after the Restoration. If they had been evicted by Cromwell, the event is unlikely to have been forgotten. If they had been ousted from Wexford before Cromwellian times, it is difficult to imagine why the West of Ireland would have attracted them at this period in Irish history. The most likely phase in which they exited from their Wexford homeland, in the aftermath of the Restoration, would have been during or shortly after the Williamite Wars when land was, once more, being lost to Protestants. Of course, this is largely speculation.

The lack of reference to a period spent overseas hints that the family came directly into Dublin from Connaught. I am reminded here of Seán Ó Neachtain's process of urbanisation which probably exhibited strong parallels to that of the ancestors of the Keoghs of Ranelagh.

David Dickson speculates that ... *there seems to have been a lower-level circular movement involving catholics between land jobbing and the less distinguished trades in the city*.[139] Seán Ó Neachtain, a Gaelic poet and scribe from County Roscommon left his native county as an itinerant seasonal labourer to work the harvest in Leinster. He had to forego the prospect of ever becoming a prosperous farmer, having lost his lands in the troubled circumstances of the seventeenth century. He entered the city, probably in the 1680s and documented his transition indirectly through his fictional writings. In relation to Ó Neachtain, William Mahon reminds us that: ... *attracted by commercial and intellectual opportunities, he settled in the rapidly-expanding capital. He had ... exchanged country*

---

139 Dickson, 1990; p. 95.

for town life. In this respect, he and his colleagues had followed a course not untypical for writers and intellectuals of the period.[140]

The contrast between country and town permeates Ó Neachtain's fiction and provides a rare first-hand commentary on early post-Restoration Gaelic urbanisation by a native writer. His protagonist, Éamonn O'Clery, hails from the *... fair, verdant and level land of Connaught*. He describes the initial impact of Dublin on his hero when coming to the outskirts of the city in Thomas Street: *... there were multitudes of royalty and nobility along the concourse, well-paying savants, base bands of rabble, and lovely, lissome ladies, all of whom Éamonn greeted affably and courteously ...*[141]

Seán's son, Tadhg, also a writer, took out a five-year lease on some rooms at Earl Street in the Liberties where he kept a school. He became the fulcrum of *The Ó Neachtain Circle*, a network of scribes and scholars in Dublin, engaged in teaching as well as the exchange and transcription of Irish manuscripts. They were an underground literary movement and happened to be Jonathan Swift's Irish-speaking contemporaries.[142]

Muiris Ó Gormáin provides a later example of Gaelic urbanisation of a man of letters. A native of Ulster, a schoolteacher, scribe, poet and collector of books, Ó Gormáin's early whereabouts are unclear. He resided for a time at Belanagare, transcribing material for the Irish historian Charles O'Conor. By 1763 he had taken up lodgings at the *Sign of the Mashing Keeve* at Saint Mary's Lane. Several years later he advertised himself as a professor of Irish at the same address. About this time he compiled the first known Irish-English phrasebook developed for middle-class and gentry clients. During his lifetime he was employed by some of the leading Irish antiquarians to copy and translate Gaelic manuscripts. He died in extreme poverty in a basement room in Saint Mary's Lane about 1794.[143]

These examples demonstrate a persistent link with native scholarship in the city of Dublin from 1680 up to the 1790s. Could it be that Thomas J. was also part of this world? It is likely that he derived his skills in accountancy within the hedge school system, the avenue through which most native Catholics obtained their education. Furthermore, the fact that he was also a librarian, and was not involved directly in trade, betrays an unusually strong relationship with the trappings of scholarship. We have seen that numerous individuals from the educated ranks became teachers. Perhaps he had been a hedge-school master? Alas, there is no proof. Nevertheless, his links, and those of his family, with learning, are verified beyond doubt.

With respect to status, the Keoghs inhabited a modest rank among traders and professionals in the city. At a higher level, were the Dermotts of Dublin. They were descendants of the distinguished MacDermots of Moylurg and became prominent merchants in the city after their marriage into the Bellews of County Louth, who had large estates and owned flour mills. Also included at this social level, were some of the Byrnes of Wicklow. About the middle of the eighteenth century one Edward Byrne, whose background was relatively

---

140 Mahon, 2000; pp. 13, 18.
141 *Ibid*; p. 12.
142 *Ibid*; pp. 1, 21.
143 McCabe, 2009; pp. 495, 496.

modest, married into the wealthy McCarthy merchants of Bordeaux. In time, Edward became the richest merchant of Dublin.[144]

The above examples show that a single model of Gaelic urbanisation and subsequent improvement didn't apply. There was a stark division between those who would not have required large amounts of capital to begin life in the city and those who had greater initial resources and/or influence. David Dickson, with reference to the eighteenth century, states: *In order to re-examine the place of catholics in the urban economy, it is helpful to break the problem down somewhat—firstly by drawing the distinction between different types of commercial and craft occupation, specifically between, on the one hand, the capitalised wholesale merchant engaged in long-distance trading, and on the other, the dealer, the shopkeeper, the factor, the master craftsman etc.; between the two sets of occupation, there was a gap in the costs of entry, the capital requirements, the opportunities for profit and, as a consequence, the social status.*[145]

In the case of the indigenous Catholics, the *two sets of occupation* represented the continued distinction between those of superior rank, who tended to be descendants of tribal leaders, and those who were petty traders, who tended to be the offspring of the professional ranks. In other words, the divide between the Gaelic lords and those with specialist skills were often maintained in the city. Of course, it is to be expected that some individuals from the lower levels elevated themselves into better positions through commerce or crafts, while others from the more influential strata experienced reversals and setbacks.

A disgruntled Irish officer abroad ... *complained in the 1690s of the advance, at the expense of old families, of "servants, shopkeepers, clerks, little attorneys, apothecaries and pedling merchants, and the like who ran away from Ireland (perhaps) with some of their creditors' money". This sour comment reflects one facet of social change. More accessible career opportunities reached a wider range of families.*[146]

The meteoric rise of John Keogh of the Catholic Committee who came from *humble beginnings* provides one of the best illustrations of the emergence of a non-aristocratic Gael as a wealthy merchant in Dublin. It has been suggested that he was probably born in the city in 1840.[147] He spent time overseas on the Isle of Man, where he allegedly made money in the smuggling trade. That island had many illicit contacts with Dublin and afforded a refuge to fugitives from Ireland, who resided there ... *in such numbers as to make a considerable part of the inhabitants of the Island.*[148]

After his alleged time as a smuggler, John Keogh surfaced as a porter and counter-boy to the Widow Lincoln in Dublin, who had a silk-mercer business at the *Sign of the Spinning-Wheel* in Francis Street. When she moved to the *Eagle* in Dame Street in 1770 she took John into partnership; two years later he set up his own business in Dame Street, where he remained until his retirement from the silk trade in 1787. He also had interests

---

144 Cullen, 1983; p. 22.
145 Dickson, 1990; p. 88.
146 Cullen, 1990; pp. 72, 73.
147 Kelly, 2004; p. 356.
148 Atholl Papers: AP 40B-16; *Reply from Dublin re Smuggling from Isle of Man, 1764*; < http://www.isle-of-man.com/manxnotebook/history/ap/ap_40b16.htm > (August, 2015)

in the brewing industry.[149] Denis Gwynn describes him as: ... *a plain businessman of extraordinary public spirit and courage and generosity, with a passionate devotion to the emancipation of his Church and of the people to whom he belonged.*[150] His education was said to be *solid, rather than elegant.*[151]

Maureen Wall noted that the Protestant Ascendency was venomous in its attacks against John Keogh, accusing him of being ... *the son of a Connaught spalpeen.*[152] They poured scorn on him in parliamentary debates.[153] Their hostility shows that the war against the Gael had already surfaced in the urban environment at this time. Protestants were doing their best to demean, prevent and frustrate the development of an influential native middle-class.

The comment that John Keogh was a Connaught spalpeen, together with the fact that he bought land in the province when the laws against Catholics owing property were relaxed, support geographical and emotional ties between his family and the West of Ireland. Wall goes as far as saying ... *it satisfied his pride of race to buy land in Roscommon where the MacEochaidhs once flourished.*[154] Whether or not he belonged to the Roscommon sept of the Keoghs is not known and the conclusion is probably conjectured on the part of Wall. When he first leased property in Connaught he did so in County Sligo and not Roscommon. Does this imply that he had greater emotional ties to Sligo? It is difficult to tell. Later however, he took long leases, or bought land in Leitrim and Roscommon.[155]

Although no kin connection has been established between John Keogh and the ancestors of the Keoghs of Ranelagh, both families came from or through Connaught. Furthermore, although John's family is not associated with Leinster, in 1782 he represented Enniscorthy for the Catholic Committee.[156] This may indicate a familial connection with County Wexford. Up to his death, he lived in his mansion at Mount Jerome in Harold's Cross. Coincidentally, Thomas J. resided in that village in 1839. Both families lived, for a time, at Drumcondra. All considered a connection between John Keogh's forefathers and the ancestors of the Keoghs of Ranelagh cannot be ruled out.

I now had a lot more information about how the native Irish were dispossessed of their properties; how they existed after losing their lands; and when and how they became the urban middle-class in Dublin. But was all this information helpful in casting light on the ancestors of the Keoghs of Ranelagh, which was the original objective of my quest? Happily, I could answer this question affirmatively.

---

149 Wall, 1989 (b); p. 163.
150 Gwynn, 1928; p. 65.
151 Huish, 1836; p. 73.
152 Wall, 1989 (b); p. 163.
153 Dr. Colum Kenny: reference provided about John Keogh mentioned in a speech in the Irish House of Commons, apparently by Sir Boyle Roche (personal communications).
154 Wall, 1989 (b); p. 164.
155 Swindale, A. Family History Notebook
< http://www.fivenine.co.uk/family_history_notebook/family_pages/keogh/john_keogh_1740_1817.htm > (August, 2015)
156 Wall, 1989 (b); p. 164.

My ancestors were former Gaelic landowners from County Wexford who were not part of the main ruling tribes of Leinster. They were tenacious linked to the lower of the *two sets of occupation* of the native middle-class of Dublin. This subordinate urban layer was derived mainly from the professional segment of native society, of which learning was its principal hallmark. The Keoghs exhibited strong links to learning.

We have seen that roughly seventy-five per cent of the Gaelic population was landless. Around ten per cent would have been numbered amongst the ruling elites.[157] All the evidence narrows the roots of the Keoghs of Ranelagh to the remaining fifteen per cent of the original Gaelic population, which was composed of septs that had specialist roles in the native professions. Without doubt, my ancestors came from this level of Irish society. I had, at last, succeeded in making a significant breakthrough and forged an important link between my forefathers' urban stratum and their roots in the Gaelic tribal system.

---

157 Based on Corish, 2009 (b); p. 374; Mytum, 1992; p. 132 and Stout, 1997; p. 110.

Native Upland Farmers

In relation to *'civilizing'* Gaelic Leinster in Tudor times, Christopher Maginn mentions that: *The imposing mountains and expansive hills where the O'Byrnes and O'Tooles resided were clearly visible from the centre of Dublin and the fires that burned there at night served to remind the city dwellers of the nearness of their enemies.*[158]

With the objective of understanding more about how my ancestors lived within the professional stratum of the Gaelic system I began to focus on existing information relating to the tribes of Leinster. But, for some reason, I could more easily imagine the Dublin Tudor viewpoint, as outlined above by Maginn, than I could visualise myself standing amongst my own people in the uplands. I was determined to reverse this mental perspective.

To step into the mysterious highland region, less than ten miles south of the city, was to enter a distinct territory, known as the *Irishry*. It had a wholly different culture and language, where the inhabitants were subject to independent Gaelic chiefs and Irish law.[159]

The Tudor horseman, who rode for the first time into these uplands with his fellow troops, had to cross the level portions of the lowland Pale—south of Dublin—where change was perceptible with every mile traversed. It was noticeable how the cultivated land around the city gave way, increasingly, to a rougher type of farming with a preponderance of pastureland. The dress of the people became more indigenous along the rough roads to the south, and use of English decreased the closer one came to the hill country. But, the ways skirted the highlands rather than plunge into them, as if to postpone the inevitable for as long as possible. The rider knew he was still on relatively safe ground as he traversed the fringes of the uplands, known as *marches country*.

Rather than a wall of linked castles, there was a clustering of defensive tower-houses at particularly vulnerable sections along the Pale's perimeter which stretched for several hundred kilometres. The construction of a stout boundary-ditch had been attempted during the colony's most vulnerable period at the end of the fifteenth century; but Dublin was becoming more powerful now and defensive works of this sort were no longer necessary.

The Tudor horseman could probably rely on the families that lived in the many tower-houses of the area to assist him if he encountered a band of hostile Irish. Some of these *marcher* families had defended the borders of Dublin for centuries, even before the Norman invasion. The oldest of them were of Norse or Viking origin and their traditional loyalty inclined towards the city. But there was always the element of pragmatism to consider. They would support the strongest side when it suited their needs. During the nadir of English rule in the fourteenth century they were more likely to befriend the natives than help a man of authority from Dublin.

At a certain point along the route, the peppered presence of fortified stone-houses declined. The wearing of native dress was now universal; Irish cabins made of wood and straw became the norm; trees were more noticeable in the landscape. But, despite the fear of

---

158 Maginn, 2005; p. 183.
159 *Ibid*; p. 3.

the inhabitants of Dublin towards the native tribes, it would soon become clear that the people of the Irishry were going about their daily chores peacefully and in their own traditional ways. Earlier apprehension might easily give way to a false sense of security. The inexperienced intruder was amongst a people who appeared neutral and friendly, but out of the apparent placidity could emerge a mob sufficiently large and well-armed to cut down a platoon of soldiers or even lay waste a city the size of Dublin. The inexperienced Englishman could, understandably, be confused. The veteran was aware that it was difficult to tell friend from foe beyond the Pale. Loyal subjects could only be recognised by getting to know, personally, the principal men of the area and their followers, rather than through outward signs like dress, behaviour or language. It was, for this reason, that every officer who penetrated the Irishry would value the presence of a native or marcher scout.

A distinct hill to the east of the uplands, which looks like a volcano, was always pointed out to the newcomer on his first intrusion into Gaelic territory. This is the present-day Sugarloaf Mountain. It represented the northern tip of the boundary between the lands of the O'Byrnes to its east and those of the O'Tooles to its West. The O'Byrnes held the seaward portions of the Wicklow Mountains; the O'Tooles' territory stretched along the middle segment and western flanks of the highlands. The hinterlands of both these tribes extended south for hundreds of square kilometres and bordered the territory of the MacMurroughs, which covered the northern half of County Wexford. The problems that these septs were causing the citizens of Dublin is put into perspective when it is revealed that the southern reaches of the Pale were, at the end of the fifteenth century, the most densely castled part of Europe.[160] What do we know about these troublesome septs?

Ignorance about indigenous society can be traced, at least in part, to the lack of adequate academic focus on Ireland's Gaelic past. Patrick Duffy and his colleagues point out that: *One of the problems has been the lack of recognition of Gaelic society as a cultural group meriting scholarly archaeological investigation, like the Vikings or the Anglo-Normans.*[161] They also tell us that: *Much of the material published on Gaelic dynasties during the nineteenth century and in the greater part of the twentieth century, although not devoid of useful references and occasional insights, tended towards romantic sentiment rather than historical accuracy.*[162] Fortunately, a wealth of fresh material about Irish society has surfaced from the academic world in recent years, which is helping to dispel the inaccurate picture portrayed in previous centuries. Every new fragment unearthed about Irish tribal life by archaeologists, historians, anthropologists and biologists becomes a valuable piece of evidence in a large jigsaw and contributes to the creation of an ever-clearer picture of Ireland's Gaelic roots.

Of course, scholars have to be careful to express authentic views about each aspect of native life based on meticulous research and avoid sentimentality. But there is a danger here of creating a sanitised effect that distorts reality in a manner that is potentially as damaging as the opposite effects generated by the romanticised notions of Irish society in former times. Therefore, when examining the evidence we must continually remind ourselves that material remains and scholarly treatises have to be interpreted in ways

160 Murphy and Potterton, 2010; p. 269.
161 Duffy, et al, 2004; p. 34.
162 *Ibid*; p. 26.

that do not strait-jacket reality in accurate academic terms but lose sight of the living individuals who created history in the first place. Just like us, they had to overcome day-to-day problems. The Gaelic people, and my ancestors who lived amongst them, had real-life narratives. They experienced anxieties, setbacks, disappointments and tragedies. They were subdued by enmity, famine and diseases; debilitated by strife; mournful in death. But they were equally reinvigorated by exciting possibilities of love and friendship; rejuvenated by triumphs and new birth.

To know more about my ancestors in the professional landowning stratum of Leinster, I had to follow the advice of Patrick Duffy and his co-authors and peel back the overlying trappings of the modern world to reveal the realities of everyday life at this level within Irish society. They tell us that to understand Gaelic Ireland involves ... *mentally stripping away modern village and townscapes, urban sprawls, late field boundaries, motorways— the entire rattle-bag of modern endeavour—in order to more clearly see surviving medieval monuments and settlement in something of their original contexts.* [163] After removing the overlying layers that cloud our view of Gaelic society, we don't often encounter the heroic warrior-class of the Irish Renaissance, traipsing about the countryside in highly decorated Celtic fabrics, carrying intricately embossed shields and swords. What we find, predominantly, are farmers.

It is clear that Gaelic society could not have maintained fifteen per cent of the population in various non-productive professional occupations without additional support or income from the land. The learned classes, therefore, would have dedicated themselves to dairy farming, supplemented by tillage. But, many details of how they pursued their various specialisations are unknown. We are on firmer ground when discussing actual farming practices, though much still remains to be discovered.

From what we know of the landowning classes, they would have possessed, at any one time, a stipulated minimum size of property. It is estimated that the lowest rank of free farmer had about thirty hectares (seventy four acres) of good land, together with rights elsewhere to pasture, timber and peat.[164] Evidence for tillage is based on pollen analysis and material remains like ploughs, associated cutting tools and drying kilns. Quern stones show how widespread the use of cereals was in the diet of native communities. Barley or oats were probably the most commonly cultivated crops. They were grown in fields bordered by fences erected to divide off the pastures and keep out cattle. There is archaeological evidence that these enclosures were conjoined to farm dwellings. Some of the fields may have constituted the *greens* mentioned in Irish texts, where sheep were grazed and where local boys played hurling.[165]

As stated above, there comes a point at which the academic groundwork must give way to human imagination in order to achieve an ultimate visualisation of a culture that no longer exists. But, imagination can also be illusory unless assisted with real-life experiences. In this respect, insights gained from living human cultures at different levels of development are props that help us to understand how society functioned in the past.

---

163 *Ibid*; pp. 60, 61.
164 Mitchell, 1977; p. 168.
165 Stout, 1997; p. 37 and Mytum, 1992; pp. 175, ff.

I was fortunate to have lived amongst rural communities as a student during forest instruction in Ireland and when I was an extension officer in El Salvador. These parallel insights into country life helped me to understand how individuals react with each other at a basic level irrespective of cultural backgrounds, and probably would have reacted in the past. Further enlightenment came from another source, too.

I already mentioned that, after returning home, having spent several years in Central America, I began writing a novel about Saint Patrick. When the opportunity arose to work in a four-year World Bank training project in Kenya, the book was not yet finished. I continued to write during off-duty hours in my new setting and was drawn into an attempt to understand the indigenous culture that Patrick confronted when he was brought to Ireland as a slave. This enticed me to read the story of Ireland's past against the living tribal background of Kenya.

Many indigenous Kenyans in Nairobi who wear a suit and tie or blouse and skirt can return to their parents' or grandparents' places and morph from their Westernised ways, linguistically and visibly, into the tribal system. A similar transformation is impossible for the Irish. Nevertheless, we can gain some insights into old Gaelic ways by examining modern-day African societies because they exhibit many aspects found in old Irish tribal systems.

I became aware of these similarities gradually, and always associate the realisation with a day I climbed Longonot Volcano, a dormant cone that rises from the floor of the immense Rift Valley close to Lake Naivasha. Below Longonot is the land of the Maasai. As I walked around the summit that afternoon the Wicklow Mountains were, for some bizarre reason, an ever-present mental backdrop in my mind. Views of the Coronation Plantation and plains of Kildare from Tonduff Mountain emerged in the African landscape. Similarities of open country may have provoked the connection and caused me to reflect on my walks in Wicklow; moreover, the strange juxtaposition of thoughts of Ireland in an African setting finds some resonance in history.

I have watched the Maasai and Samburu pasturing their herds and flocks on the plains of East Africa and could not escape the feeling that, in these and other tribes, we are witnessing the closest living examples to ancient Irish pastoralism. Leaving aside obvious differences in climate and wildlife, the iconic image of a herder, clutching a spear as he stands in grassland amongst his cattle in the Rift Valley of Kenya or Tanzania, would have fitted comfortably into the summer pasturelands of Ireland's Central Plain in pre-Norman times.

I obtained a photograph of a reproduction Irish roundhouse and asked my African counterparts to distinguish what tribe it belonged to. They guessed it was Luo or Kikuyu but were taken aback to find it was an Irish design. The dwelling in the photo was a component of the iconic ringfort or *rath*. The rath was not a real fort but a palisaded enclosure of timber or brushwood surrounding an open space or *lis* where one or two round or rectangular houses stood. I have seen similar structures in Kenya. Surprisingly, the construction and occupation of ringforts was not prominent in the medieval and later landscapes of Ireland; they tapered off well before the coming of the Normans in the twelfth century. However, in Wicklow a number of ringforts continued as dwellings well into modern times, probably because of the ready availability of timber. Elsewhere, in place of the rath, unprotected rectangular buildings were preferred.[166]

The Irish pastoralists lived with their livestock and fed on milk, blood and other products of their animals, much like today's Maasai. Charles McGlinchey describes some of these practices in an Irish context. He writes: *In my father's time and before it, people went in greatly for bleeding cattle in the summer-time ... A rope was tied round the animal's neck and a vein would swell till it would be as thick as a man's thumb. The spur was put on top of the vein and the man gave it a knock with a stick. The blood came out and was capped in a piggin.*[167] At that time farmers had to sit all night with their livestock for fear that others would come and steal the product, bleeding them to death.

Traditionally, Maasai herds move to the more humid highlands during the dry season and back to the lowlands in the rainy season. These movements are not unlike the semi-nomadic practice of Irish pastoralists, called *booleying*, a system of husbandry in which communities followed their herds to summer grazing lands in the mountains, returning to the lowlands in winter. I found further confirmation of similarities with Gaelic culture in John Galaty's *Maasai Expansion,* which underlines what he calls the *constellation of factors* that go into the traits of the pastoral Maasai and include *congeniality and hospitality, respect and obedience* that go hand-in-hand with *intemperate bravery, ambition and self-sacrifice.* Constant reference has also been made to the aggressiveness, bellicosity, self-reliance and assertiveness of the Maasai. Similar comments have been made about the native Irish who were, in the main, cattle herders. These traits have been ... *attributed to herding experience engrained in a 'pastoral personality' and codified in a pastoral culture.*[168]

Above the Rift Valley escarpment are natural forest habitats and the territory of the Kikuyu. Here tribal huts were marked out, according to the desired size, by making a circle of a certain radius around a stick that was placed in the ground.[169] Old Irish roundhouses appear to have been laid out in a similar manner.[170] Many other characteristics were shared by the early Irish and contemporary African cultures, such as the acceptance of polygamy and the use of festivals for renewing friendships, strengthening political alliances and arranging marriages. The tenacious beliefs in taboos; the use of sacred groves; the methods of avoiding direct conversation in making deals; the close association of the blacksmith to the spiritual world are additional examples of similarities.

A characteristic that was peculiar to the Irish was their season of greatest abundance in late summer and autumn when the cattle herd was culled to reduce pressure on winter pastures. Culling took place because the farmers didn't know how to store animal foodstuffs in bulk to feed their livestock during the winter months.[171] The culling of the herd gave rise to great banquets, explaining the importance of the fest of *Samhain* from which the present-

---

166 Mitchell, 1977; pp. 167 ff. and Stout, 1997; pp. 24, 32.
167 McGlinchey, 1987; p. 28.
168 Galaty, 1993; p. 80.
169 Kenyatta, 1991; p. 80.
170 Stout, 1997; p. 14.
171 Mytum, 1992; pp. 183, ff.

day celebrations of Halloween are derived. Late winter and early spring were times of increasing need, or even famine, particularly when the previous growing season was poor or after a consecutive run of bad harvests. The Irish annals give us an idea of when the worst of these events occurred. We can begin to construct something of the lost minutiae of the lives of the native Irish through these sources.

Duffy and his co-authors reveal that as recently as the early 1990s, the details of the medieval economy of Gaelic Ireland remained virtually unknown. It is now clear that native farmers ran a subsistence economy, meaning that primary production and processing of the agricultural output satisfied basic needs. But it is also true that there was always some form of surplus which was used for social requirements. The potential of this surplus was not necessarily recognised in terms of economic profit. A positive margin above basic needs for physical survival was not a desirable luxury but essential to maintain position in society. Harold Mytum explains that: *Failure to maintain social position could be just as physically dangerous as lack of foodstuffs; therefore surplus to fulfil social obligations above basic subsistence needs was required, and this should be considered as part of the subsistence economy.*[172]

Irrespective of the particular size of property that the farmer possessed, it would have been an integral part of a wider geographical and political building-block, known in ancient Ireland as the *tuath*, which literally means "a people". There were about 150 of these small kingdoms in the country; each one equated roughly to a modern barony and each was sufficiently large to merit being ruled by a king. The consistency of the dimensions of the tuath underlines the fact that, once boundaries were established, they tended to endure and subsequent changes in the landscape and its inhabitants took place within these established frameworks.[173] Each tuath contained perhaps 3,000 men, women and children, providing an estimated population of half a million for the country as a whole, in Early Christian times.[174]

It is generally recognised that towns were lacking in Ireland. Nevertheless, there were dwelling sites called *bailes*, which seem to have been plebeian settlements of many hovels, often closely associated with the houses of free farmers. These collective structures were the sources of the Gaelic workforce. In Cavan, under the O Reillys, some sort of town grew up and may have developed through the initiative of the Gaelic merchant family of MacBrady who traded with the Pale.[175] In Ossory, a prosperous native centre or trading post existed at Aghaboe. A well-travelled road or *greate waye* linked this centre with Durrow in County Kilkenny and it contributed to the world of trade until Jacobean times, *when it probably declined following the political eclipse of the local MacGiollapadraig lords.*[176]

This overview provides an initial peep into what life must have been like for native landowning families. Many more details concerning agricultural and economic aspects of Gaelic society could be explored. However, turning to their professional roles, the existence

---

172 *Ibid*; p. 166.
173 Duffy, 2004; pp. 121, 122; MacNiocaill, 1980; p. 28; Mytum, 1992; p. 141.
174 Stout, 1997; p. 110.
175 Nicholls, 2005; p. 140.
176 Edwards, 2004; pp. 81, ff.

of Irish septs—like the forefathers of the Keoghs of Ranelagh—that dedicated themselves to learning and teaching, reinforces the reality of specific tasking and specialisation within the tribal economy.[177] Unfortunately, relatively little is known about the breakdown between specialist pursuits and work on the land. How many professionals, for example, were exclusively dedicated to writing, teaching and legal matters; how many spent most of their time on the land; did the majority of men of a professional rank divide their day, equally, between their vocational activities and farming; did the balance shift according to age? Presumably, a clever poet could gain a reputation that would hold him in good social standing and endow him and his family with material support without working the land.

It is not possible to answer many of these questions. Nonetheless, the level of learning required by native specialists can be appreciated through a cursory understanding of Irish Brehon Laws. These tracts represented Ireland's indigenous system of legislation that developed from custom, and governed everyday life and politics. The laws dealt with the intricacies of: rank; profession; fosterage; property-rights; offences; fines; the disadvantaged; contracts-and-pledges; procedures and punishments. The legal tracts recognise some regional variations but these were *relatively minor and merely emphasise the essential unity of the whole*.[178] The laws were passed on orally from one generation to the next and were only finally written down about the seventh century.[179] At that stage Ireland was Christian and therefore its edicts were heavily influenced by the Church, but they maintained a great deal of ancient tradition.

An idea of the complexity of the law tracts is revealed through the studies of two nineteenth-century scholars, Eugene O'Curry and John O'Donovan. They were the first since the death of the hereditary Irish antiquarian Duald Mac Firbis in 1670 to penetrate and understand the difficult and highly-technical language of these ancient documents. *From the labours of O'Donovan and O'Curry the Government published in the Master of the Rolls series five great tomes and a sixth containing a glossary. But these five large volumes do not by any means contain the whole of Irish law literature, which, in its widest sense, that is, including such pieces as the 'Book of Rights', would probably fill at least ten such volumes*.[180] Brehon Law survived until the middle of the seventeenth century when it was finally supplanted, under force, by English Common Law. A basic understanding of Irish law would have been an important constituent in the training of the professional learned classes.

177 Breen, 2004; p. 425.
178 Mytum, 1992; p. 102.
179 McMahon, 1980; p. 27.
180 The Catholic Encyclopedia. *The Brehon Laws*. < http://www.newadvent.org/cathen/02753a.htm > (August, 2015)

Tribal Roots

Christopher Maginn informs us that a representative of the MacKeoghs, a learned poet class, was always present at the inauguration of the chiefs of Leinster.[181] Further to their role in the ceremonial investiture of kings and lords, it is widely acknowledged that they were petty chiefs, and hereditary bards to the ruling family of O'Byrnes.

I was conscious of the possibility that my surname could have been adopted rather than being part of the "true" MacKeogh (*MacEochaidh*) sept of Leinster. It is always possible that families who carried the designation of a particular tribe were accepted into it by adoption, fosterage, accident or illegitimacy. Until I had proof I could not be certain that the story of my ancestors necessarily coincided with the history of the "real" MacKeoghs of Leinster. On the other hand, incorporation into a sept—by any means or under any circumstances—would render the descendants of that person indistinguishable from the "original" members of the tribe. For the moment, therefore, I could safely assume, at minimum, some overlap between my ancestors and the bardic septs of Leinster.

The most probable region of County Wexford in which the forefathers of the Keoghs of Ranelagh held property would, according to the historical literature of Gaelic tribes in the area, have been its northern segment, which remained largely in native hands, at least up until the plantations of 1610-1622.[182] Coincidentally, northern Wexford was the main seat of the MacKeogh sept in the province. I was closing in on the actual area that my ancestors came from.

But, I have no way of knowing the size of my forefathers' farm. If they maintained it after 1622, according to Henry Goff, it had to have been over one hundred acres because farms with less area had been confiscated. [183] Unfortunately, I have also no way of knowing how long they held on to their lands; Goff tells us that in the troubled period of the plantations the bards ... *usually got short shrift in the distribution of land.*[184] Now I realised that it was highly unlikely I would ever be able to pinpoint the specific parcel of farmland that they had owned. I had to reluctantly relinquish the long-standing ambition of revealing the very ground on which they lived and worked. However, I came across the following reassignment of a holding that related to north Wexford: In 1613 Thomas M'Keagh (MacKeogh) was assigned two hundred acres of land.[185] Perhaps this was—by some marvellous coincidence—my ancestor and his property. I could at least claim it to be a surrogate farm. As we have seen, the Keoghs probably moved to Connaught after the Restoration. They later adopted their knowhow, honed within the Gaelic system, to suit their urban environment. I had now succeeded in clarifying the identity of the family in as far as it would ever be possible.

Although I had acknowledged that I would never succeed in joining the Keoghs of Ranelagh, in an unbroken line of forefathers, back to their tribal homeland, it occurred to me that I could

---

181 Maginn, 2005; p. 8.
182 Colfer, 2002; p. 23 and Canny, 2009; p. 178.
183 Goff, 2001; p. 138.
184 *Ibid*; p. 144.
185 Russell and Prendergast, 1877; p. 454.

construct a genealogical device to assist in visualising each individual ancestor. In place of unknown names, I set numbers. Thomas the Elder was the oldest known name in the Keogh family. His father was the first unnamed Keogh and I gave him the designation *Keogh-1*; his father, in turn, became *Keogh-2* and so on. The actual span per generation between me and Thomas the Elder was more than thirty-six years. I therefore assumed that Keogh-1 was born about 1730, some thirty six years before Thomas the Elder. However, the interval between generations was likely to have diminished in previous periods. I therefore assumed a standard thirty years as the generation-span before 1730. On this basis Keogh-2 was born in 1700, thirty years before the birth of his father, and so on.

In constructing this ancestral device, I had to decide on a starting point. I was happy to probe back to a period before the Norman Conquest when my forefathers lived on land that they would have occupied since time immemorial. Surprisingly, this land was nowhere near Wexford, but on the plains of Kildare. The Normans were responsible for their dislocation from the midlands in early medieval times.

In the immediate period after the Norman Invasion, both Gael and foreigner learnt an important lesson. Irish warfare was superior to that of the invaders when practised in dense forest, in the mountains and on the boglands where the landscape was unfavourable to foreign cavalry. The Irish horsemen were skilled skirmishers but could not take on their enemies in the open.[186] The English were forced to avoid hostile areas outside the mineral soils of the lowlands. Thus foreign and Irish territories divided along ecological lines between the open fertile plains that the English dominated and the forested flanks of the uplands, combined with the humid boggy areas of the midlands that remained in Irish control. Therefore, it was no accident that the native Irish moved into the Leinster uplands from the plains of Kildare.

On the eve of the Norman Invasion, my forefathers inhabited what I considered to be their true niche in the Irish landscape, when their culture exhibited its maximum expression of Irishness, uncomplicated and uncontaminated by later incursions of foreigners. They lived in equilibrium with their environment on the plains of Kildare. In other words, they had established a balance between themselves and the existing natural flora and fauna of the lowlands. This, I fancied, was their *Idyllic Period*, when the bond between them and the natural world was at its strongest. Indeed, I felt that the best chance I would have of achieving a completely satisfactory understanding of their true identity was by increasing my knowledge of this 'pristine' period.

Roughly twenty of my forefathers embraced the interval between the eve of the Norman Conquest and the birth of Thomas the Elder. I reversed the numbers to provide an ascending chronological sequence and gave each man a Roman numeral from I to XX, Keogh XX being the father of Thomas the Elder.

Using the genealogical device I had constructed, I divided the period between the Norman Conquest and the birth of Thomas the Elder into four phases. The first phase, the *Idyllic Period*, ended when the Normans began their active colonisation of Kildare in 1178. Indigenous tribes that had held the fertile lowlands for centuries represented obstacles to

---

186 Heath, 2008; pp. 38 ff.

the newcomers' insatiable appetite for power and wealth and, as a result, the Gaels—at least the troublesome ruling classes and their retinues—were driven to the less-fertile uplands.[187] The O'Byrnes, O'Tooles and their related septs, including the MacKeoghs, found refuge in the hill country of Wicklow and Wexford.

The second or middle genealogical phase of the Keoghs lasted from 1178 to 1610 and I termed this the *Upland Phase* because, during this 400-year period my ancestors lived on the flanks and foothills of the Leinster highlands. They used the Gaelic form of the surname at the time. I therefore applied *MacEochaidh* instead of *Keogh* to all my forefathers who lived during and before their Upland Phase.

Their third phase was initiated in 1610, when the colonisation of the northern segment of County Wexford began. It is likely that they suffered in the general disruptions, though they may not have forfeited all their land at this time. They eventually moved to Connaught, probably after the Restoration; were likely to have begun to lose the use of Gaelic as their main language; accepted an anglicised version of their name and decided to move to Dublin. I called it the *Transitional Phase*. The current *Urban Phase* commenced when the Keoghs started to live in the city. As we have seen, the beginning of this stage is imprecise.

The ancestral device I had constructed helped me to structure my understanding of the lives of my people over several hundred years. Although it will never be possible to recreate the personal details of my twenty male ancestors over the turbulent years since they left their ancestral lands in Kildare and eventually came into the city, the broad outline should correlate fairly strongly with the real thing in the manner that pixels in digital cartography reflect the underlying terrain.

MacEochaidh I, who was born around 1160, was the last man to have experienced the family's Idyllic Period. He would have witnessed the wrenching of his tribe from their "true" ancestral homeland and their natural environment that they had inhabited for generations; he would have experienced exile into the uplands of Leinster.

In terms of social order in the Irishry, much continued unchanged in daily life for the fourteen men who existed in the Upland Phase of my family's past between 1178 and 1610. Fourteen times during this phase an infant male ancestor had his first memory, which had some association with domestic activities or scenes within and around his dwelling house. It might have been the image of the straw roof above his cradle where the smoke curled as he kicked his legs, moved his arms and hands and exercised his vocals cords in the joy of new life.

Memories grew. The perpetual movement of people about the heart was prominent in his memories. His mother was always doing something or giving her children something to do. There was firewood to be brought in; pots to be filled with water; milk to be turned to butter in wooden barrels. Stoking the fire; grinding wheat; cutting pig-meat; submerging pork into water; swinging the black pot into place over the hot fire. Everything she did generated a different sound. The swirl of the quern gave a stamp of identity to the day in which grinding took place; the initial scraping sound of stone against stone would

---

187 O'Byrne, 2003; pp. 16, 17.

accelerate into a hum that was interrupted with brief pauses as the flour was gathered and new grain added. The bubbling cauldron; the hot stone flag; the spit; each gave off their own delicious smells before a soup; a roast; an oatmeal cake materialised. Events happened at the same pace every day; never faster, never slower.

Every task was sure to be interrupted by someone who would darken the entrance before coming inside to sit down and talk. Some were greeted with enthusiasm and lots of humour; others with courtesy or nervousness; some were roared at and quickly retreated from the opening. The noises of the children echoed the atmosphere of the visitors; lively on good occasions; silent against the stranger. Some acquaintances came with gifts like honey and venison and carried off a cut of pork. At times there was great excitement as eels or sea cod were carried in. These times of excitement could result in a new or coveted taste, provided the produce was shared; sometimes these delights were reserved only for the men.

The atmosphere of the place and the subjects that were talked about always changed when the men came in and stored their knives and other implements they had been using in set places in the thatch overhead or on nails driven into wooden beams. Inevitably, they hovered about the fire to see what was made ready for them. The smell of ale was strong when men gathered in numbers. If the weather was good and problems light, their humour was ebullient. If things were not running in their favour, there was much silence. The women continued in their own set ways whether the men were humoured or not. In time, each boy grew into manhood and began to understand his future role in the professional ranks of his society. He also learned about the contemporary political and historical context in which his people found themselves.

MacEochaidh II witnessed the emerging of new land-ownership patterns at the turn of the twelfth and thirteenth centuries, which were dictated largely by strength and advantage between Normans and Gaels. His son and grandson would have observed, at first hand, the expansion of Norman territory to its zenith. His great-grandson was present to watch foreign strength wane.

MacEochaidh VI remembered when it was not easy for his mother to fill the cauldron with meat or stew; or find grain for the quern. He was seven in 1315. It seemed never to stop raining. As spring turned to summer the other children grew quiet; eventually they spent time huddled together watching the adults. Children commonly died; but this was different; they never passed away in such numbers. The following year heavy snows covered the land; the older men said they had never seen the like before; again he was hungry all the time. In later life he always divided the events that occurred before the time of the great hunger and the deep snows from those that happened after.

Having survived the ravages of the famine of 1315, MacEochaidh VI lived to witness the cattle plague of 1322 and endured the smallpox outbreak of 1327 when he was a young adult. Despite these setbacks, he and his generation perceived the new feelings of confidence amongst the upland clans during the first decades of the fourteenth century when the indigenous re-conquest of foreign-held territory began. His son lived through the Black Death that came to Ireland in 1348, though this disease was not as common amongst the Gaels in the uplands as it was in the towns and cities of Ireland. His grandson, MacEochaidh VIII, lived to see the visit of King Richard II to Ireland.

Richard became the first king to visit the country since 1210 and the last to do so before the 1690s. He came to Ireland in 1394 and made a second ill-fated trip in June 1399. The significance of his first visit was a meeting of the Leinster tribes and an agreement that they would surrender their lands to the crown and obtain them back under English law through a re-grant. The tribes didn't take such things seriously; but the English used the agreement against the Irish after unearthing it hundreds of years later in the early seventeenth century at the time of the Wexford plantations.[188]

For most of the fifteenth century and up to the reign of the Tudors in England, an uneasy balance of power had been maintained between the Gaels and the Old English in Leinster. Henry VIII became king during the life of MacEochaidh XII and relations between England and Ireland deteriorated considerably from then on. A much more aggressive approach was taken against the Irish under Henry and his daughter, Elizabeth. The three following generations after MacEochaidh XII lived through this period. At the beginning of the Tudor dynasty, the Gaelic lordships were still powerful. However, MacEochaidh XIII observed newly arrived Tudor soldiers enter his territory more frequently and it made him uneasy. When Elizabeth died in 1603, the last great native counter-attack and defeat had occurred at Kinsale, opening the way for the final dissolution of the tribal system. MacEochaidh XV was the last to have experienced freedom under the independent chiefs of Gaelic Leinster more than 400 years and fourteen generations after MacEochaidh I.

Four generations separate me from Thomas the Elder. The same number of generations separated him from Keogh XVI, the first man who experienced the beginning of the Transitional Phase of the family. This gave me a good idea of the interval in time back to my tribal roots. Few, if any, material objects could have survived long after the end of the family's Upland Phase was over; it was a different story for family memes.

Unlike the study of archaeological changes—that are measurable through tangible objects—pinpointing modifications in ancestral memes that have been passed on amongst the native Irish in response to devastating and long drawn-out attacks against their culture would be a difficult and highly complex task. The exact nature of each modification in the long sweep of Irish history is almost impossible to trace. But the overall processes, which retained a tenacious though shifting core, is an intriguing story. An alternative way of expressing this view is that the outlook of the original tribal culture, from which its modern urban counterpart sprang, was completely transformed and, if placed side-by-side, the similarities between the old and new would be unrecognisable. On the other hand, the modern Gaelic offshoot in the city would be completely dissimilar if its base had been different.

Most of us are unaware that, irrespective of our origins, old influences are at work within us and remain to be discovered. A flavour of ancient memes have come down to modern times and it fascinated me to think that, even before delving into family history, I had succeeded in picking up something—no more, perhaps, than a distant echo—of the essence of indigenous culture in the residual presence of former generations in my grandfather's house at Beechwood Road. The realisation that some current influences have emerged from deep within native society fully satisfied my desire to link myself intimately to

---

188 Goff, 2001; pp. 135, 137.

Gaelic Ireland. The overall experience has been like the uncovering of a long-lost tapestry that now hangs as a permanent image on the walls of my mind. The image has the same effect as an intricate and enlightening work of art; there is always something new and refreshing to see in it.

A similar history could be written for the entire indigenous middle-class community in the cities and towns of Ireland, at least with regard to its development up to the beginning of the twentieth century. But, the quantitative nature of its growth in Dublin, as demonstrated earlier, implies that it was a relatively small entity amongst middle-class urban ranks, an uncomfortable fact that questions—once more—the legitimacy of applying an official Gaelic identity to the entire Irish nation after independence.

III. The Wider Perspective

Idyllic Illusion

Anthropologists recognise the fascination we have for the intimate relationship between man and nature. Writing about the Maasai, Thomas Spear and Richard Waller acknowledge that ... *it is precisely the apparent 'primordiality' and 'naturalness' of ethnicity that provides its evocative power.*[189] An extension of this concept is the view that these qualities reach their maximum expression within a pristine biological environment in which the primeval society is embedded. Earlier, I conveyed the opinion that there is something of the *noble savage* in the notion of primitive man in nature; something of the perfect fit between humans and their surroundings: the ultimate definition of identity. In other words, we cannot attain a satisfactory understanding of ourselves until we uncover the essential links between mankind and nature, which must have reached their most intimate level of intertwining in early societies. If this is true, it follows that identity in all later cultures must be judged against this *basic natural standard*. We must always ask the question: How far are we from the idyllic? And our answer provides a measure of the remove between the ideal and our present condition.

At this point in my quest, I held the notion that ancient Gaelic society lived an ideal form of existence in a pristine environment. It is understandable, then, why I would apply the term *Idyllic Period* to the family's phase of existence on the plains of Kildare in pre-Norman times. I was not unique in harbouring the view of a faultless bond between a Celtic people and their natural surrounds. The concept was central to the outlook of former generations. It was a powerful precept in the minds of those who chose the evocative symbols of the young Irish State.

I now felt that I was approaching a more succinct expression of the real underlying motives for my inquiry. I was seeking something deeper than a simply link between the Keoghs of Ranelagh and their Gaelic past. Instead, I had been trying to forge a connection to a Celtic people who had been embedded in an unspoiled environment. The next step was to achieve a clearer perceptive of the meaning of "identity" by understanding what is meant by the term *basic natural standard* which defines it.

Two things helped me in this process. I was able to draw on the experience I had as a young forester in Latin America and the knowledge I gained from a consultancy assignment in Ireland at the opposite end of my career, which involved defining what is meant by *high conservation value* in existing native woodlands. Forest was the predominant natural vegetation of Ireland. Defining high conservation values involved studying elite biological woodland in the context of interference by man. These elite sites are the showcase forests of the country; the best that exist in terms of Irish biodiversity.

My desire to experience the reality of the rainforest at first hand and gain insights into a primordial culture was a large part of the reason why I was attracted to Latin America in the first place. As a young forester I was trying to answer questions that would arise

---

189 Spear and Waller, 1993; p. 137.

later in more articulate terms. I was really trying to clear up the perception of what I conceived to be environmental and cultural purity or "originality". I felt that firsthand experience of a primordial tribe would provide me a clear view of what life was like for humans freed of all subsequent contamination and modernisation. In this manner, I would have a benchmark— now defined as a *basic natural standard*—against which all cultures, including my own, could be judged and I would understand how far humanity had drifted from the "original" over subsequent generations.

A reappraisal of the journey that Henning Flachsenberg and I made to South America from El Salvador, those many years ago, in the context of a contemporary understanding of the relationship between mankind and nature, challenges many of the views I held. Before undertaking the journey I surmised that some of the oldest and most original cultures of Latin America were to be found where the natural environment was still conserved and where the local Indian populations were living in harmony with it. It followed that the authentic cultures of the region must still be preserved intact in areas of remaining tropical forests—the primary natural vegetation of much of the sub-continent.

When planning our expedition, we considered travelling up the River Orinoco and Rio Negro, then crossing into the Amazon, eventually coming out at Manaus. Around 1560 a Spaniard named Aguirre ascended the Amazon into the Rio Negro. He and his men noted a strange change in the flow of the waters, which had been moving against them in a southerly direction. Now the currents flowed with them towards the north. Aguirre discovered that they were no longer moving upriver. They didn't realise that the Amazon and Orinoco have a common source in this area and that the waters of both rivers spout out of the same catchment. We wanted to do this journey in reverse.

It was fortunate that Dr. Leslie Holdridge, whose ecological mapping system is used widely in Central and South America, was working in our project in El Salvador. He advised against crossing from the Orinoco to the Amazon, suggesting that all we would see, for much of the journey, would be two banks of trees on either edge of the river at a great distance from each other. It would be more interesting and productive to pick a smaller river, which would offer much more variety close at hand. In response, Henning and I turned to an atlas of South America and picked out a river called the Ventuari in Venezuela, a tributary of the Orinoco, which seemed to fit what we were looking for. We put all our accumulated leave into the venture and set out for Caracas without making any booking, beyond the return flight to El Salvador.

I liked to call our venture an expedition. However, it was far from a professional investigation; it was more a curious peep, by young foresters, into the jungles of South America. But for me it was to become a life-changing experience and offered pointers to where the ultimate definition of human identity might lie. Enlightenment percolated through daily occurrences that appeared commonplace, but the backdrop of the jungle against which they happened steered the underlying contemplation towards an unexpected conclusion.

Several days after arriving in Caracas we were exhilarated to be in the air over the Orinoco in a twin-engine DC-3, having left Ciudad Bolivar airport, a place that reminded me of Collinstown in Dublin in the 1950s. Even the style of the airhostess seemed to be of a previous era.

Down below the broken clouds were the great plain or *llanos* of Venezuela. In the distance a mix of light and dark patches stretched out like a modern artist's abstraction to fill the earth to the horizon. Directly underneath our path of flight a brown, green and kaki tableland of grass and low vegetation, dotted with bushes, gave way abruptly to trees along the margins of the river. Islands, partially covered in scrub or composed totally of sand, lay like resting monsters in the water. Swamps and reeds covered the wetter banks of the river.

Soon the aircraft dropped altitude to several hundred metres and the Orinoco went out of sight. Cattle were dotted on the great prairie. The river briefly came into view again before the plane landed at Caricara, a small town built beside the river with a tiny airport the size and shape of a seaside cottage. It was about as dead as Brittas Bay out of season. Some passengers alighted and became part of an existence whose pace of vitality was several dimensions slower than Ciudad Bolivar, which, in turn, was a good deal slower than Caracas, the capital. They became lonely figures in a lonely landscape and I wondered how they existed in such a deserted place. However, the only way we have of appreciating the wealth of other cultures and forms of existence, particularly those that run at a slower pace than ours, is to allow ourselves to seep slowly into the local tempo, with ample time to adjust. When accomplished properly, we can often emerge from the experience to criticise our former state of existence.

The plane was airborne again. After some time it descended and landed at the airport of Puerto Ayacucho. A local taxi took us to the Hotel Amazonas. The taxi was a multi-use truck that had been employed to carry animals; it was now filled with people. The driver tried to cheat us into paying the fares of some of the passengers he was acquainted with but we resisted.

In the hotel we met a *Señor* Barletto, an Italian who told us that there were restrictions preventing foreigners making contact with local Indians because some groups entered the area with the objective of photographing forest tribes to use in the pornographic trade. We decided to approach local authorities in case of difficulties and, armed with blue UN passports, went to the *Guardia Nacional*. The local commander gave us a letter asking all civil and military groups to give what co-operation they could with respect to our passage through the region.

Next day we visited the offices of the Ministry of Agriculture to talk to local forestry staff. They provided some information on the vegetation of the Orinoco. One officer agreed to transport us by Land Rover to Samariapo to catch a boat into the interior. In the distance, in our direction of travel, blue mountains seem to hold out the promise of the primeval. But on arrival at Samariapo, a dirty little river port with many boats, the atmosphere changed. We wanted to go to San Fernando, which would bring us to the mouth of the Ventuari and our gateway into the forest. However, we were told that it would be difficult to get a boat. Eventually, the name of a local man emerged. He might be able to take us there—at a price. We bargained and got a bad deal. But at least we were moving again. National flags abounded around Samariapo to ensure a clear distinction between the Venezuelan and Colombian sides of the Orinoco.

The journey to San Fernando, or *San Fernando de Atabapo* to give it its full grandiose title, took over four hours instead of the promised two and a half. This little town, which was founded in 1756 by Don José Solano, was the real gateway into the interior, but a gateway that schemed against our progress. San Fernando offered with one hand and took with the other—an unjust comment, though that is the way I felt at the time. My gloom was aggravated by an uncomfortable night. We were to blame for staying on an outside passageway of the Guardia Nacional compound. It was provided because of our letter of support from the commander in Puerto Ayacucho.

If I am in a place without facilities I like to be alone. If I am with people I like to have privacy and running water. I had no privacy there and facilities were dismal. The toilets in the Guardia buildings were badly kept and the water system was not functioning properly. To make matters worse, a soldier, returning from the town late at night, used them to ditch the contents of his stomach and the remains stayed all night. The smell was nauseating. Worse again, my hammock was missing two cord separators, with the result that I was so squeezed the blood would have stopped flowing in my limbs. I transferred to the concrete floor of the passage but slept badly under the vigilant eye of the sentry.

In the morning, after a restless night, I woke feeling very sore. Then came dismal news. It would be difficult to get upriver unless we hired a craft and a boatman to steer it. This meant paying his fee as well as the costs of hire and fuel. Having been swindled out of money at every step so far, we felt that we were going to be swindled again and were reluctant to fall into another trap. We had organised the trip badly. What would we do now? The whole venture looked as if it would collapse. There were several options: abandon the project, buy a small canoe and paddle along the river ourselves or hire a boat with a driver. The notion of paddling was criticised by local boatmen, who said this would be a foolish act. The people that we saw travelling in small paddle canoes were Indians who knew the currents.

We went bathing in the river; then had breakfast consisting of six scrambled eggs cooked over a camp stove. Water and some juice from a can washed them down. Even the food we bought in the town was sold at an exorbitant price. We were being tricked at every stage and this would surely burst our budget. I fell into a state of depression. Henning and I sat apart in our own thoughts. This was the lowest point I had reached in many years. I was so close to achieving what I had wanted for decades—observing, at first hand, the natural forests and the authentic cultures of the Orinoco basin. All the hopes I had put on this expedition were so close to being fulfilled but, because of a shortage of money, we would have to turn back. Desperation and logic fought an uncomfortable fight on the banks of the river in that mean little town. I would prefer to face the risks of paddling by canoe than turn back now. If I was prepared to risk my life, I should be prepared to risk my money.

We had to do something. We had to come to a decision. Finally, we opted to pay a man and hire a boat; it was the only realistic way forward. We then began to negotiate with a boatman and agreed a price to carry us up the Ventuari, providing we would leave within the hour. In this manner we were released from that little town I hated.

The easiest way to move through the rainforest was by boat. Our small craft, a *bongo*, made out of a single piece of ceiba tree with a roof of palm straw and an outboard motor attached to the stern, sat low in the water as it made its way upriver. The pen-line on the atlas of South America that represented the Ventuari was now translated into a gushing force of water against the bow between two riverbanks of tropical forest.

We came ashore on the first evening having travelled east from San Fernando for much of the day. There was a cluster of empty huts in a grass-covered opening, abandoned by slash-and-burn cultivators. We stayed in the huts. These were no more than simple wooden frames covered by palm leaves. First we pounded the upright posts to dislodge any snakes that might have been lurking in the roof. Thankfully, none appeared. It was turning very dark when we strapped our hammocks to the cross poles and divided the space under the roof into areas of separate functions.

We lit a fire to prepare our evening meal. Just then the sky dislodged a torrent of rain and we had to race to untie our hammocks and change them to a drier part of the hut. At times I saw Henning's silhouette, his shirt blowing hard in the wind, as he worked partly in the downpour against the blue and white flashes of lightning. Rivulets of water began flowing on to the floor of the hut and we successfully guided the flow away from the area where we had placed our possessions. Then, when we had won the battle against the elements, we prepared the evening fare, a mix of soup into which peas were dumped. The soup was followed by biscuits and tea and good conversation. The storm cleared, the stars appeared between the clouds and we relaxed. Sleep came swiftly and easily.

It was still dark at 5.15 a.m. when we packed our things in preparation for another day up-river. Light came to the Ventuari and revealed our solitude in a forest clearing. In the area around the huts there was no evidence of human life. Facilities were non-existent, but it was luxurious. The sense of freedom and isolation was exhilarating. I walked on my own through the grass. In such a place there is a peace that is unequalled in town or city. I listened to the eternal music of the forest: sounds like the tapping of a woodpecker and the roar of howler monkeys coming from the vicinity of tall trees nearby. Are these, I wondered, the sounds we all long for in our deep heart's core, irrespective of whether we live in city, town or countryside?

We were moving upriver again. As we journeyed we spent time filtering river water from a plastic bucket with the help of a ceramic hand pump, then added purifying tablets to ensure that it was drinkable; at least stomach problems were avoided. We wrote observations in our diaries or just sat back and watched the boat throw up a screen of spray from the bow as it cut against the current. The hypnotic throb of the motor, the continual swish of water and the motion of the passing treescape lulled us into a drowsy state at the edge of sleep.

The forest canopy is the only skyline along the river in flat country and any elevated ground is striking. Two blue mountain peaks became very noticeable on the horizon. Slowly they grew in size till they dominated the entire scene. These were the twin peaks of Cerro Moriche. We passed under their bulk at their very base; then watched them recede as slowly as they had come. This gave us some idea of our speed and progress and a sense of the immensity of the area through which we travelled. Our sense of time and motion was beginning to slip downwards to the pace of the river and the jungle.

The term *jungle* conjures up a terrifying picture of lurking hidden dangers. It is just a great extension of trees and vegetation. There are dangers within, but if nature is treated with respect they are minimised. The one who is travelling through the forest without compass or tree markers is begging to be lost. The one who wears sandals and walks through the grass at the edge of the *selva* and savanna is inviting snakes to bite. But it has to be admitted that there are important differences that made past expeditions unique compared to modern ones. When no malaria tablets existed; when no snake-bite serum was available; when water filters or purifying tablets could not be purchased; when there were no airstrips for flying doctors; when vaccinations were unknown, things were completely different. It requires little imagination to calculate how long it might take for one's health to collapse if anything went wrong under primitive conditions.

I admit to something of the same craving for adventure that Peter Fleming expressed in his *Brazilian Adventure,* which detailed his expedition to Mato Grosso to solve the mystery of Fawcett's disappearance in the State in 1925. He said that he secretly yearned for the *Lost World*, a reference to Conan Doyle's story of exploration and exciting encounters in the jungles of South America.[190] But there was, apparently, a lack of real danger for us and this removed the spice of adventure from our expedition; in a way I was playing the game of explorer. I felt I had no opportunity to really prove myself capable of meeting the challenges of nature in raw form.

I was as close as ever I would be to savouring what previous explorers faced in South America. As I watched the forest pass I became conscious that ours was the same visual experience as that beheld by Humboldt, Solano, Fawcett, Fleming and all former explorers of these regions through the ages. Large parts of the landscape were the same then as now, thus the element of time, as a factor that divided us, was at least partially removed.

At a distance the jungle appears to be endless and totally monotonous. But closer observation shows it to be highly complex. Here, a vine drapes over the river. There, a tree has fallen into a watery grave. In one location palms are abundant, while further on they appear to be completely absent. Sometimes there is only a single layer of vegetation. Elsewhere, layers of vegetation rise one above the other. Here, the treetops are low; there, the canopy is too tall to observe. In places the trees are of a large diameter, while in another they are many and their stems are small. Where pockets of forest have been undisturbed, which is rare in this area, the oldest trees are venerable relics of times past and have stood for centuries. To the trained eye, all these signals provide clues to recent and past historical events. Most of the evidence pointed to the scars of man on the landscape. There were few signs that the people were living in harmony with nature.

The bongo reached a small town called Las Carmelitas. *Plantains,* a type of banana, grew about the place which was relatively well organised but, like all towns along the river, it gave the impression that there were fewer people than houses to accommodate them. I wandered around while the boatman removed the motor to adjust it, with the help of a storeowner and a man who had emigrated from Spain to live amongst the river people.

The Spaniard joined us on the next part of the journey upriver and the entire flavour of the enterprise changed. The Spaniard turned out to be a *campesino* who later became a night

---

190 Fleming, 1957; p. 107.

watchman in Madrid. We figured he was in his fifties. He drew us into conversation about the Spanish Civil War, the church and things of his own world. He told us he had helped some people on the wrong political side and, for his trouble, was given a gaol sentence. We christened him Robinson Crusoe because of his rugged appearance. He was thin, weather-beaten and wore a battered straw hat, an unwashed shirt, a pair of rugged trousers and runners without socks. His feet were a mass of mosquito bites. This was the unlikely owner of 300 head of cattle from San Juan de Manapiare. His openness and outgoing nature enabled us to make close contact with the Indians in the locality.

We had come to the Ventuari as strangers and outsiders but were becoming, little by little, part of the river people. We penetrated further into the interior. At each identifiable place we made deeper breaks with the world we had come from. Now we reached an area of very few people and I had the distinct feeling that we were passing a great invisible divide between civilisation as we knew it into a world that early cultivators and hunter-gatherers of past aeons would recognise.

Robinson Crusoe was trying to make contact with some Guahibo and Maco Indians because they had borrowed his boat and had not returned it. We met two Guahibo canoes—miniature Noah's Arks carrying men, women, children, dogs, a cat, chickens, a parrot and luggage of all sorts. They were moving their slash-and-burn forest location. A child sat placidly under an enormous hat amid this heap of life's essentials. One of the oarsmen gave an occasional shout as if of joy though there seemed no occasion for it. Robinson Crusoe got into conversation and one Indian said they were making for the Isla Vapor, a place of the Maco tribe, which lay a little downstream. Our boat turned about for this place.

The Maco didn't appear when we first reached the shore, but we could hear their sounds—something like the subdued shouts made by the Guahibo paddler. Then the men appeared one by one. There was mention of a fiesta going on. The conversation changed and revolved around the Spaniard's problem. The women appeared and they behaved like adolescent schoolgirls. Our presence gave rise to smiles, nods, giggles and comments. On the surface they appeared to be a very innocent, content and curious people.

We left Robinson Crusoe on Isla Vapor to sort out his problem and turned upriver again. After some time we came upon a canoe paddled by a *mestizo*—a man of mixed Indian and Spanish race. He was accompanied by a woman and, I presumed, their child. Our boatman wanted to procure meat and a discussion ensued between him and the canoeist, who said he would provide the desired goods if we would come to his house. We then came alongside the small boat, tied it to our bongo and towed it to an island upriver where the family had a hut. The canoeist carried a bow and arrow in his craft. The arrowhead was small and made of metal. He also had a worn armament, like a blunderbuss. These old implements were concrete evidence of the time-warp in which the river people lived.

Our boatman bought a turtle that was about half a metre long. It had a sharp bite and the canoeist demonstrated how the animal could split sticks in its mouth. The sticks severed with a single crack. Our boatman also bought meat of a wild pig, which he paid for in Bolívares and matches. We left the family on their island and, once more, made our way between the walls of forest until we came to a settlement called La Vuelta de Araguato an insect-ridden place which was to be our stop for the night.

The inhabitants, who would not have numbered more than ten, were friendly. At each resting-place we had to unload the bongo before dark and reload it in the morning. There was a danger not only of theft if we left goods in the boat but also of anacondas. After arriving on the shore, the first thing we did was tie up our hammocks to a wooden frame that had a roof of straw. The Ventuari was dotted with such structures and it was acceptable for those who travelled on the river to use them without paying. This meant that our budget was in better shape than anticipated. Hotel rates on the river were zero.

We lit a fire and settled down to make our evening meal consisting of spaghetti, tinned meat and tea. My stomach continued to behave well but grew tired of dried and tinned food. One may eat fairly well along the river; there are ample supplies of meat and fruit. Bartering was common; batteries and Bolívares could be swapped for pineapples and eggs. When, next morning, I heard I could obtain bananas, I jumped at the opportunity. I was happy to swap tinned food for fresh fruit and the river people were happy to add the novelty of something out of a can to their jungle diet. But not all was fresh. I bartered some spaghetti for three eggs. I dropped one; the other was bad, which spoilt my appetite for the third. Henning had no scruples and ate the last egg.

Robinson Crusoe arrived from Isla Vapor and joined us on our journey to Yamara. This place appeared to be nothing but a name and when we entered the tributary beside it, the forest was not well developed. The canopy height had dropped considerably; more evidence of man's scars on nature. Though it was a peaceful location, two years previously a *caiman* had attacked and killed a man here. A duck now swam on the quiet surface as if it were on a pond in Stephen's Green in the heart of Dublin.

At another point along the river we spotted a small sandy beach, with a tributary nearby. Henning and I went ashore; then entered the *selva* to explore. There were animal tracks through the undergrowth here. We walked for some time before finding a solitary place where we sat down and listened, in silence, to the sounds of nature. Evidence of recent human activities was absent. There was little movement until a large black vulture settled itself in the branches of a tree overhead. We watched the large bird and took photographs of it. After some time we grew impatient and walked further through the undergrowth. There were sounds of a large animal moving through the vegetation. But we saw nothing. On the river, freshwater dolphins jumped and turtles lay in the sunshine on a bough over the water. At another time, two highly-coloured macaws appeared, flying majestically overhead. The shock spectacle of colour in a world of greens can be electrifying, whether it is birds in flight or the unexpected appearance of a tree fully-draped in purple sunlit flowers in the midst of eternal monochrome.

The feeling of a lack of danger can lull the traveller into a false sense of security. At one point our boat came to an area of forest where the trees were well developed. I wanted to see what lay beyond the jungle at this spot. I wanted to check if there was a band of forest along the river banks beyond which lay savannah. We were not far from open country. I suggested to Henning that we go ashore. He was not in the humour, so I decided to go alone. I consider myself to have a fairly good sense of direction. But, as a precaution, I took a machete and marked the trees as I went.

There were no paths here and I was becoming conscious of the danger of being lost. Despite some misgivings, I continued and soon came to water. I was convinced that I had reached a pond or a lake. Then I heard voices nearby and went in their direction. To my amazement it was Henning and the people of our bongo. Without saying a word about my experience, I climbed aboard and spent the next hours contemplating how this could have happened. I became convinced about how easily one can get lost in the forest within a relatively short distance if there are no landmarks to guide one's path. Within a few days I took a photograph of a place, indicated by our boatman, where a man went into the forest and was never heard of again. This was a chilling reminder to me of what could have happened.

We made a brief stop at Morocoto, place of the Piaroa Indians whose traditional hut is cylindrical with a conical straw roof. Only one such hut existed in the village. The settlement was comparatively large and the occupants were highly amused by our appearance. The women looked at us from a distance and, like the Maco, often peeped from behind a secure object. If they were near they would pretend to ignore us totally or scurry away quickly.

Again, there were few signs of man living in harmony with nature and no evidence of anything approaching a pristine forest; on the other hand, there was plenty more evidence of scars on the natural vegetation with associated indications of recovery after repeated wounding by the acts of man. The best example I had that man and nature live in conflict, rather than harmony, came at a most unusual location. It was a lonely cutting high on a riverbank where a Greek intellectual had turned to the solitude of nature for his existence and spent seven years as a hermit beside the Ventuari. The river people called him mad— but who knows the truth. He, apparently, had been a university professor who had a problem with the government. It seems he may have been a communist, but the story was far from clear. We inspected the site and found a small area planted with mango, guayaba, pineapple and lemon and we carried off some fruit. The remains of the house, which consisted of clay walls, was only barely distinguishable from the soil from which it had been constructed. The legacy of the hermit was visible in old cans, a rotting shoe, a battered metal packing-case and an area cleared of jungle. Even this lone man left a visible scar on nature that was only in the first stages of recovery.

I began to change my views about man's ability to live in harmony with nature. Man lives at the expense of nature. On our journey of over 300 kilometres upriver on the Ventuari I realised that our hope of finding the pristine forest was an elusive goal. Our species cannot live in the natural environment without affecting and changing it; and most of the riverbanks had been heavily disturbed at one time or another.

On the other hand, it is hard to deny that an emotive image comes to mind when the term *old growth* forest is used. *To many it describes a forest that has grown for centuries without human disturbance and now is a stand of massive, towering trees with jumbles of large decaying tree trunks; deep shade pierced by shafts of sunlight; and dense patches of herbs, shrubs, and saplings that may conceal rare species. Such a forest is as awe-inspiring as it is biologically rich. It may contain the largest trees, the oldest trees, the most at-risk forest species, and the largest accumulation of carbon per acre of any forest type on earth.*[191] This is probably what most of us have in mind when we talk about a pristine forest, an ancient forest, a virgin forest, or any of the myriad of other widely-used but loose terms to describe the majesty of these ecosystems.

Conservationists now prefer to avoid contentious, inexact or emotive terms, which engender nature with qualities that are passing or never existed in the first place. It may come as a surprise to the non-biologist that scientists have difficulties in defining what is meant by *naturalness* when pertaining to ecosystems. *Natural* and *nature* must be amongst the commonest words used in biological sciences, yet their meaning is frequently uncertain and the implied values can be contentious, especially when applied to systems that were interfered with in any way by man. And what ecosystem has not been modified by humans, either directly or indirectly? Mankind has played a major role over the centuries in moulding the ecosystems of the world so it is difficult to recognise any area that has been completely untouched. Hunter-gatherers were around in Europe when the forests started to expand after the Ice Age, and were probably responsible for the spread of many species across the treeless wastes as woodlands took possession of the areas to the north of their Alpine refuges. Therefore, the process of natural colonisation in the wake of the disappearing ice sheets was not fully an act of nature devoid of man's interference.

A more satisfying way to view ecosystems is in terms of *processes*. Old-growth is a relative term; and old things die. Unless younger forests are allowed to become older, then ancient woodlands disappear. Today when scientists talk about *restoring naturalness* to areas that have been damaged, like the woodlands of Ireland that have been modified many times since they covered the country before the arrival of man, the goal is to ensure an ongoing sustainable supply of ecosystem goods and services from these areas. The goal has become one of allowing restoration processes to take place to augment and protect the intrinsic values of the woodlands, rather than re-establishing particular patterns or structures of vegetation.

It is now clear that natural ecosystems and the development of human cultures both involve processes. A different set of dynamics is at work in nature where humans are present or absent. Recognition is thereby given to the special powers that humans have, unlike other species which are part of their ecosystem or set of ecosystems, but do not have our abilities to transcend, dominate and modify them.

Before I came to the Orinoco I was searching for an elusive and static condition in which nature and mankind were living in an original and pristine condition of existence. I was seeking a steady-state in which man and nature linked together in a single harmonious unit and in which human identity found its perfect meaning. This elusive state doesn't exist and didn't exist. Human cultures are in a condition of continual change, and fundamental change was set in motion at an unknown point in the past. Therefore the *basic natural standard* against which all subsequent changes can be identified in mankind is an illusion. To comprehend a culture at any particular moment, it is necessary to understand how it developed to that point in time. Even the Amazon tribes that maintain little contact with modern life came to the region from outside; they were not truly indigenous to the region. Their origins are to be found elsewhere.

---

191 NCSE, 2008; p. 5.

My forefathers who inhabited the plains of Kildare during their so-called Idyllic Period had reached their particular stage of development through a long process of cultural and ecosystem change and, therefore, this was by no means their true natural or ancestral base. By then they had eliminated much of the natural forest in favour of open-grazing lands. They had imposed a pastoral landscape on what had been a natural forest. It followed that the expression *Idyllic Period* was no longer appropriate to describe their condition in pre-Norman times; I dropped the term in favour of what I now call their *Lowland Phase*.

Having dismissed the notion of a steady-state harmony between man and nature, a new question now arose. I wondered how far into the past do major influences penetrate. In other words, how far back should we go, either individually or on the collective cultural level, to understand how the principal processes of the past impinge on our present identity? I reached an instinctive conclusion that it would be artificial to define *any* particular point or stage as the base of our ancestral and natural influences. By reaching this conclusion I made a significant step forward, which would eventually allow my inquiry into the nature of human identity to be unfettered by artificial definitions of who we are.

White Feathers

In the aftermath of the Orinoco expedition and its reappraisal, I understood clearly that we cannot arrive at a true definition of identity if "any" factor—past or present—that impinges on our makeup, is omitted. I had been reluctant to acknowledge and examine the full range of cultural forces that emanated from all sides of my family; I had been, for too long, avoiding the influences coming from my hybrid nature and this was an obstacle to defining my true identity. I was not pure Gael but a mix of Gael and Old English; a mix of old enemies. It was time to face this uncomfortable truth.

The hybrid nature of the descendants of the Keoghs of Ranelagh comes to the fore when Finola Keogh discusses her mother, actress Evelyn Lund. Ernest Blythe once said that Evelyn could not be employed in the Abbey Theatre because she was an Englishwoman. Finola agreed that her mother came from Yorkshire but lay emphasis on the Danish origin of the surname and pointed out, furthermore, that Evelyn's mother was a Dillon of Norman-Irish origin. She then revealed that this family had *turncoated* to Protestantism, probably to hold onto their lands. But what is most revealing is that Finola states her mother ... *fitted into no convenient camp.*[192] This is the precise response generated in cultures without clear-cut identities and I instantly recognised the parallels created in my own family through the mixed nature of its Gaelic and Old English backgrounds.

I began to examine the set of ancestral memes that arose from the British associations of my mother's people by considering the anecdotes, stories and traditions that had been handed down to me through my mother or, more especially, through her own mother. These memes represented a completely separate cultural pathway out of the past compared to those of my native ancestors. It was obvious how much they conflicted with the idea of Gaelic purity, lauded in Ireland in the 1950s and praised by Irish schoolmasters, politicians and presenters on Radio Éireann and celebrated in events like *An Tóstal.*

Examining my Old English roots gave me a radically new perspective in terms of defining authentic family identity. This exercise has a particular relevance in Ireland where many of us are, likewise, of mixed cultural backgrounds. The new direction in my journey was not undertaken without pain. But for the first time I faced what I was avoiding: the source of cultural tensions that had weakened my sense of identity.

One evening in the early 1940s my father happened to attend a dance in Ashbrook tennis club. So did Aileen Goulding. She was in no mood to go out that night but her friend, Sylvia, encouraged her. Under these precarious circumstances so began a romance that culminated in the marriage of my parents in Harold Cross Church. This event represented the social merger of two urban Catholic cultures—the Dublin nationalist Gael and the Old English loyalist. Two streams, two viewpoints, two outlooks coalesced under an unwritten treaty. My mother's interest in Britain, in contrast to my father's silence on the subject, was blatantly obvious. He was indifferent or silently antagonistic to her enthusiasm about the accession to the throne of Queen Elizabeth in summer 1953, while she bought every newspaper that covered the event. The wireless became an object of reverence, around which she listened, in hushed silence, as the BBC commentator, in a deep Oxford

---

192 Keogh, 1992; p. 59.

accent, described each scene on the developing pageantry from Buckingham Palace to Westminster Abbey.

Although the Keoghs tended to marry into families with broadly similar backgrounds, their sets of inherited memes were often dissimilar. This provided each subsequent generation and new family with a unique distinctiveness. In the case of my parents the contrast was particularly stark and helped me to distinguish the residual traits that originated from separate traditions. My father was a dormant nationalist, but he was more interested in economic realities and the world of business survival than politics. And perhaps it was more prudent for him to avoid the issues than arouse the defensive mind-set of my mother. If she felt her Old English identity threatened she would attack the Irish State as a travesty or speak as a martyr beleaguered in a foreign land.

The atmosphere emanating from the house of my grandfather, Bartholomew, was totally at variance to that generated in my mother's family. The inhabitants of Beechwood Road were more likely to relate stories about the 1916 Rising in Dublin than the Boer War, and names like Churchill or Lloyd George were more likely to be spoken of in derogatory terms than as allies. Yet the tone of these conversations could not be described as extreme republican, though they did have a definite nationalistic flavour. Still, Bartholomew's outlook heavily contrasted the essence of the world that my mother came from. She was a child of the British Empire; Bartholomew was Irish with a lean towards America. These basic contrasts in cultural perspectives resided side by side in my home. My mother and father accommodated them separately in their unspoken truce; however, the anomalies made me uneasy because, it seemed, a complete commitment to one particular set of inherited values, with the exception of religion, necessitated a rejection of the opposite set. In other words, it appeared that I had to make a stark choice: I was an Irish nationalist or Old English; I could not be both.

My grandmother Bride Gough—mother of my mother—epitomised the essence of the Old English culture but she held it without the same level of defensiveness that my mother exhibited. She grew up in an Ireland that was linked intimately to Britain and, unlike my mother, didn't feel that her identity was under threat. In subsequent years, when independence finally came to southern Ireland, dramatic changes in her life relegated Irish-British politics to the backstage.

One of my grandmother's outstanding skills was her ability to bring history to life through her many stories, an art that she kept alive beside the heart of our suburban household in Clontarf during the 1950s. She was a teacher by profession and knew well how to communicate. In fact, she ran a private school in Waterford after the First World War. It is understandable, then, that she was also highly influential in awakening me to the realities of the invasive past in our midst.

Though I was unaware at the time, the perspective which she portrayed embodied powerful ancestral memes; everything she was handing on was tinged with the ethos, atmosphere and attitude of a family with a particular British distinctiveness. Her recollections were of instances at the fringes rather than in centre-stage of human history, but these snippets reinforced the reality of time in a way that no historical analysis could do. Embedded in her anecdotes were echoes of great events and the trauma of many conflicts like the

Crimea War, the South African Boer War and the First War. As a direct consequence of her interpretative skills, whenever I come across symbols of these events in memorials and statues in London or in documentaries, they evoke an indefinable emotion of chilling familiarity.

My grandmother shared with me the memory of the shock, and the shock of people around her, on learning of the sinking of the Titanic after striking an iceberg on her maiden voyage in April 1912. In many ways it was the equivalent to the worldwide disbelief aroused when President Kennedy was killed in 1963 or when the 9/11 terrorist attack happened in the US in 2001. My grandmother told me of the cold boast of those who put their confidence in the Belfast-built vessel: *Not even God could sink the Titanic*. It was a tragedy of enormous proportions and a serious dent to engineering confidence. Before dawn on 15th April, the unsinkable plunged to its death four miles below the icy surface, taking with it more than 1,500 passengers and crew and all its treasures.

Bride Gough was born above her father's leather business in George's Street, Waterford, in 1879 into a large family. She jokingly said she disliked having to celebrate her birthday with Hitler. Her father's house was a landmark in the city and built partly of imported pitch pine of which he was very proud. It would last a long time, he said: it did. Up until the 1980s the premises carried his name *Richard Gough* above its main entrance.

This was the house from which Bride witnessed a baton charge in the town square outside the main front door. She saw an old bystander, who was dealt with as harshly as the young agitators. He received a blow from a truncheon—an incident probably emanating from coercive legislation under Prime Minister Gladstone during the late nineteenth century.

Hers was the house from which her father refused to hang out a flag for Parnell after his fall from grace in 1890. Richard Gough, who was staunchly Catholic and conservative, is reputed to have said: '*He will know what side I'm on.*' Parnell's affair with Katharine O'Shea, the wife of Captain O'Shea caused the division. The most likely date for Richard's action was January 1891 during the final hectic months in which Parnell tried desperately, but unsuccessfully, to claw back power for himself and his party. Because of his dramatic influence on Irish politics in the second half of the nineteenth century Parnell comes into our family history on all sides but in different guises.

My grandmother lived in our house when I was young. We called her *AB* because she hated the Gaelic name Bride or Bridget that she had been given. She had a particular daily routine beginning by attending Mass, after which she had ample time for her grandchildren. In the afternoon, when my mother had completed the housework and had finished dinner, the two ladies would sit together and talk and smoke in the kitchen. If the weather was clement during summer, the event was transferred to deck-chairs in the back garden. Their conversation was laced with incidents linked with cities like Waterford, Cork, London and Glasgow, where they had intimate connections through friends and relations both living and dead. They joked; they shared joyous and sad moments.

After tea at around 5.30 in the evening AB would retire to her room before my father came home so that my parents could have time for themselves and their children. All this I took for granted. I had few glimpses of how she spent her evenings alone in her room.

She prayed often and had several prayer books with pictures of Christ and other gospel events, and text in black and red type. It is now, much later in life, that I begin to imagine the profundity of her memories and what she must have being going through.

AB was born sixty-eight years before my birth, bringing the direct oral memory of the family back to the early political years of Parnell. Though she was born after the Crimean conflict her descriptions of it carried a definite stamp of account handed on from her parents' generation. Her own fireside in Waterford was the source of many snippets of history, which she passed on to us. In her anecdotes were contained allusions to the social realities of her people. It is difficult for me to separate her experiences from instances emanating from her parents' and grandparents' times. Nonetheless, assuming that the memory within her household stretched back into the past in a similar fashion to mine, this would bring the indirect oral history of our family another sixty or seventy years before her birth, reaching to the Napoleonic era. The echoes of former generations; the expression of her feelings and attitudes to history; and the associated behaviour of her family constituted her ancestral memes and they are essential components of mine.

AB's sessions were laced with poetry and exotic themes from Kipling and Scott and Wordsworth and Longfellow. Her stories were peppered with nursery rhymes which, in turn, held snippets of past events. Many of these rhymes came from the essence of English history. *Humpty Dumpty* was a colloquial term used in the fifteenth century to describe someone who was obese. In the famous rhyme, reference was being made, not to a person, but a huge cannon that was placed on the protective wall of a church in Colchester during the Civil War between Charles I and Cromwell. A shot from a Parliamentary cannon dislodged Humpty Dumpty, and all the king's horses and all the king's men could not undo the damage. Another rhyme like *Ding Dong Bell* ended when the cat was saved by Little Tommy Stout. It tried to encourage children not to harm animals. *Hickory Dickory Dock* was a nonsense-rhyme first published in 1744 and helped children to learn onomatopoeia. The joint authors of *Twinkle Twinkle Little Star* were two sisters called Ann and Jane Taylor. It was first published in 1806 and popular for the use of language. In all, nursery rhymes were valuable tools to teach history, to appreciate language, to provide moral lessons and to have fun. They were as relevant in the 1950s as they had been for tens or hundreds of years previously.

Nursery rhymes set the mind alive with images and I was fascinated to hear AB tell us that she went upstairs to bed in her father's house with candles, just like the characters out of the rhymes themselves. There was no central heating and no running water in her house. Chamber pots and jugs and ceramic bowls were used in place of toilets and wash-hand basins. Many aspects of the daily routine she faced were exactly the same as those encountered by Jane Austen. In her early childhood many of the basic modes of transport had remained unchanged since prehistory. The horse was still the main means of haulage overland and sail was the main method of propulsion for ships. However, fundamental changes were taking place. Trains allowed journeys to be made that were unthinkable in former years. It was possible to travel from London to many other cities and towns in hours rather than days at a consistent speed of sixty miles per hour. The invention of the screw propeller in the 1830s, which came about in tandem with metal hulls and steam-driven motors, revolutionised shipping. Steam ships were becoming a more frequent sight in Waterford in the last quarter of the nineteenth century. AB remembered running out of her house to see the first cars and the first aeroplanes—forms of transport that were about to transform the world.

My grandmother's family was cosmopolitan rather than insular. She talked about her brother who travelled through northern Australia. He narrated his experiences to her in a letter describing an encounter in his tent when a snake came in and crawled over him. He could only lie still until the danger had passed. AB was in boarding school at the time. Therefore, he must have gone to Australia before the turn of the twentieth century. Letters that arrived at her school were opened by the nuns and censored if they felt it was necessary. The nun who presented the letter complimented her for having such a brother. Unfortunately, AB burnt the note and we will never know what other novelties it contained.

AB was born and lived her early life in the Victorian era. She had many sayings that reflected the philosophy and attitudes of that time, like: *A stitch in time saves nine*; or *early to bed early to rise makes a man healthy, wealthy and wise*. Note the Victorian emphasis on *man*. Women could not vote then. Nevertheless, AB carried her Victorianism easily and not as a burden as one might expect from subsequent commentary about the period. In many ways, her upbringing and the memes that she was handing on to us, with the exception of her religion, would be totally familiar to middle-class Protestant children in England.

The Victorian era was punctuated with strife during the heyday of the British Empire, like the Crimea War in the 1850s, an Indian rebellion in 1857, a Zulu war in 1879 and the Boer War during which the long reign of Victoria came to an end. On 14th January 1901 the Queen had an interview with Lord Roberts, who had returned victorious from South Africa a few days before. After the audience she collapsed. On the following day her medical attendants recognised that her state was hopeless; and yet, for two days more, the indomitable spirit fought on. But then she stopped working and the last optimism of those about her broke down. She died at eighty-one years of age, after a reign of sixty-three years. The Victorian era gave way to the Edwardian. The very old reluctantly relinquished influence to the old; a generation of eighty-year-olds passed the torch to a younger generation of sixty-year-olds.

When it came to education, AB's father sent her to England and Scotland because he felt that an education abroad would give his daughter the best foundation he could possibly provide. Britain was the natural political hub for a family that maintained loyalty to the crown despite the anti-Catholic bias of the monarchy and despite the fact that their own religious centre of gravity was Rome. AB's outlook reflected a British worldview from an Irish centre on one particular spoke of the Union Jack that radiated out from London, the heart of the British Empire. Though her outlook bore a distinct British bias, her use of the word *them* to describe Irish and British politicians betrayed an ambiguity in her identity. My mother jokingly said that the real fulcrum-point of her psychological makeup lay somewhere in the Irish Sea.

When on mainland Britain AB was not taught Irish history, perhaps because it was an embarrassment to the establishment or not becoming for the education of young ladies.

In this way hundreds of years of tension between Ireland and England and the conflicts over land were all glossed over. Yet, when she was at home she did pick up, inevitably, something of the flavour of the traditional conflict between the neighbouring islands and amongst the different social orders in Ireland.

AB related to us her memories of elegant horse-drawn carriages near Hyde Park where she watched gentlemen lift top hats to salute each other as they passed; they were accompanied by their well-dressed women-folk. These scenes of yester year occurred during her stay in London. She related many other snippets that gave colour to the era. For example, it was customary during the Edwardian period for a young a man, who wished to dance with a single girl at a social occasion to formally request, in writing, to do so before the event. This tradition reflected the strict social codes that were in place.

But the occasion, at which AB met Michael Goulding, her husband to be, was somewhat different. It was a card game at which both came last. Once more, the precarious and random incidents of attraction are the stuff on which the golden threads of life are often woven. He was a civil servant who worked in Somerset House and played rugby for London Irish. His mother was Irish and his father had worked in the government services in Ireland. He was a Catholic and shared much in common with AB's Old English outlook. It is easy to understand why my mother was so unapologetically West British.

The world of AB and her fiancé was about to undergo a massive transformation; humanity was on the brink of a plunge into an abyss of unprecedented conflict that would dramatically change all aspects of social life. In 1914 the First World War broke out. In 1915 Germany started its air raids on British cities and by the end of the war 250 tons of bombs had been dropped, causing thousands of civilian casualties. At first, Zeppelins began raiding London in sporadic attacks but these escalated into squadron-size forays by numerous Zeppelins, always at night and in the light of the moon. Daylight bomber raids followed in June 1917. That month AB and Michael were married in Shoreditch in London.

AB was caught in an early daylight raid and described the scene in the street where an ashen-faced man ran in fear; it was totally unnerving to see a man frightened; that was not meant to happen. She had to seek shelter in an unknown household in the city—something frowned upon for a young lady in London under normal circumstances.

She recalled another incident at the time: Michael failed to come home after playing a rugby match. She was distraught, but in those days before telephones, the first news about him came in the morning newspapers where she read that he had suffered concussion and ended up in hospital. This was a mild incident compared to what lay in store for the couple.

AB talked about trainloads of soldiers on the move. She spent time travelling between Britain and Ireland and talked of her journeys by boat, weaving a zigzag path on the Irish Sea to avoid German submarines but, because she was such a poor sailor, always sick at sea, she had more to preoccupy herself with than German torpedoes.

Conditions along the front-line trenches in France were appalling and, apart from the onslaught of enemy shot and shell, soldiers suffered numerous diseases, such as trench-foot or foot-rot caused by continual damp. Besides, body lice spread trench fever and typhus. News of the horrendous sacrifices that men were making on the front spread home.

Nonetheless, pro-war propaganda incited a show of nationalistic fervour. As the Germans invaded neutral Belgium in August 1914, the patriotic calls grew and the jingoistic spin changed from an accusation against the Germans of treaty violation to a chronicle of both real and fictionalised war atrocities. Appeals to duty, conscience, patriotism and sense of honour modified and became a plea for the protection of the family. The war was portrayed as *a battle between good and evil* to be fought against the enemy of the home. The imagery that permeated wartime propaganda began to reflect itself in British recruitment efforts.

In the first two years of the war the British Army depended exclusively on voluntary enlistments. However, in the changing atmosphere Admiral Charles Penrose Fitzgerald organized a group of thirty women to help persuade the men of Britain to join in the fight against the enemy. It was the tactical objective of this group, called *The White Feather Brigade,* to shame civilian men into joining the armed services. This campaign was to be accomplished by public humiliation: the women handing out white feathers to any young man who didn't wear a uniform. The pressure to enlist became inescapable.

Because Michael was a young man and not in uniform, a woman of The White Feather Brigade threw these plumage symbols in his face. This incident happened one day as he was walking in London. It had the desired impact. He felt that the honorable and patriotic thing to do was join the armed forces and, as a result, he spent time in the Royal Navy in Jamaica. A powerful symbol of little physical weight transformed the lives of Michael Goulding, AB and their offspring. When he left for Jamaica his young wife was pregnant. She was in Ireland when she gave birth to my mother.

Unbeknown to the world at large, a sinister development was taking place on mainland Europe, which would also have a devastating effect on her family. British soldiers destined for the trenches usually landed at the French ports of Le Havre and Boulogne. They were then transported to the main base camp just outside the French town of Etaples. Huge numbers passed through this camp, either going to or coming from the war zone. Many of those returning were sick and dying from war wounds. Unnoticed, an invisible enemy lurked within. Etaples was a massive site. Approximately 10,000 troops a week would pass through. Feeding all these men was a problem. The British Army sent in supply trains of food each day. But there were other ways in which the men could be fed. A small farm was set up in the middle of the camp with poultry and other livestock. Most importantly, there was also a large piggery attached to the farm.

In 1916 men fell sick in the camp with a strange illness that had flu-like symptoms. In the late stages of the infirmity the colouring of the skin changed to lavender, an almost grey-blue hue, before taking its victims. It is now thought that a virus mutated from a poultry strain of the illness, then crossed to infect pigs and finally passed into humans. All the ingredients for the mutation were present in Etaples. In the summer of 1917 the flu seemed to abate. But this was the calm before the storm. In 1918 it reappeared and reached pandemic proportions. Known as the *Spanish flu* it continued through three successive waves that circled the world, breaking out apparently simultaneously in many different places. Eventually the virus burned itself out; but not before some forty to sixty million people, mostly the young and healthy, were carried off.

A peculiar aspect to the epidemic was the speed of death. Victims grew weak suddenly; some fell down in the street. AB recalled these incidents herself, describing how many were becoming reluctant to pick up the fallen for fear of infection. People began to carry handkerchiefs laced with disinfectant to keep away the germs. There was a theory that the world turned faster than its atmosphere and that the disease arose from dead war victims on the field of battle in France. This explained to them how farmers in out-of-the-way places could collapse and die. Widespread fear turned to panic and schools and factories closed. The virus killed more people than any other single outbreak of disease, surpassing even the Black Death of the Middle Ages.

My mother succumbed to the Spanish flu and, at the height of her sickness, a doctor stayed by her side till the fever broke. AB knew, then, her child would be safe. More good news followed. One can only imagine the celebration by AB and Michael of the armistice on 11th November 1918. The separated couple that were so deeply in love knew they would soon be reunited. Michael would be coming home safely. He never saw action in Jamaica.

Unfortunately, on his return to England in February 1919, like many other soldiers and sailors, he caught the flu during its third wave. It was said that troops returning in winter were badly clothed and ill-prepared for the cold, particularly men coming home from the tropics. Michael eventually died. I say "eventually" because it appeared that he had recovered but didn't allow himself enough time to convalesce. He was about to leave the forces and was on his way to Chatham Royal Navy base when he collapsed in the street. He died later in hospital. If Michael had not been humiliated into joining the forces and spending time in Jamaica, perhaps this tragedy would not have happened. His young wife was left to fend for herself with her baby.

Although the initial recruitment efforts of the White Feather Brigade were deemed patriotic, their nasty methods came to be considered—at the very least—extremely poor taste. As the carnage was calculated in the clear hindsight of the post-war period, people took pains to distance themselves from any participation in these kinds of recruitment efforts. But for Michael and his young family, the damage had already been done; a great vacuum was left behind; a wonderfully-deep relationship was substituted by a terrible emptiness.

The shrill notes of a single bugle in a cold graveyard represented AB's final farewell to Michael. For her, the metallic sound of the bugle playing the last post was chilling; with it was buried her hope and the father of her young daughter. She was left so numb that she could not cry. An indifferent commemorative plaque in Somerset House bears Michael's name, along with other compatriots. Few today can comprehend the significance of it; do they even recognise it as a monument to real and ordinary people? A photograph of Michael's London-Irish rugby team exists—young men in the prime of their lives. Perhaps two of them survived the war.

After the elegant words were over there followed a terrible silence around the grave of Michael. The burden was now for AB alone to carry. She never remarried. As I mentioned, I did not appreciate, until later in my adult life, what a horrific memory she held all these years. It accompanied her in the silence of her room in our house but I was completely unaware.

The burden of war did not end with the armistice, nor was it confined to one generation. My mother recalled to me the lonely chill she felt as she watched the desolate and isolated Comeragh Mountains pass by as she travelled by train from Waterford, where she lived with her mother, to boarding school in Fermoy. She feared the potential loss of AB, who was the only person with whom she really shared her life. My mother didn't like to dwell on death. Nonetheless, she listened faithfully with AB to the BBC commentary from the Cenotaph in London on Britain's Remembrance Day each November. She did it for her father whom she never knew and to empathise with her mother. The icy notes of the last post brought back the final goodbye to Michael. The poignant stillness of the two-minutes silence; the cold autumnal breeze moving coats and scarves against a people immobilised, fixed the minds of loved-ones on the emptiness of the moment and the fullness of their memories.

Old English Identity

At some point, as we weave back into the past, the origin of a particular family outlook enters the zone of fading domestic memory and confused influences. We barely discern the distant echoes of former generations in us or in our immediate ancestors, but they are present, and only distinguishable if we pursue them deliberately. My parents' perspectives originated in their respective homes and these homes were moulded by the societies from which they had emerged. The more I considered the topic it occurred to me that, as a general principle, family memes do not spring equally from all sides. In other words, my existing memes didn't arise evenly from the principle families in my makeup. Unequal influences were absolutely clear in my mother's case. Her father died when she was in her infancy and her mother's influences—from the Gough family—were therefore a much more powerful presence than that of her father's family (Goulding) though some influence cannot be ruled out. I resolved to unravel the story of the Goughs to its origin to see if I could trace the sources of their ancestral memes.

Prior to her death, my mother spent much time researching her Old English background. Before she passed away she bequeathed her papers to me and from these I gathered that the family's origins in Ireland can be traced to a certain Garret Gough who arrived from Wales in 1530 under orders of King Henry VIII. The king wanted to regain the allegiance of the original Anglo-Irish or Old English who had attained a level of independence bordering on rebellion. The monarch also wanted to establish peace and generally ... *reduce this land to obedience and good order*.[193] He felt that the most convenient way to win Ireland over was through concessions, bribes and bullying. However, he was informed that to suppress Ireland would involve correcting the ways of the Old English as well as dominating the natives. He would have to raise and pay for an army of 6,000 and create a new infrastructure of castles throughout the land in order to bring it to complete submission. Henry didn't follow this advice. England would learn the hard way that Ireland would need special methods if it were to be fully dominated.

In 1530, matters other than Ireland were competing for the king's attention. He was planning to separate from his first wife Catherine of Aragon because she failed to provide him a male heir. Henry turned to the pope to grant him an annulment. The pope opposed the request, causing Henry's break from the Church, thus opening the way for his marriage to Anne Boleyn.

After Anne was crowned queen, the English Protestant Reformation began in earnest. In Ireland, a religious rift commenced between the monarch's loyal Protestant subjects on one side and the Old English settlers combined with the Gaels on the other. For convenience, the Old English can be thought of as colonists that had come to Ireland since Norman times onwards and were Catholics. The *New* English were Protestants. The chasm that formed between Catholics and Protestants created an irrevocable tripartite division in Ireland that has lasted to the present day.

Sometime after arriving in Ireland, Garret Gough's descendants developed an intimate association with County Waterford. Edward Gough became mayor of the city in 1600

---

193 Ellis, 1998; p. 119.

and three years later he was knighted. Edward's son James was granted, among other possessions, the manor, castle, and lands of Kilmanahan, near Clonmel. He was also granted a licence to hold a market in the local town on Saturdays and, like his father, was knighted. He became a member of parliament for Waterford.

By 1641 the combined Old English and Gaelic entities in Ireland had lost about one third of the land area to the New English settlers. We saw earlier that the rebellion, which broke out that year in Ulster, fused the Catholics of the whole country into a single force, known as the Confederation of Kilkenny. They came together to prevent further loss of property and erosion of their power-base.

The descendants of Garret Gough became part of this movement. Patrick Gough rode out from his manor at Kilmanahan to join the rebellion. But he could not have foreseen the consequences he was bringing on himself and his offspring by his actions. The Catholics persisted in their claims that they opposed the government and not King Charles I. But by spring 1642 it became clear that the king did not support the revolt and he called on the Catholics to lay down their arms. The Protestant Government, however, was bent on confiscating rebel lands and drew up plans to seize one million hectares (two and a half million acres) in the aftermath of the disturbances.[194]

It was not until after Cromwell arrived in Ireland in 1649 and had gained the upper hand over the combined Catholic forces that he could begin to take revenge for the rebellion. He executed the main culprits and drew up plans to banish others to Connaught or force them into exile. Contrary to the popular belief that only the Gael was affected, the Goughs and many other Old English families were transplanted during the Cromwellian confiscations.

Patrick Gough, who had taken part in the rebellion, was dead. But, he was deemed to have been a Papist and because the family was unable to prove *constant good affection* to the Cromwellian Parliament, they lost their property at Kilmanahan. Patrick's mother, Dame Mary Gough, and her relations were banished to Clare in the West of Ireland. All owners whose lands were due for confiscation had to move west of the Shannon by May 1654 or face execution. The Goughs joined the long straggling lines of evicted Irish moving westwards with their meagre belongings. This exodus was subsequently dubbed *To Hell or Connaught*. The troublesome Irish were to be confined, like native North Americans, to a reservation, which was surrounded by sea and the River Shannon, with only one stretch of land some ten miles wide that was to be closed up by a line of forts.[195]

Much later, when Catholic King James II was elevated to the throne of England, the Old English sensed that they would be supported by the monarchy. As a result, Garret Gough—grandson of Dame Mary and son of Patrick who had lost the family property at Kilmanahan—exited from confinement in the West of Ireland. He joined Tyrconnell's new army, was made a captain and raised a company of foot at his own expense. He returned to County Waterford with his small force of men and seized his late father's estates, which he held on behalf of the king.

---

194 Foster, 1989; p. 90.
195 Berresford Ellis, 2000; p. 89.

Garret confiscated the lands from a certain John Greene. Greene requested Garret to allow him a pass to remove his family and some possessions from the castle to the town of Clonmel. The pass was obtained and Greene left nothing of value behind him ... *but some lumber of old chairs, stools and tables not worth removing, and some small quantity of corn, which he and his wife Catherine removed from time to time by degrees* ... without any control from Garret or any person under his command.[196] The following year, Garret received title to his lands under the Act of Repeal. Like many other Protestant families, Green sailed for England.

It was at this stage that forty-year-old Dutch Prince William of Orange became King William III of England in opposition to James II. As we saw, the two kings came to Ireland and faced each other on opposite sides of the River Boyne. Garret Gough left his estates at Kilmanahan for the last time on 16th June. He served in King James' army under Colonel Thomas Butler at the Boyne.[197]

With the demise of King James, the fortunes of Garret changed abruptly. Although the Act of Repeal had permitted him to reclaim his father's lands at Kilmanahan, a separate Act of Parliament now declared this null and void.

John Greene returned to Ireland to reclaim the estates for himself. Nonetheless, in February 1704 Garret made an appeal in the Court of Chancery. He claimed for goods removed by Greene from his former estates including, amongst other things, eighty barrels of wheat; seventy barrels of barley; seventy barrels of small barley and five dozen Russia leather chairs. He pleaded that the court would take into consideration that he had treated Greene well when he reclaimed his lands under King James. Garret further pleaded that all his witnesses were either dead or had gone to foreign or remote parts overseas, and that their testimony could not be obtained. He also pleaded that he be ... *comprehended and adjudged within the articles of the Treaty of Limerick, and he prayed the Court to compel John Greene to give him relief.*[198] But his plea was in vain; John Greene and the court were not obliging. Garret lived for a further eighteen years and died in 1722. The historical trail of my ancestors becomes wafer-thin at this point. My mother told me that Garret Gough had a son, Patrick, who went to sea.

After the Williamite wars, the Goughs emerged as tenant farmers in Carrigsaggart, a townland in the most easterly barony of County Waterford. They may have been there as early as 1726 and remained in the vicinity for generations. Richard Gough, my great-grandfather and father of AB, was born there. He moved into Waterford city as a young man and in 1863 was shop assistant to his relative Edward Walsh, one of the largest and wealthiest merchants in the city. In time, Richard opened a business for himself and became a leather merchant and grocer .

Kevin Haddick-Flynn summarises that, in reference to the Williamite wars: *The Jacobite defeat destroyed the Old English community as a political force. They had been the original Anglo-Irish and had kept their distinctive identity intact for five centuries,*

---

196 *The Goughs of Kilmanahan.* The Nationalist. 21st December, 1940.
197 D'Alton, 1855; p. 685.
198 *The Goughs of Kilmanahan.* The Nationalist. 21st December, 1940.

during which time their loyalty had been to England. Since the days of the Reformation they had strained to reconcile their Catholicism with their allegiance to a succession of Protestant monarchs. But the strain had been too much. In the years ahead they would share the same religious disabilities as the Gaelic Irish and in time both would become indistinguishable.[199]

I disagree vehemently with the last part of Haddick-Flynn's conclusion. It is incorrect to suggest that the Gaelic Irish and the Old English became indistinguishable. It is true that when the Old English first came to Ireland they intermingled with the Gaelic Irish, particularly outside the Dublin Pale. The process of intermixing and adopting Irish traditions, known as *gaelicisation,* was so widespread that it was said the Old English *became more Irish than the Irish themselves.* This is a convenient mistruth, coined in the late eighteenth century, which played along with twentieth-century Irish nationalism to incorporate the Old English within the Gaelic identity of the new state.

Despite adoption of Irish ways and even intermarrying, the Old English never lost sight of their origins. They always saw themselves set apart from the Gael and knew their status to be on a higher pedestal—and therefore more privileged—than the native Irish in contemporary English eyes. They used this advantage to their own aggrandisement. Their instinct of superiority showed up again and again in the actions and attitudes of families like the Kildares and Ormonds who acknowledged themselves to be the legitimate representatives of the monarch in Ireland. It showed up in the stubborn Old English refusal to join O'Neill in the Nine Years War; it appeared when they ignored Gaelic interests in the Confederation of Kilkenny; it was revealed in the tensions that erupted in the Catholic Association in 1763 and it emerged again in opposition to Daniel O'Connell in later years.[200] Catholics in Ireland were clearly divided into two nations since the beginning. Their differences certainly became less noticeable in time but tensions erupted periodically.

The historical record reiterates that, although maintaining their fidelity to the Catholic religion, the Old English remained loyal to the monarchy, whether Catholic or Protestant, but manifested their opposition to Protestant governments and adopted a standoff-cum-co-operative position towards Gaelic entities. This was the "precise" cultural position of the Goughs of Waterford and was reflected in the outlooks of AB and my mother, confirming that their intellectual and emotional inheritances—or family memes—emanated from deep ancestral roots. Their history clearly reveals the reasons for their pro-British attitudes.

Here is confirmation of the incompatible nature of many ancestral memes in my family. I cannot claim cultural purity. I am a hybrid; a mix of Gael and Old English; a blend of opposing cultures that created a stark landscape fracture on my mind. This was the base of my cultural discrepancies. The degree of underlying tensions that I experienced highlights the reality and strength of conflicting ancestral memes in one Irish household. Despite this, my parents got on well; it was left to their children to resolve their cultural contradictions.

199 Haddick-Flynn, 2003; p. 198.
200 Ellis, 1998; p. 347; Corish, 2009 (a); p. 312; Gwynn, 1928; p. 22, ff. Geoghegan, 2008; p. 145.

A Dangerous Pastime

If anyone doesn't understand the deep traditional animosity between the Irish and the English, it is because they don't know the history of Ireland. These are sentiments that my mother would never have expressed. She would tend to present Irish history as a misunderstanding between cultures, and place as much emphasis as she could on the positive contribution of Britain in Ireland. My tendency, in our family conversations, to deal with the Irish/English divide with raw emotion, exposes the depth of the competing sets of memes in our family. I acknowledge that the reading of Irish history is a dangerous pastime for me because it often engenders bitterness emanating from a stubborn Gaelic outlook. But herein lies a great inconsistency; I fully understand and even sympathise with the Old English attitudes of my late mother.

The reason why I had formerly dismissed or avoided facing my Old English inheritance was the deep distaste that I felt for what the foreign intruders did to my people—the native Irish. It was with great discomfort that I eventually admitted that my ancestors were amongst the invaders. I now feel that the best way to deal with divisions, animosities, inconsistencies and cultural contradictions—and to reach beyond them or break through their limitations—is to acknowledge these realities rather than pretend they don't exist. Therefore, I feel obliged to freely express my uncensored viewpoint before I can deal with its limitations. However, I have always tried, in as far as possible, to approach the subject of Irish history with the disposition of fairness. I have not always succeeded, as will become obvious.

In the late sixteenth century, when the conquerors were developing a plan for the final submission of Gaelic Ireland through the planting of new blood from outside—with a strong preference for English blood—they attempted to justify their actions in terms of a civilising mission to a barbarous and degenerate people amongst whom they would spread *true* religion. This attitude of superiority had a long history. Their predecessor—the Normans—had scant regard for Gaelic culture. Their chronicler, Giraldus Cambrensis who was a medieval clergyman, demeaned the Irish in his writings. He held the contemporary British view of the racial inferiority of the Gael. He observed that ... *although they are richly endowed with the gifts of nature, their want of civilisation, shown both in their dress and mental culture, makes them a barbarous people.*[201] This tradition of division between the native Irish and the peoples of the neighbouring island with their views of English superiority began with—or even before—the coming of the Normans and has lasted up to the present day.

During the seventeenth century, the monarchy didn't want to overburden itself with costs so it agreed to approach the task of "civilising" the country in a way that would minimise the financial burden on the crown. Ireland had been a continual drain on the resources of the English exchequer and this situation would have to change. Conscious of the need to appease the king, the English authorities in Ireland came up with an attractive proposal: they suggested that the very process of reforming the island could be a source of revenue for the monarchy, not to mention the benefits that would accrue to themselves.

---

201 Giraldus Cambrensis. *The Topography of Ireland.* Translated by: T. Forester. Medieval Latin Series. Cambridge, Ontario 2000; pp.68, 69. < *http://www.yorku.ca/inpar/topography_ireland.pdf* > (August, 2015)

In their quest to bring the country to "their" version of civility the English exploited every means at their disposal, including the threat of rebellion and risk of invasion from Spain, to increase their military strength in Ireland. To keep costs down the army would be supported from local resources. Schemes were devised to show weaknesses in land title. These titles were, of course, based on English law which was not recognised in Gaelic territories, unless under duress. When the English began to plant and take over the island with new Protestant settlers they increasingly turned to more uncivilised and barbarous means to achieve their ends. They demeaned the Gaels as no better than "brute beasts", for if they recognised them as humans they could not get away with the underhand means whereby they rooted out opposing elements in their own self-interest. So the English answer to the Irish was to classify them as inconsistent, ambivalent and exclusive, and denigrate them as wild, savage, rude, lazy and uncouth. Unfortunately, most of what was written about Gaelic society came from the pens of English visitors, the majority of which had little sympathy with Irish culture. The English simplification developed out of a combined frustration at the incompatibility of Gaelic society with theirs and as a device for soothing consciences on the brink of mass confiscations of lands and wealth.

English and Gaelic polities had comparatively little in common in terms of language, law, customs and governmental institutions.[202] Ireland's history is to a large extent one of conflict and interaction between two separate civilisations. The English were grossly ignorant about Gaelic society and had no wish to learn. They even goaded the Irish into controlled rebellion so that they could then demand the forfeiture of their properties; they provided them with mortgages they could not repay and then confiscated their possessions in foreclosures. Naturally, the Irish refused to conform and rose in uncontrolled rebellion. The English then executed, evicted or exported the troublesome elements to Virginia and the Caribbean. They did all of this with one eye fixed firmly on the resources of the country. They became asset strippers, exploiting the forests for their timber as soon as they gained control over Gaelic woodlands. Yet they masked their avarice as a concern for the common good.

It is the self-righteous stance of the English which ignores historic facts that is singularly infuriating and this attitude prevails in modern times in some, albeit decreasing, circles. Such people often feign surprise that the Irish are still living in the past and retain their old anti-English hostility against the great civilisation that gave parliamentary democracy and fair-play to the world. Those holding such attitudes refuse to stand aside and objectively examine their own history.

I am reminded of the myopic comments made by William Piers who demeaned the ... *rotten and ruinous clay houses and cottages* of the Irish. Anything that the Gael put their hands to had to be debased. However, after a storm in 1615, his fellow Englishman George Canning lamented that his two-storey timber houses at Coleraine were ... *stripped of some of their slates, while the temporary thatched houses constructed by the English workmen were 'torn almost naked.'* Meanwhile the Gaelic houses were untouched.[203]

It goads me that I obtain a measure of immature glee on discovering historic examples that show the proud English in such poor light. On reflection, it is a reaction against what

202 Ellis, 1998; p. 11.
203 Canny, 2009; pp. 90, 218.

I see as the injustices against my Gaelic people whose history and land were stolen by the newcomers. The tragedy is that these emotions against the English can so easily transform themselves from harmless insults to violence given the right conditions. I remember the fury generated in Dublin after the killing of thirteen civilians by British troops on Bloody Sunday in the North of Ireland on 30th January 1972, which resulted in the burning of the British Embassy in the city. This type of reaction is easy to provoke in Ireland because of the treatment Ireland received at the hands of the crown for so long. It is at the base of much Irish/English tensions.

Parallels between the white man's treatment of the natives of North America and the English behaviour towards the Gael are striking. Indeed the colonial plantations of Virginia in the seventeenth century were based on the blueprint developed in Ireland at that time. In an incredibly arrogant posture, Europeans and their descendants felt themselves ... *ordained by destiny to rule all of America. They were the dominant race and therefore responsible for the Indians—along with their lands, their forests and their mineral wealth.*[204] But, the real intent of the English in Ireland and the Europeans in America occasionally slips through the cracks in their pretence to be upright and righteous. The plain fact is: mention of civility and responsibility were glossed messages for the unleashing of activities that were driven by full-blown greed for material gain. As with the English in Ireland, the real motivation of the outsider in North America came through when they admitted to coveting a land which was ... *waiting to be dug up, dammed up, and properly deforested so that fortunes could be made in the process.*[205]

A key irritation to the English planter and American homesteader alike was the lack of sedentary agriculture practised amongst the native people, and their high level of local mobility. When a census of the Utes was to be taken in 1875 it was stated by the Indian agent F. F. Bond that: *You might as well try to count a swarm of bees when on the wing. They travel all over the country like the deer which they hunt.*[206] Likewise, the Gaels allowed their horses to run wild about their territory, and cattle and sheep appeared to move at the whim of their owners within fixed borders.[207] The English saw the *pastoral personality* in Ireland as an easy-going way of life leaving plenty of time for mischief. Wealth was mobile in the form of cattle rather than stable in the form of land. Gaels and native Americans alike were expected to accept the *civilising* and sedentary ways of their enemies.

The pragmatic Gael easily entered into and dissolved treaties with the royal government and with each other and the whole system appeared to the newcomers like the celebration of anarchy. On the other hand, Roy Foster observes that ... *Gaelic society was measured against a 'standard of outlandish reference' ... The English saw the world of cattle-raids, Brehons and poets as arrogantly archaic and deliberately mystifying: a world at once bogus and perverse, which could only be civilised by means of plantation.*[208] But when the Gael did adopt the ways of their enemies they were often rejected, like the Earl of Thomond in County Clare whom we will encounter shortly. In a similar manner the natives of North

204 Brown, 1991; p. 8.
205 *Ibid*; p. 388.
206 *Ibid*; pp. 371, 372.
207 Edwards, 2004; pp. 84, 85.
208 Foster, 1989; p. 32.

America were rejected, like Ely Samuel Parker who became a civil engineer but was not allowed to practice his skills in the Union Army and elsewhere because of his ethnicity.[209]

Gaels who resided in the poorer uplands of Leinster were the most rebellious of enemies against the English Crown and were the ones mainly responsible for the recurring raids on Dublin city. Interesting similarities with regard to violence are found amongst the natives of North America like those of the South Carolina interior. Lowland Indians ... *like their lowland Gaelic counterparts, relied increasingly on agriculture and trade, while the Indians dwelling in the uplands almost exclusively hunted for their foodstuffs and earned a particularly war-like reputation among European settlers and Indians alike.*[210]

It has to be admitted that not all of the English in Ireland or Europeans in North America automatically debased the native people with whom they made contact. For example, the presence of white men like Tom Jeffords and John Clum helped maintain peace in Apache country simply because they accepted the indigenous people as human beings rather than savage killers.[211]

Likewise, one of the most successful English Tudor governors in Ireland was Anthony St Ledger, who made remarkable progress towards a peaceful settlement between the Irish and English during the reign of Henry VIII through conciliation rather than militarism. He even included a measure of power-sharing for the Gaels in the form of the unprecedented representation of their Lords in parliament.[212] He recognised that the upland Gaels lacked sufficient arable land, which would reduce their wants and decrease their tendency to violence at the same time. How Irish history would have differed if men like him had represented the monarchy. On the other hand, the Gael was not all benign. We have the example of General Patrick E. Connor, who was born in rural County Kerry in 1820 and who was responsible for the butchering of over 270 Paiutes on Bear River in 1863 and much more besides.[213]

Reaching a fair understanding of Irish history is to acknowledge that biases exist on all sides and that we must be open to distinguishing where the actual dividing line between right and wrong, truth and fiction should be drawn. New research should not attempt to couch historical happenings within revisionist histories that pretend the past was, in fact, diametrically opposed to the perspectives of history held by opposing entities.

Despite the bitter emotions that often arise when I read Irish history; and despite my feelings of anti-English sentiments when I consider the disruption that my ancestors suffered under the invaders, something prevented me from taking part in the demonstrations against Bloody Sunday in Dublin on 2nd February 1972. At the time I was unsure about who was telling the truth. My hesitation was more closely aligned with the reaction of my mother's outlook than with popular sentiment. She assumed that the British Army was in the right and held an innate belief that it could not have behaved dishonourably. In hindsight and in

---

209 Brown, 1991; p. 179.
210 Maginn, 2005; p. 186.
211 Brown, 1991; p. 217.
212 Ellis, 1998; pp. 149; 154.
213 Brown, 1991; p. 104.

view of the Saville Report which exonerated the victims and condemned the British Army, I had clearly made a wrong judgement. It became crystal clear to me that I harboured incompatible sets of ancestral memes in my psyche and that the Old English set had gained the upper hand on this occasion.

Love of Enemy

Another insidious dimension of the British in Ireland was their imposition of Protestantism over a population that was mostly Catholic. They forced those in public life to take the oath of supremacy, thus segregating anyone out of the system who conformed to Catholicism, a religion which, according to them, was steeped in idolatry and superstition. Even in modern times this attitude was continued within Irish society. A relation of mine was seen emerging from Westland Row Catholic church in post-independent Ireland and was asked by his Protestant firm to remove himself from their employment forthwith.

When walking about Saint Patrick's Cathedral in Dublin, which is a bastion of Protestant Ascendency, I find myself incensed by the honourable titles bestowed on the men who disinherited my ancestors. Consider *The Most Noble George Grenville Nugent Temple, Marquis of Buckingham* who became Lord Lieutenant of Ireland on two occasions but maintained his position by resorting to bribery on a large scale. Equally out of place in the Cathedral is the chair used by King William III when he came to Saint Patrick's to give thanks to God for his victory over King James at the battle of the Boyne in 1690 and which is juxtaposed against the meek vision—in stained glass—of Jesus who commanded us to: *Love your enemies.* How can these walls be draped with the regimental flags of the British Army in a glorification of war, suppression and tyranny in Ireland and other countries around the world? And how can the tricolour, a symbol which *they* once hated, be allowed to adorn the rear of the high altar? The whole edifice is a contradiction in terms.

I could desist from writing such thoughts, but—and I repeat myself here—I sense that in all human conflicts, it is better to face such feelings and confront divisions in order to find ways around them or through them, rather than hide behind politically-correct verbiage, weak smiles and limp handshakes that maintain the *status quo.*

Conflict over belief brings to the fore the old axiom that religion is responsible for human divisions and wars. But, in the case of the English in Ireland, the truth reveals itself behind a thin veneer of religion. Peel it back and the raw lust for power and wealth is once more exposed. For example, Protestants imposed fines upon recusants (Catholics who broke the law by refusing to attend Church of England services). This was ... *the coercive instrument most immediately available to enforce conformity. It was also advantageous because if fines failed to bring people to church they would, at least, become a considerable source of revenue.*[214] The imposition of fines on a nation that was mainly and stubbornly Catholic was, potentially, a lucrative business. It didn't work out quite as planned. Collection fell to minor officials who accepted bribes from the better-off Catholic landowners and merchants, leaving the poor to do the paying or go to gaol.

Even if the Irish did conform they were not guaranteed an equal footing on a par with the invader. The local O'Brien leader in County Clare is a good example. He felt that the best way to maintain his ancestral estates and his power was to bow to the wishes of the English and become Protestant. As it turned out, not even his family was free from discrimination. On the death of the Fourth Earl of Thomond (the title which the O'Briens had been given by the English in reward for their conversion), it was recommended by the authorities that

---

214 Canny, 2009; p. 307.

they should not continue to be lieutenants of the county because it ... *gave onto them a greater dependency than in reason of state ought to be afforded to any of the natives of this kingdom.*[215] What is clearly revealed here is that power rather than belief was the force driving the English who wished to maintain an ethnically-pure society at the top.

A monument to the German mercenary Duke of Schomberg, who fought on the side of King William at the battle of the Boyne, was erected close to the high altar of Saint Patrick's by Dean Jonathan Swift. Swift wrote two ponderous odes in celebration of the king's victory and this clearly places him as an enemy of the Jacobites and the majority of the Gaelic and Old English Catholic populations in Ireland. Alas, nothing is that simple with Swift. Despite his many eccentricities, he is not valueless as a representative of the Protestant society he came from.

For me Dean Swift is a bridge over a great chasm between the New English and my Gaelic people in Ireland. Saint Patrick's Hospital for the insane is living proof of his desire to help those less fortunate than he. It was here that my great-great-grandfather Thomas J. resided because Swift saw fit to help him, though he never knew him. Our lives entwined at that place. We became part of a unique story. The desire of Swift, the illness of Thomas J. and my longing to trace the golden threads of my ancestors linked us together in the same space but in separate time. Though time divided us, a fleeting moment of sorrow joined our three lives across the centuries.

For me Swift is the redemptive aspect of Saint Patrick's Cathedral and his story merits a brief examination. When I was young I had, for reasons unbeknown to me, a fascination and an interest in his life. Whenever I was near the Cathedral I tried to place him in the landscape about the edifice but failed. I knew he lived somewhere in the vicinity but could never find exactly where. Perhaps he lived in the area that is now enclosed by the adjacent police station? I was wrong. I read several books on the man but they didn't provide the answers I was looking for. Then I bought his biography written by Victoria Glendinning. Because she provided information on the man, his times and details of the places he moved through, my questions were at last answered. The deanery is on the opposite side of the road to the Cathedral and faces Kevin Street. It stands proud and in good condition. It was here that Swift spent the last seventeen years of his life after the death of his beloved Stella. He was doomed to a lonely existence and ended up walking around the deanery up to ten hours per day. Towards the close of his life he struggled as crippling infirmity took hold. He was eventually declared unfit to manage his affairs. He was of *unsound mind.*[216]

Swift's grandfather—Reverend Thomas Swift—was the vicar of Goodrich in Herefordshire. Several of the Swifts who came to Ireland were lawyers. Victoria Glendinning in her elegant biography of the man points out that prospects were particularly good for lawyers in frontier Ireland because ... *lands were annexed, restored, sequestered, allotted, and fought over in retaliation or response to every rebellion of the native Irish, and every change of English administration, religious-political upheaval, or policy shift.*[217]

---

215 *Ibid*; p. 285.
216 Glendinning, 1999; pp. 270, 291, 292.
217 *Ibid*; p. 18.

Swift was born in Hoey's Court Dublin in November 1667. His father was dead at the time of his birth. His mother appears to have abandoned him to his uncles in Ireland when she left to live in Leicester in England. Uncle Godwin was his main guardian. It may well have been his odd relationship with his mother that caused his eccentricity and frustration. Swift himself put it this way: *I remember, when I was a little boy, I felt a great fish at the end of my line which I drew up almost to the ground. But it dropped in and the disappointment vexeth me to this very day and I believe it was the type of all my future disappointments.* Glendinning adds: *He was a disappointed man. Disappointed by the circumstances of his birth, which led to his youthful poverty. Disappointed by the powerful patrons who could have furthered his career and did not. He harboured grievances and resentments.*[218]

Swift was generally recognised as a man of rude wit and manner. He became the Dean of Saint Patrick's, a post he attained in 1714. However, in the period 1689 to 1727 he availed of several opportunities to visit and reside in England. He was hopeful that periods spent there would be the steppingstones to his lifelong ambition, which was an appointment as bishop in an appropriate diocese in England. When in London he was never presented to Queen Anne, which he desired. She and some of her influential advisers distrusted and disliked Swift because of ... *the virulence of his personal satires and his apparent godlessness.*[219] He wrote copiously on the human condition with savage wit. Even friends suffered the acid drops of his sharp pen. He never compromised the frankness and bitterness of his satire. Many were wounded by it. Yet he would not or could not see the damage it was doing to himself.

Swift's relationship to women was odd to say the least: intimate yet distant; gracious yet cruel. Stella, whom he met when she was eight in Moorpark in England, was his clear favourite and followed him to Ireland but she came with a chaperone—Rebecca Dingley— and the two ladies lived together in Trim, close to his early parish centre at Laracor.

Swift damaged his reputation by befriending another woman around 1707. Her name was Vanessa. Her father, Bartholomew Vanhomrigh, a Dutchman who had become a revenue commissioner in Dublin and eventually rose to be the Lord Mayor of the city, had considerable property in Ireland. His position came about as a result of the peaceful Dutch invasion of Britain and Ireland under King William III which allowed such men to occupy all sorts of employments in these islands at the time.[220]

Vanessa desired to be Swift's wife and, like Stella, came over to Ireland. She moved into one of her father's houses in Celbridge in 1714 to be near Swift. He was terror-stricken for fear of scandal. At first he avoided her company but, being infatuated, he renewed their friendship. He spent many hours with her; he wrote part of *Gulliver's Travels* in the garden of her house on the banks of the Liffey. But two rival women in and around a small city like Dublin was a powder keg waiting to go off—and it did. Vanessa knew of Swift's fondness for Stella and rumours of his marriage to her were the live sparks that caused detonation. Rumours still abound about his possible marriage to Stella, but there is no proof. They never lived together openly as man and wife.[221]

---

218 *Ibid*; p. 6.
219 *Ibid*; p. 12.
220 *Ibid*; pp. 44, 124, ff.
221 *Ibid*; pp. 194, 199, 236.

Circumstances reached crisis point when Vanessa wrote to Stella asking her if it was true that she was married to Swift. He got hold of the letter through Stella and was so angry that he rode out on horseback from the deanery of Saint Patrick's to her house in Celbridge. Without saying anything he threw the letter down on a desk before his former love and retreated—never to have anything to do with her again. This literally broke her heart. Within a short time she was dead. To Swift's misfortune, Stella was also ill and, within several years, also died.[222]

Swift provides a totally different perspective on Ireland compared to the outlooks of the Old English or the Gael. He felt that Catholics in Ireland were ... *altogether as inconsiderable as women and children. Their lands are almost entirely taken from them, and they are rendered incapable of purchasing any more ...*[223]

Swift's community was the Protestant opportunist who helped confiscate land from Catholics. His life affords a revealing vista on Irish history from the point of view of an invader family during the seventy-eight years of his life that straddled the turn of the seventeenth and eighteenth centuries.

In examining Swift's life I stare directly into the face of the enemy of my people but I have no anger. This is because he has several redeeming features that I can relate to. He was vulnerable rather than pompous. He was honest despite his glaring faults and prejudices. He was benevolent towards the most vulnerable in society. Before leaving the world, he made a final gesture that sealed his reputation. He bequeathed his estates to the foundation of Saint Patrick's Hospital for idiots and lunatics in Dublin. Cruelly, Lord Orrery intimated that Swift set up an asylum and was the first proper inhabitant of his own hospital, which of course was untrue because Saint Patrick's was set up after his death.[224]

Swift's interest in madness goes back at least to his days in Moorpark. Between 1696 and 1698 he wrote a *Tale of a Tub* that deals with the subject. At that time, social sightseeing in London included visits to the madhouse at Bedlam and the zoo. Both shared equal interest on the itinerary. The inmates of Bedlam were lepers of the mind. However, in his visits to this madhouse Swift took an alternative view. These people were different, he observed, not outcasts. His attitude to madness elevates him above most—in his time, or even in ours—because he perceived his more unfortunate fellow man as not being decoupled from society by mental infirmity but under a strange influence of some sort that merited understanding. Nonetheless, Glendinning reminds us that his attitude was not sentimental; *his generosity was dispassionate.*[225] It is not clear if Swift's conciliatory views on madness had anything to do with his religious background, which appeared to be relatively weak.

Unfortunately, it is difficult for me to decouple the chilling coldness I feel towards the trappings of Protestantism and associated attitudes of Ascendancy domination, superiority and exclusion. A bitter aftertaste remains against the type of Protestantism that still maintains an undercurrent of superiority in Irish society. The feeling arises from deep-

---

222 *Ibid*; p. 202, ff.
223 *Ibid*; p. 50.
224 Malcolm, 1989; p. 4.
225 Glendinning, 1999; p. 264.

seated family memes that have been handed down from generation to generation. This is a cultural rather than a religious or belief response. To be frank: residual pockets of Irish Protestants and, without doubt, many loyalists in Ulster have an equally chilling disdain towards the cultural trappings of Catholicism. Breaking through such intolerances takes time; they do not automatically melt away because we acknowledge their existence.

Fortunately, men and women of good conscience were and are numbered among the ranks of all rival denominations in Ireland. The second wife of Swift's acquaintance Lord Orrery admitted to abhorring Presbyterians and Catholics equally. But she was finally able to say that ... *I have so far got the better of these wrong prejudices as to see the merit of persons in both these sects, and to pray to God Almighty that he will be pleased mercifully to break down the middle wall of partition between us.*[226]

The long-standing cultural tensions dividing traditional enemies in Ireland and the British mainland are latent. They awaken at times of heightened stress. This means that some memes can become dominant under certain circumstances and be submissive in other cases. As a result, behaviour may appear to be inconsistent. For example, in my case, the Old English memes dominated on the occasion of the demonstrations against the events of Bloody Sunday in Northern Ireland; this may appear inconsistent or at least unexpected considering the opinions I have express towards the behaviour of the English conquerors in Ireland. Perhaps. Yet this is understandable within the reality of competing family memes.

Returning again to the suggestion about religion being largely responsible for human divisions, I contend that, in my case, the cultural and political landscapes of former historical periods are stamped firmly on my mind. I carry the baggage of those times though I desire to be rid of the worst of it. As I suggested previously, it would be unnatural to say that, when reading the history of Ireland, my attitudes towards the Protestant Ascendancy that were responsible for the demise of most of our family estates, is impartial. But, Swift and people like Lady Orrery are, for me, bridges into the minds and hearts of the old adversary and, as such, make the steps on the road to reconciliation and eventual love of enemy a great deal easier.

---

226 *Ibid*; p. 51.

Destiny

The twists and turns of Grafton Street in Dublin follow an old *boreen* that led from Stephen's Green to Trinity College. As we walk along this thoroughfare we are swayed, physically, by the meanderings of former times. In like manner, we are touched by the reality of the past in various other ways. We may barely discern these elusive forces; but they are amongst us. Identifying historic influences that impinge on our reality requires effort on our part. In return we obtain the keys to understanding the present. Furthermore, knowledge of the past and present provoke us to face another dimension of self: our destiny.

We sometimes encounter the reality of the past by accident, as I did during one of the most humble yet memorable tasks I undertook as a student. In the summer of 1970, I was working for a company called Irish Forest Products and was assisting its forester, Michael Mallin, to mark and select old oak trees for felling on the Ballinacor Estate at the mouth of Glenmalure Valley in County Wicklow.

Our task might be dismissed as menial till it is realised that these trees were destined to re-roof an old abbey in County Tipperary. According to William Hayes in his booklet *Holy Cross Abbey*, the building was probably well under way when Prince John arrived at Waterford in 1185. By all accounts the first monastic buildings were sufficiently advanced shortly after 1200 to attract the Archbishop of Cashel to retire there.[227]

The early fifteenth century was significant for the abbey in that an ambitious rebuilding was begun. One hundred years later, after Henry VIII broke from the Catholic Church, thirteen religious houses in the Pale and nearby centres were suppressed and their properties put into the hands of the crown. Holy Cross, on the other hand, evaded the general sentence by becoming a secular college. Nonetheless, like other monasteries in Ireland it was eventually abandoned and declined. In 1572 parts of the abbey were intact, but by 1626 most of the building was damp and uninhabitable.

Another attempt was made to renovate the buildings by Abbot John Cantwell in the early decades of the seventeenth century. A native of Thurles parish, Cantwell studied in Bordeaux before entering the Cistercian Order in Spain, returning to Ireland in 1633. *He took care to cover in the whole church which through the inclemency of the seasons and the cruelty of the heretics had remained without a roof ...*[228] It appears that Cantwell's efforts were only partially successful. The Cromwellian invasion brought his endeavours to an end.

In the late 1960s local moves were made to restore the abbey church and in 1971 the actual work of restoration began. The oak from Irish Forest Products was the first on the scene and was put into the tower. It was policy to use unseasoned oak, as the fresh timber was easier to work, fashion and fit. William well recalls the assembling of the tower roof on the ground before being taken apart and finally fitted in place. He believed that some of the

---

227 Details of Holy Cross Abbey derived from: Hayes, 1973 and Hayes, 2011.
228 From an English translation of Br Malachy Hartry's *Triumphalia Chronologica Monasterii Sanctae Crucis* (c. 1640) by Rev Denis Murphy, S.J. (1895; p. 219); personal communications, William J. Hayes, 2011.

oak for the adjoining part of the roof—that of the north transept—came from a different woodland source through Abbeyleix sawmills. Nonetheless, at least in the tower and parts of the north transept, boards from the glens of Wicklow play their part in protecting the church.

There are many dimensions to the abbey, the most central of which is the domain of faith. In addition, the very *raison d'être* for the church was, and still is, a celebration of wood. Holy Cross was built to house the relic of the "true cross". The original relic was given to an O'Brien king in recognition of his patronage to the church on the eve of the Norman invasion of Ireland. This piece of wood marked time in the relative widths of its annual wood rings. Where did it come from? Was it a section of the wood given to Constantine The Great's aged mother in Jerusalem or a medieval hoax? One way or the other, it carried its own intriguing story. Other time-signatures are found in the abbey. They are written in the annual rings of the oak boards of the tower roof, made from the trees of Wicklow, and these beams reflect spring and summer weather patterns between the first half of the nineteenth century and the 1970s.

When I considered the links with time that Michael and I had, through the church, I realised that we had become direct counterparts of long-forgotten medieval and early-modern workers who carried out the same task of selecting, from oak copses, the trees for the previous roofs. Roofing and re-roofing must have taken place on at least four occasions: firstly, round 1200; then between 1400 and 1450; next, in the 1630s and, finally, in 1971. We all inhabited very different worlds. The earliest woodlanders were men who were experiencing the calamitous events of the Norman invasion. The next group who selected the timbers lived in a country that was still recovering from the ravages of the Black Death. The discovery of the New World was at least half a century away. The early-modern woodlanders talked about the English and Scottish plantations that were afoot from Munster to Ulster. Our Ireland was undergoing a profound modernisation after independence and was separating from the ways that had held sway in human cultures for centuries. The internet was less than a quarter century into the future. The religion that had given rise to the abbey was about to experience a period of deep discomfort in Ireland. Indeed, Christianity itself would suffer the beginning of a new phase of turbulence as its tenets clashed with modern secularism.

Michael and I participated briefly and at the margins of a long human and spiritual story but were linked momentarily and intimately into the activities of past generations. Who, I wonder, will be around for the fifth roofing and what will their world be like?

Holy Cross was and is a symbol of Catholic faith that spanned the whole period from the arrival of the Normans in Ireland up to the present day. Catholicism was a badge of identity for most of my ancestors. And religion was a core factor that divided or united the three main traditions in Ireland. It united the native Irish and Old English when it suited them; it created a permanent divide between these Catholic entities on one side and the Protestant Ascendancy when the Penal Laws were in force. As such, religion was strongly aligned with the interests of each cultural group. And the interests of each group, in turn, equated with their particular desires for influence and material gain. Therefore, several forces were at work at the same time, making it difficult to understand what people actually believed in, outside their political and cultural contexts.

However, the essence of religion is belief and has much to do with purpose in life. Our origin is one pole of identity; our fate or our destiny is the other. Therefore, the realm of what we believe in—or don't believe in—is a vital dimension of self-discovery when we refuse to put limits on our process of inquiry. When considering my relationship with Catholicism as a component of identity, I found it important to make a clear distinction between its cultural and belief dimensions. I have maintained my faith into adult life despite the many obstacles thrown up against it. Obstacles against Christianity have changed many times since the abbey was first built. Today, it is often claimed, the major force against traditional belief is science.

For long I applied scientific methods when trying to understand the world and the universe. That is how I was trained. But I remained unsatisfied because there are two perspectives on knowledge. I persisted in the outer perspective where we deal with understanding from the objective point of view only. Later I became aware that exploring the nature of our universe exclusively through science is as limiting as trying to comprehend the spirit of Christmas by chemically analysing children's presents. The non-scientific, mystical or spiritual domain is ultimately subjective and intuitive, but almost limitless thought is possible here.

Daniel O'Leary says: *The mystical experience is like the mirror image of science, a direct perception of cosmic oneness, an inside window into the mystery that science grapples with from the outside.*[229] It is a different way to decode the universe. However, unlike science, religion or belief may derive theories about the nature of the supernatural but it is impossible to test hypothesis; it is impossible to replicate experimental design and repeat tests in the same way as science can do because we are dealing with a different medium. With no way of testing the truth of belief, anything is possible. Religions can, in theory, concoct any belief and hold it up as reality. No one can contradict. There are enormous risks for self-delusion. Ironically, in a world that respects the rigorous discipline of science, relativism finds no base for any particular principles for moral guidance in the domain beyond science. For these reasons, possibly the most positive aspect of an institutionalised religion is the measure of collective thought and the desire for objective morality it brings to the world.

Being open to the non-scientific, yet retaining the scientific approach is a holistic way to explore the nature of things. Nonetheless, the quest to understand the origins and reasons for the universe seems destined to continue until we can answer a deeper question: *Why is there anything at all instead of nothing?*[230] Our reality may be that we are no nearer or further from the truth the more we progress. Truth moves away like a rainbow as we advance. James Frazer is probably right when he speculates that ... *advance of knowledge is an infinite progression towards a goal that for ever recedes....*[231] The limitations of science in answering philosophical, metaphysical or religious questions are becoming clearer. Could science be a transient apparatus associated principally with the current phase of human development?

---

229 O'Leary, 1998; p. 276.
230 Shiga, 2007; p. 33.
231 Frazer, 1996; p. 854.

Frazer says that ... *the history of thought should warn us against concluding that because the scientific theory of the world is the best that has yet been formulated, it is necessarily complete and final. We must remember that at bottom the generalisations of science or, in common parlance, the laws of nature, are merely hypotheses devised to explain that ever-shifting phantasmagoria of thought ... In the last analysis magic, religion, and science are nothing but theories of thought; and as science has supplanted its predecessors, so it may hereafter be itself superseded by some more perfect hypothesis, perhaps by some totally different way of looking at the phenomena ... of which we in this generation can form no idea.*[232]

That science will reach its limitations in answering questions is a possibility, given the suggestion that our universe is only a tiny part of an unimaginably large and diverse multiverse. Cosmologist George Ellis considers the multiverse concept to be a potentially dangerous idea in that it postulates the existence of unobservable universes. The role of science is diminished in a situation where material is not testable.[233] For example, contemporary science can only speculate or theorise about what happened before *Planck Time*, which began at an extremely small interval after the *Big Bang*. If what happened before this event cannot be determined in an empirical manner, then science will have reached an impasse.

Whatever about the future of science, we are and always will be plagued, through our intelligence, to search for answers to our condition. The question about our reason for existing is always posed, will always be posed and we must respond. But will we ever have enough information to solve our riddle?

This question reminds me of an experience I had in Kenya. I was preparing to co-ordinate a training course for a group of all-male forestry managers. Their outlook was, understandably, macho. The chosen training company provided an assertive male trainer and a female teacher of rather delicate appearance who was not a day over twenty-five. Before the course began I was approached by several managers. They didn't want to be trained by the lady. I was concerned and made contact with the company director to discuss the situation. *'Don't worry,'* he said, *'she has trained all-male groups before and is used to such situations.'*

'But these are foresters,' I said. He insisted that I should not worry.

The training was to take place one day a week over several months. I attended the events as co-ordinator. The male director supervised the sessions on the first two occasions. Then the young lady appeared. Her first presentation passed off more successfully than I had anticipated. But on the second session she presented a mathematical puzzle and asked her audience to solve it. A discussion ensued and soon became heated, bordering on aggression. My concerns were being realised. She would not be able to control the situation now. However, after allowing the debate to go on amongst the participants for a little time longer she then told them that, although it appeared doable, there simply was not enough information provided to solve the puzzle. Total silence followed with much

232 *Ibid*; p. 854.
233 Gefter, 2010; pp. 28, 29.

slipping back into protective shells. This is what the director had in mind when he told me not to worry about the female teacher. From then on she had the audience in the palm of her hand.

There may be a direct parallel in this example in relation to our knowledge of the universe. Perhaps we don't have sufficient information to solve our riddle. In like manner, any inference about the presence or absence of a divine being—based on scientific results—is premature, because we don't have the means to prove or disprove this hypothesis with the present materials to hand. Taking the view that God is a primitive or medieval fantasy that we have grown beyond is also premature; the issue about whether a creator actually exists or not has not been brought to a final conclusion. It is a matter of individual inclination to believe in something or nothing. We may or may not "sense" a watchmaker behind the universal timepiece. Ultimately, we have no way of knowing if a supreme being exists, unless it is revealed to us. Revelation, of course, is a basic precept of Christian belief.

In the absence of a final proof, we have to remain dumb or take one side or the other. We have to believe in something or be neutral; even atheism is a belief. Like the bell curve of a normal distribution, most people tend to shift along the gradient, sometimes going to one extreme or the other but with no final conclusion. There are some who genuinely believe in nothing beyond the material. There are others who hold an unshakeable religious faith. The vast majority, it seems, slip from one camp to the other depending on circumstances. Their prevailing sentiment is doubt about which camp they are in. For many, doubt is kept unanswered and well in the background as they get on with living life. But to evade the question does not bring them any closer to uncovering self-understanding.

Questioning our place in the scheme of things originates from within. Whether we believe or disbelieve in a divine presence, or a set of religious dogmas, or nothing, the way we reach our conclusions takes place in the same compartments and in the same manner within our brains. In other words, our cognitive processes provoke us to ask the question about our reason for living and our purpose in life. We must try to satisfy our yearnings for answers or evade the deep promptings of our nature. To run from our craving to understand our predicament is to live in perpetual twilight. The continual development of our perspective of the world and universe is a personal pilgrimage in which raw truth is our best compass. Unfortunately, raw truth can often be uncomfortable, particularly when moral implications entail restrictions and responsibilities on us. But, irrespective of the outcome, this quest is our most worthy undertaking because it influences all we do and who we become. Exploring our destiny is, therefore, an essential element in the quest to determine who we are.

Bison Hunting to Bib Manufacturing

The ultimate aspiration of the family historian is to collect information about the totality of our ancestors on every side. But this exercise inevitably ends up with tattered edges as we run out of leads. Nonetheless, having become convinced that my enquiry was still too narrow, I widened it as far as I could to accommodate my known surnames. I now felt that I could, in theory at least, break through to a higher level of understanding if I could see identity in terms of the origins of all my forbearers. But I was forced to limit the scope of this investigation to an arbitrary four generations because, beyond my great-grand-parents, some family names were uncertain or missing and would give rise to a lopsided analysis.

Including Keogh, I boast eight surnames over four generations. Six of these would be recognised as Gaelic Irish, including Keogh; Delaney; McDowell; Moran; O'Neill and Sheridan. But the others—Gough and Goulding—would be deemed foreign, or at least non-Gaelic. The result of this exercise was: on the basis of surnames alone, I am not a pure Gael. I could claim to be seventy-five per cent native Irish, assuming, of course, no contamination from non-Irish sources in my Gaelic surnames. To what, then, does the non-Gaelic portion belong? Gough was probably Welsh in origin. But the Irish Goughs could not qualify, in their present context, as being British because of their remote detachment from the UK. Goulding was a mystery and may have had a Jewish origin. However, in contemporary terms these surnames "are" Irish but not Gaelic. The term *Irish*, therefore, embraces a wide spectrum of possibilities. I became dissatisfied with this outcome because it included all-comers, based only on long-term residency in Ireland and this diminishes distinctiveness. I concluded that it was difficult, if not impossible, to create a unique identity based on surnames alone.

An alternative way I had to comprehend my identity had nothing to do with surnames. It entailed how other people perceived me. This approach, I felt, would be more objective. When I lived in County Galway during my practical year in forestry instruction, an old countryman referred to me as a *Jackeen* (Dubliner) in a disparaging manner that carried with it a hint that I was less than him. He, not I, was the genuine representative of Ireland. Compared to him I was a foreigner in demeanour and accent. Many rural people, particularly in the past, perceived Dublin people in this way. On the other hand, whenever I left Ireland I was accepted as being one-hundred-per-cent Irish. When I was overseas I was not less or more Irish than anyone from any segment of the island's population. Depending on other people's perceptions to define one's identity, therefore, means that, as views change, one's identity modifies. Identity must be based on something more solid and lasting. Indeed, identity has to do with the quality or condition of being or remaining the same.

Another approach in determining identity is to consider ancestral numbers. Each of us has a mother and father; each of them, in turn, had a mother and father. In other words, the numbers involved in the reproductive process is doubled from generation to generation. As we widen our search to include the entirety of our ancestors, the numbers of reproductive events and their geographic spread increase accordingly. But the further back in time we go the fewer people there were on the face of the earth. If we take the process to about nineteen generations, the mathematical numbers surpass the total possible population of Ireland at the time. How are the two sets of numbers—the reproductive events and the total population—reconciled? The apparent contradiction underlines the fact that a particular conception is often shared by many descendants and shows that the population of a certain geographic area is highly inter-related. It does not necessarily mean that former descendants were evenly distributed across a particular geographic territory like the island of Ireland; it is more likely that they came from clusters of people. Defining identity in this manner, therefore, means being able to identify these ancestral clusters and understand their dynamics through time. Given the lack of information about Gaelic culture in Ireland, cluster analysis of this type is well into the future.

Attempts at determining identity through surnames, oral family history and cluster analysis are severely limited. Genealogists are inevitably confronted by *brick walls* despite whatever number of new breakthroughs they make. No matter how far into the past we trace our origins, we are, at some point, confronted by a wall of emptiness. History can assist in providing a contextual background but is, at best, generic. Yet, despite these limitations hindering the understanding of our wider family identities, modern science has opened an exciting new window into our ancestral past through human genetics. I turned to this emerging field to take the process further. The tenor of the entire investigation was changed by this shift in direction and placed the context of the story of my ancestors as a whole into a dimension I could not have imagined at the outset.

To appreciate something of the power of genetic fingerprinting it was necessary for me to have at least a basic understanding of modern genetics. Perspectives in this relatively recent discipline are changing rapidly as new techniques are being applied and as new information is being analysed, which means that current results must be accepted as part of a work-in-progress.

Stephen Oppenheimer states that: *We are the products of our genes. The secret keys to this Edwardian truism were traced and cut out on bits of cardboard by two adventure-scientists, Jim Watson and Francis Crick, in 1953.*[234] These scientists revealed the role of the biological chemical called deoxyribonucleic acid (DNA). This double helix of entwined crossbars, or base pairs, is the chemical code for any organism, including us. The different patterns of bases give rise to the totality of organisms from toadstools to sequoias; from earth worms to brain surgeons.

DNA can be thought of as a long word made up of chemical letters; these letters provide the written commands for the creation of the body's chemicals and their resulting order. DNA is found mainly in the operating room of the cell: the nucleus. DNA does not *do* anything except send out commands to messenger molecules, which ensure that the various proteins or building blocks of our bodies are created in the right places and in just the right amounts.

DNA is the fundamental code that makes us biologically who we are. In reproductive cells, the double helices unravel into two in anticipation of a new combination. The father's DNA is stored in the sperm. In the mother it is stored in the egg. What happens next, during fertilisation, pin-points the instant in which the individual comes into existence.

---

234 Oppenheimer, 2004; p. 35.

This is described succinctly by Condic (2008)[235]: *Following the binding of sperm and egg to each other, the membranes of these two cells fuse, creating in this instant a single hybrid cell: the zygote or one-cell embryo ... Cell fusion is a well studied and very rapid event, occurring in less than a second. Because the zygote arises from the fusion of two different cells, it contains all the components of both sperm and egg, and therefore the zygote has a unique molecular composition that is distinct from either gamete. ... These modifications block sperm binding to the cell surface and prevent further intrusion of additional spermatozoa on the unfolding process of development. Thus, the zygote acts immediately and specifically to antagonize the function of the gametes from which it is derived ... Clearly, then, the prior trajectories of sperm and egg have been abandoned, and a new developmental trajectory—that of the zygote—has taken their place.*

That is to say, the separate functions of sperm and egg are modified and the new cell, the zygote, with its unique molecular base, is immediately protective of itself—a state that will be conserved in the individual until the death of the whole organism. The instant the zygote is produced is the precise moment that the golden threads of life become the new generation. In biological terms, the embrace of the inherited bases from both parents, thus forming a new and totally unique set of double helixes, is the code-birth of the individual. The set of instructions for skin pigmentation, eye colour and other genetically dominant characteristics is now present. From then the process of development continues as the first cell divides into two, then four and so on. A pattern emerges, reflecting the DNA commands. The initial ball of cells keeps on growing, then sends out appendages, and begins the process of complex expansion, segregation, differentiation and infolding over a period of nine months, at the end of which the baby enters the world.

The sex-determining DNA genes are located on what are called the X- and Y-chromosomes. Sperm cells carry both. The female carries only the X chromosomes. At conception one chromosome from each parent enters the first cell. If the X- and Y-chromosomes end up in this cell, the baby is male. If, on the other hand, the resulting union is XX, the baby is female.

Fortunately for ancestral research, scientists have identified part of the male DNA (Y-chromosome) that remains the same for hundreds of generations. Therefore, if certain markers are identified for a man on this part of his DNA, then the same is automatically determined for his father and his father in turn and so on for thousands of years without change. Over the last decade genetic research has gradually defined the deep-rooted relationships between male DNA throughout the world and what emerges is a pattern that connects all men of our planet. A total of fifteen *clusters* or *clans* have been identified worldwide based on a very stable genetic system of markers or slow molecular changes called mutations. Only men can undertake a study of their paternal line. This is because, as mentioned, no female carries the Y-chromosome. Females must determine their paternal lineage from their father or a near relative who has inherited a Y-chromosome from the same source.

To follow the female line we need a different foundation. Tiny bodies called mitochondria are found in each of our cells. They function like batteries within the cellular fluid and are

235 Condic, 2008; p. 3.

the powerhouses of the cells. Aeons ago these tubular bodies were probably free-living organisms with their own control DNA. They invaded other single-celled life forms and developed symbiotic relationships with them. Eventually, through the process of evolution, they became an important part of our own makeup. The DNA of the mitochondria is not part of the cell's control nucleus and it arises exclusively from our mothers. The father's mitochondria, contained in the tail of the sperm, are jettisoned just before conception.

This process of jettisoning is fortunate for ancestral research because mitochondrial DNA contains markers that are stable and are not interfered with in any way by the male genes. In effect, if these female markers are determined for someone, then the same set is automatically determined for that person's mother and her mother in turn and so on for thousands of years without significant change. In fact, only one mutation takes place, on average, once every 20,000 years within these female markers, or once every seven or eight hundred generations.

Over the last ten to fifteen years the sources of different female markers have been gradually clarified and this has resulted in thirty-six clusters worldwide. Seven women have given rise to most native Europeans that exist today and these have been christened *The Seven Daughters of Eve* by Dr. Bryan Sykes.[236] Oxford geneticist Sykes has named these women: *Helena, Jasmine, Katrine, Tara, Ursula, Velda* and *Xenia.*

Tiny and more rapid mutations also occur at random on other parts of our female and male genes and these steadily accumulate as different molecular markers. The changes are then passed down through the generations and allow us to refine our links into our biological past. If mutations took place too frequently or too infrequently, they would not be much good for ancestral research. Through the combination of stable and more rapid marker mutations we have a mechanism to help us advance, in an unprecedented way, the story of male and female human genealogy.

The mutations on our Y-chromosome and mitochondrial DNA allow each of us to reconstruct a genetic family tree, which is written in our bodily chemistry. This reconstruction provides us with a picture of male and female genealogy of the entire species. Not only can we construct the tree itself; the resulting mutations tend to be found in varying frequencies across the surface of the earth and we can determine approximately where and when they occurred. Through this process it is possible to trace the migrations of modern humans around the globe from our beginnings in Africa. Although still in its infancy, genetics has provided the best insight into the story of human development and has forced a rewriting of early history and pre-history.

It turns out that it is difficult to correlate what we term "tribal" or "ethnic" groupings with human genetic patterns. This is not to say that there are no such relationships; otherwise we would not be able to use genetic markings to trace the movements of people around the world. But, it is best to visualise the entire human genome as a continuum, which has arisen from a common base (our ancestral singularity) and which is now composed of clusters of certain genetic markers that have arisen as "appendages" on the human genome derived from isolation—deliberate in the case of Jews—or environmental in the case of

---

236 Sykes, 2007; p. 105.

several remote peoples. However, there are no clear-cut frontiers between these clusters, which put pay to any attempts that try to define tribal or ethnic groupings in specific genetic terms.

I engaged a number of scientific laboratories to determine my male and female genetic bases. Each of these posted me a small multi-bristled brush or plastic rod. After rubbing the instrument on the inner part of my mouth, I returned it for analysis. The reply, which took about a month, always felt longer. I could not wait to scrutinise their findings. The detailed laboratory analyses I was given influenced my understanding of the nature of identity as answers that eluded me for decades began to emerge. In addition to confirming my Irish roots, Oxford Ancestors laboratory stated: *Your DNA sequences shows you to be a direct maternal descendant of Tara.* This lady was one of the *Seven Daughters of Eve*; she lived in the region of Tuscany about 17,000 years ago. I carry her ancient signature within my being.

I knew two females who bore Tara's markers. The closest of these was my mother, followed by my grandmother, AB. Her mother, Elin Sheridan, and her mother in turn, Bride McGrath, are known to me in name only. Roughly sixty women with the same marker genes take me back to the Early Christian period when the domestic scene was played out within ringforts and crannogs made of wooden palisades and straw-covered roundhouses. Some seventy or eighty females take me back to the time of Christ; one hundred and fifty to the megalithic builders of Newgrange and more than three hundred to the first people who came to these islands, which is about halfway in time to the origins of Tara's mutation near Tuscany. Each of these women bore at least one baby girl; each girl awoke in the arms of the preceding generation and, as she grew up, gleaned her view of the world and the universe through a multitude of domestic activities and gossip around the hearth. Each girl had a partner and produced her own children. If she was lucky she watched them grow, bereaved the loss of her parents, then watched her offspring become adults and form new relationships before she died. In this way, the golden threads of life were passed on in simple or complex domestic scenes that changed against a background of shifting landscapes and technological developments.

Oxford Ancestors laboratory informed me that my male DNA was compared against their database, which contains thousands of signatures from Britain and Ireland. The report stated: *There are intriguing genetic connections between Y-chromosomes such as yours and those found in the Iberian Peninsula, especially among the Basques.* Much research has been devoted to the genetics of these Iberian people and various conflicting theories have been proposed. One view is that there is evidence for continuity with the Palaeolithic period. The present-day Basque country may have become one of a few European refuges during the severe cold spell of the last Ice Age and ... *managed to preserve more of its original genetic diversity than did other parts of Western Europe.*[237] If so, according to another school of thought, this could only have been for its womenfolk. Descendants of the first agriculturalists—the Neolithic culture of the Middle East—fanned out like a gigantic, slow-spreading infection, conquering all before them. This epidemic-like wave of humanity, composed mainly of men, overran every culture before it with new technological knowhow, eventually suppressing and then eliminating or diminishing

237 Oppenheimer, 2004; p. 138.

the older male genetic varieties throughout Western Europe and dominating the female population. As a result, one set of genetic determinants or male markers is found in very high frequencies in Western Europe, reaching over eighty per cent in parts of Ireland.[238]

The story of my male ancestors is becoming clearer, though much has yet to be determined. They belonged to the R1b haplogroup and were the victors; at least for the time being.[239] The particular "clan" that gave rise to my male DNA markers has been named *Oisin* by Dr. Sykes and it had its origins tens of thousands of years ago in the Middle East.[240] Through the means of genetic fingerprinting I can trace my male DNA line to a particular mutation, some 1,300 or 1,400 generations below the upper rungs of my genetic ladder.

I knew James and Bartholomew—my father and grandfather—who carried my male mutations on the long march out of the past. I sensed something of James, my great-grandfather, through oral family history. I gleaned knowledge of his father Thomas J., and of his father in turn, Thomas the Elder, through the existing records. As seen previously, twenty-five men take me back to the eve of the Norman Conquest when the Keoghs inhabited the plains of Kildare. Roughly fifty or sixty separate me from the time of Saint Patrick.

Comparative studies of Irish Y-chromosomes have confirmed a genetic association between the Keoghs of Ranelagh and the surname in Wexford. The results endorse family oral history and all previous assumptions I made about their authentic links to the Gaelic tribes of Leinster. Here was the final proof that the family belonged to the MacEochaidh sept of that province. Their unusually strong relationship with learning, as demonstrated by Thomas J.'s professional activities, lends further credence to their possible links to a bardic past. Unfortunately, without documented evidence, it is not possible to take that last step and assume that they had been the poets and inaugurators of the kings and lords of Leinster; yet there is no evidence to the contrary.

How ironic it is that, previously, I felt a weak cultural affinity to Ireland. I may now rightfully consider my male ancestors as genuinely Irish; not first-nation Irish—because we probably eliminated them—but Neolithic or Bronze Age Irish. The long stretch of time from the present into the Palaeolithic incorporates male ancestors whose occupations ranged from bison and deer hunting to the manufacturing of shirts, kiddies' bibs and bias binding.

We have seen that all men in the world sprang from one of fifteen clusters; and all females originated from one of thirty-six genetic nodes. These, in turn, emerged from a shared ancestry in Africa for modern humans. The common paternal ancestor of living men is our DNA Adam. Each female genetic clan, in turn, traces its own markers to other ancestral women, eventually arriving at one Mitochondrial Eve. Every person alive today, therefore, has inherited his or her female markers from one single woman. This female was not the only woman alive at that time. She was part of a core of some 2,000-10,000 African

---

238 Sykes, 2007; p. 160.
239 The R1b people may have been associated with Bronze Age rather than Neolithic cultures.
240 Results from Oxford Ancestors genetic laboratory (2005).

men and women who lived around 200,000 years ago.[241] The historical and pre-historical background of male chromosomes was similar. The male lines also sprang from a core of African men and women. A fundamental truth is that each and every human being alive today, irrespective of their background, traces themselves to a common point: our ancestral singularity in Africa. Ultimately, we are all Africans.

Of course, the real picture becomes more complex if we consider our complete genetic makeup (autosomal DNA) rather than focus on our male and female chromosomes alone. Whatever level of complexity we choose, it is tempting to draw a line at a convenient point in pre-history—in which humans reached a particular level of development—and declare this to be our true ancestral base. In other words, we may feel that we have gone far enough to satisfy our yearnings for self discovery if we can determine at what stage modern mankind emerged. But no matter how human development is defined, it is, along with its environment, in a constant state of change and, to comprehend its state at any particular moment it is necessary to understand how it reached that point in time. Earlier I wondered how far back we should go, either individually or collectively, to comprehend the principal influences of the past that impinge on our present circumstances. I concluded that it would be artificial to define *any* particular point as the base of these influences. The significance of this assumption came to the fore at this juncture. It allowed my inquiry into the nature of human identity to be unfettered by artificial definitions of who we are.

Most scientists recognise that several distinct genera evolved before our species (*Homo sapiens*) emerged and most scientists agree that there were several shifts in dimensions between the first walking primates and users of high-tech computers. But the farther back we go, the less we are sure about what we are dealing with—human or animal? Some of the earlier human types are well-known names, like the *Homo neanderthalensis* or *Homo erectus*. Anthropologists talk in terms of *fully modern humans* or *human in the fullest sense*, or *real humanity* to distinguish us from our evolutionary cousins. The results, regrettably, are unsatisfactory. Outcomes depend on the arbitrary range of attributes chosen to distinguish hominids. Do we define humans by their ability to walk upright; or do we depend on their capacity to use stone tools; make fire and cook meat; paint on the wall of a cave; participate in long-distant exchange—or is it a combination of these traits?

For some scientists, humans as such are not recognisable until about 200,000 years ago; for others they are distinguishable only some 30 or 40,000 years in the past when the most evocative expressions of the human mind emerged in cave art. But the dating of cave art is in dispute. This inference reinforced my instinctive feelings against determining any particular point as our ancestral base. To comprehend ourselves as a species or organism we cannot put synthetic limits on a process that has been taking place over aeons; we are part of a continuum. Our golden threads of life extend back in time without the break of a single day or single hour to the beginnings of biological time. There was no "next stage" without a previous "live" stage. Furthermore: since we are fairly sure that all living organisms on earth are genetically related, it is highly probable that every living thing on earth has descended from a first organism.

How can we rest happy, then, to imagine ourselves as hominids if, in fact, we sprang from walking primates? In this case the question—when did we become fully human?—is

241 Oppenheimer, 2004; pp. 46, 47.

irrelevant, at least in physical terms. How can we declare our origins in primates if these, in turn, sprang from lesser terrestrial animals? And how do we rest our origins in lesser land animals if, in fact, our early terrestrial biology came forward from the waters of the planet?

Using this perspective, the emergence of life from water is every bit as important as the development of upright posture. We must continue backwards and seamlessly into biological and cosmic processes in order to define ourselves properly. Ultimately, we are derived from the core of nature itself . In a process of becoming, there are no frontiers. We are an intimate part of every development that had anything to do with our emergence because all these steps were vital in our creation. By liberating our thinking in this form, we are drawn inevitably from earthly time into universal time because the entire process of the development of the universe was necessary for the emergence of life on earth.

The naturalist view of human emergence, expressed here, has implications. It appears to suggest that there is no difference between man and the animals and would also appear to clinch the argument against the faith that I have maintained into adult life, because the foundations of this belief-system are based on Judeo-Christian principles as found in the Bible; and the Bible contains the Book of Genesis, which appears to support creationism as the origins of the human family.

However, a conclusion of this sort would assume that no developmental thinking can be tolerated in a faith-system. It also resides on the narrow assumption that the Bible must be taken absolutely literally and is not open to interpretation. Of course, Genesis was written long ago for a people who had no idea about the intricacies or theory of evolution. The first book of the Bible may have emerged from oral tradition out of the Iron or Bronze Age, if not before, and was only expressed in written form round half a millennium before Christ. On the other hand, it may even be argued that phrases in Genesis like: *let the waters bring forth* ..., which is related to the emergence of fish and birds or: *let the earth bring forth* ... , which is related to the appearance of plants and animals, are decidedly evolutionary terms.[242] But, all considered, it would be ridiculous to seek concrete affirmation of modern scientific theory in this ancient biblical text.

Besides, using the theory of evolution to explain every aspect of reality stretches science well beyond the frontiers of its own discipline. The mechanism of human development may be explained by science; the "why" of evolution is a subject for philosophy or theology. Perhaps we have no way of determining the presence or absence of the human soul—which is the essence of what differentiates man from animals in Biblical terms—through the scientific apparatus. As stated previously, being open to the non-scientific, yet retaining the scientific approach is a holistic way to explore the nature of things. Our innermost beliefs emerge from evidence, combined with intuition. However, reaching a satisfying conviction is not a static or smooth process and never will be. My personal faith is alternatively challenged and illuminated in the light of new scientific, philosophical and theological findings and, the older I get the more I am open to the unexpected. However, it was my perspective on identity, rather than my faith, that was about to undergo a fundamental and relatively rapid shift in outlook given what I had discovered about human genetics.

---

242 Christian Bible; Genesis, Chapter 1

Tip-toeing Round Eggshells

Knowledge of my genetic base has had a stark effect on my sense of identity. I had, once more, broken through a significant genealogical brick wall and felt, for the first time, a particular bond with the distant Iron, Bronze and Stone Age peoples of Ireland. When standing before a replica Neolithic thatched house in the Newgrange interpretive centre, shortly after receiving the first laboratory results, I had a novel experience. I was in the presence of the familiar. The depictions before me represented "my" people. They existed in the intimate setting of the Irish landscape and took on the vibrancy of real characters. But this was a small change in outlook compared to what I was about to experience. I now had the means to examine cultural contradictions from a completely new perspective.

It is thought that modern humans had been confined to Africa for perhaps 100,000 years or more. But, dwindling food resources on the coasts of Eritrea and attractive shorelines, holding the promise of more ample food supplies along the southern Arabian coastline, were powerful stimuli prompting groups of people to leave the Old Continent. Fortunately, a ford had been developed across this stretch of water. It was created by the fall in sea level due to expanding ice sheets at the poles during a major cold event probably around 60-80,000 thousand years ago. At its coldest, this glaciation plunged the world's seas one hundred metres below today's ocean surfaces. The way was now open for modern man to exit Africa. But, at that stage present-day Yemen was still inhabited by an older human species that appears to have threatened and therefore delayed the entry of modern man into Asia. Eventually our ancestors overcame their fear and crossed the water by way of the *Gate of Grief*, the narrowest point at the southerly end of the Red Sea.[243]

A small number of groups from Africa thus made their way into modern Yemen. After many generations the genetic lines that entered Asia became totally detached from their homeland and drifted down the coastline leaving permanent or semi-permanent colonies as they went. These people were dark-skinned and looked like other Africans of the time. Most of the ancient tribes that left the Old Continent can trace their origins back to this exodus, which may have led, directly or indirectly, to the wiping out of all earlier human types around the globe,[244] despite the probability that some hybridisation occurred before the elimination of all rivals.

The first modern humans outside Africa moved forward along a shoreline at the southern end of the Arabian Peninsula. They then pushed onwards towards the Gulf of Oman. The route turned and twisted along a connected beachfront, which is currently submerged offshore from India, Sri Lanka, Burma and Indonesia. The low sea levels allowed strips of land that are now separated to be joined, providing a walkway to Australia, with limited areas of shallow waters that didn't interrupt progress. This movement was not a planned operation but a slow addition to the last—then remotest colony on earth. The most adventurous were encouraged by a variety of factors to move beyond the populations behind them. They literally ate their way down to Australia within 10-15,000 years, leaving new colonies as they went.

---

243 Based on Oppenheimer, 2004; pp.74, ff.
244 *Ibid*; p. xx and Dutchen, 2014.

Even today, all along the route that modern humans followed between Africa and Australia, remnants of the first beachcomber colonies of so-called aboriginals are encountered in small communities. They are people whose appearances have features in common with Africans, such as frizzy hair and very dark skins. They are found, for example, in the Hadramaut of the South Arabian coast. Also, the Kadar and Paniyan ethnic groups of India and the Veddas of Sri Lanka fall into this category, as well as the Jarawa and the Onge people who live in the most southerly Andaman in the Bay of Bengal. The Aboriginal Malays; the New Guineans and the first Australians all share a modified semblance of the principal beachcomber and island-hopping generations of modern humans outside Africa.[245]

From the first settlements left behind as a string of beads on the main route between the Red Sea and Australia, new tributaries of human adventurers moved inland into the heartland of Europe and Asia. The process of splitting off of groups of people from the original colonies resulted in the development of amoeba-like tentacle flows of pioneers that eventually separated out-of-Africa man into different entities. One of the main breakaway colonies was located somewhere between the Gulf of Oman and India. It moved into lowlands parallel to the Zagros Mountains and made its way into the *Fertile Crescent* centred on the Rivers Tigris and Euphrates. However, these settlers were forced to wait until areas further to the north became sufficiently hospitable to allow them to migrate out of Mesopotamia. The delay imposed on the colony permitted others of their cousins to reach Australia over 60,000 years ago and become the aboriginal tribes, well before mankind moved north into Europe.[246]

Around 45-50,000 years ago, when the climate improved, the peoples of the Tigris and Euphrates valleys spread outwards, moving in northerly and westerly directions, arriving in the Levant, the central plains of eastern Europe and central Asia. Re-encounters after thousands or tens-of-thousands of years were inevitable. For example, the groups that split away from the beachcomber shore on the Arabian Sea, round 40,000 years ago, and made their way up the Indus River—in time arriving north of the Himalayas—encountered other groups that had come north on the far side of the same mountain mass. It is anyone's guess how the meetings turned out. After such a long period of segregation, strangers would not recognise that they were distant cousins. Such unions were no different from the best and worst of later historic encounters between peoples. If the populations could help each other to their mutual benefit they would; if not, they would either go their separate ways or fight over possession of the best hunting grounds, after which the weaker group would retreat. In this case, before parting, payment was demanded by the dominant group, including the pick of young women. Whether the encounters were friendly or antagonistic, genetic intermixing probably occurred.

As temperatures increased at the end of the last glaciation about 10,000 years ago melting ice left great swathes of open country that were colonised by tundra and grassland in which big game, like bison and reindeer, became abundant. Forests began to spread into what came to be known as the *Mammoth Steppe*, which contained the world's largest grassland area. At its maximum extent this Steppe stretched from the Atlantic coast of Europe in the

---

245 Oppenheimer, 2004; pp. 157, ff.
246 *Ibid*; p. 130.

west, passed north of the Himalayas and reached Hokkaido in the east.[247] Trees continued to invade parts of this enormous area from refuges on its southern margins, eventually shrinking the non-forest area to its current ecological extension.

Humans who had been detained in the Pyrenees by the ice sheets were now on the move. France became their hunting grounds on their slow migration in the direction of Britain and Ireland. They snaked across the plains, hugged the coastline of Western Europe and sailed along its shores. Amongst them were female descendants of Tara—women who bore her mitochondrial mutations; the same as those I carry in me today.

The mutations that gave rise to the Y-DNA markers of my ancient ancestors occurred, as we have seen, in the Middle East within what Dr Brian Sykes calls the *clan* of *Oisin*. These mutations generated the R1b people, whose genetic haplotype I have inherited. Descendants of mammoth and bison hunters, they were the first to domesticate cattle in northern Mesopotamia 10,000 years ago. They spawned a movement that travelled north, crossed the Caucasus and descended onto the vast Pontic-Caspian Steep, where they found excellent grazing grounds. Over the following centuries they rounded the Black Sea by way of Ukraine then penetrated into the heart of Europe along the route of the Danube and other areas of easy access, eventually making their way to the western extremities of the Continent.[248] They were highly successful because they had advanced faster in technological terms and took advantage of the less-developed phases of the peoples they encountered.

Given that my forbearers depended on a wide geographical expanse for their existence, I can no longer confine my roots to one island or even one region. The newfound clarity about my ancient peoples, both male and female, forced me to conclude that it is artificial to limit my *belonging* to the immediate area in which I find myself. I come from Ireland; Britain; France; Spain; Italy; the Danube; Ukraine; Armenia; Turkey; Persia; the Gulf of Oman and all the areas my ancestors trekked through after their exodus from Africa.

I, like all human beings on earth today, am part of the living rim of a species that traces its origins, through the dead spokes of its ancestors, to a common hub. Every living human has arisen from the same protoplasmic flow over the surface of the globe. Our unique hub is our ancestral singularity that came about in Africa some 200,000 years ago. It appears, furthermore, that this common centre was a bottleneck in which the numbers of human survivors had dwindled to near-extinction. As a result, our genetic diversity is relatively narrow.

Despite limitations in the variability of our DNA, an incredible acceleration in capability took place within our species. Although we are derived from the core of nature itself, this leap in capacity—however it is described—marks an outstanding division in aptitude from the rest of the living biological kingdom. To downplay humanity's meteoric rise in ability or somehow diminish its importance would be to falsify reality.

What becomes more difficult to determine or demarcate, than divisions between mankind and the rest of the living world, are differences within the human species. Unfortunately,

247 *Ibid*; p. 215.
248 For example, see:< http://www.eupedia.com/europe/Haplogroup_R1b_Y-DNA.shtml#origins > (August, 2015)

we often classify humans on appearances, which can be deceptive. A case in point is skin colour. Over long periods of time certain genes were turned on in the peoples who wandered inland and north across upper latitudes; others turned off. Pigments disappeared in those who travelled farthest from the sun and selection forces tended to grade our hue according to distance from the equator. For this reason ... *our colour may have more to say about where our ancestors lived over the past 10,000-20,000 years than about their genetic divergence over the previous 60,000 years.*[249] Changes occurred, like the introduction of small amounts of DNA from other non-modern humans (e.g. Neanderthals and Denisovans) who shared many of our attributes and have contributed some of their genome to our species. However, we are the only survivors of this evolutionary trajectory. More importantly, the sum of modifications were never enough to sever the basic genetic links between all humans; they were never enough to create barriers to reproduction; they were never enough to make any of us into a separate species.

The disassociation between our basic underlying genetic structures and our superficial—and often incorrect—understanding of human differences, questions the entire bag of judgemental tools we use to classify ourselves. Human genetics is the new classifier and necessitates a radical shift in thinking: a major change in paradigm.

In recent years, the Human Genome Project gave us, for the first time, the ability to read mankind's complete genetic blueprint. Every individual has an exclusive genetic structure, which is a distinct pattern of DNA sequences. This basic pattern is measureable and constitutes an objective description of an individual's deep-seated physical makeup. Furthermore, it is left essentially unchanged throughout all stages of growth, development and degeneration. The foundational DNA sequences remain the same from the beginning of an individual's existence as a zygote to his or her last breath. The fundamental pattern does not depend on cognitive abilities or consciousness. The victim of Alzheimer's disease, who has lost most of his or her memory, contains the same genetic configuration he or she had as an infant without self-awareness or as a fully-functioning adult during the peak of a successful career. As such, it lends itself to an objective definition of identity.

Being relatively new, the understanding of the human genome was outside the comprehension of social scientists from the time of John Locke or David Hume right up to the present day. The difficulty that they and others had in verifying whether one physical body at one time is the same thing as a physical body at another time is overcome in the human genome. We can now ground persistence of personal identity in the continuous existence of our basic DNA sequences, irrespective of epigenetic changes which happen during cell differentiation or which cause certain genes to turn on or off over one's lifetime and can occur as a result of dietary and other environmental exposure. Personal identity is also persistent irrespective of exceptional changes to DNA in differentiated (somatic) cells; the exceptions hereby proving the rule. It is persistent irrespective of damage to DNA due to random accidents, or the losing and gaining of different material particles in our bodies over time. The permanence of the abiding substance—our basic underlying genomic pattern—can now be empirically determined and verified, even as all else changes.

---

249 Oppenheimer, 2004; p. 199.

Personal identity is the product of sexual reproduction that generates new and unique DNA sequences.[250] In other words, the identity of the individual involves a male and female that have—in their turn—originated from the organic substratum of the human species. A species is defined, in biological terms, by a group of living organisms consisting of similar individuals capable of exchanging genes or interbreeding. Ability to reproduce with our own is, therefore, the essential unchanging constant that distinguishes us as human. Reproductive events can happen, in theory, anywhere within the wider human genome. In other words, human reproduction defines the identity of the group in a comprehensive manner.

Human reproduction is—at one and the same time—the factor that defines our communal identity and gives rise to our personal identity. It is the organic link between both; the common bond, without which neither exists. Therefore, a common definition to cover both identities is possible to devise and may be expressed as follows: *Identity is the sameness of "A" at all times and in all circumstances; the condition or fact that "A" is itself and not something else* ("A" may be *"the individual", "the group"* or both). The late sixteenth-century origin of the word "identity" (in the sense *quality of being identical or the same*) is also conserved in the definition. We now have succinct, measureable and objective ways to define personal identity, communal identity, or both together.

Applicability of the term "identity" to sub-communities within the human family is not possible. The inherent identity that defines our species is and was identical for every sub-set that can possibly be conceptualised. Every sub-set is permeable to the "other" through interbreeding. Therefore, unity within the human race, based on its common origins and ability to intermix, resists the notion of fundamental internal divisions. The differences that we observe are one of grade rather than essence and, though helpful in the study of human behaviour, they do not constitute separate "identities".

"Identity" cannot be applied to phenotypical, cultural or imagined differences that have arisen as a result of changes due to location, environment or time. To take one example: our cultural divisions are merely the collective and temporary expression of particular segments of people derived from similar urges and mechanisms within a similar object: the human brain, which—in turn—is a product of our common genome. The processes that give rise to our cultural differences are, therefore, identical. Besides, all cultural traits arose from a common base: our ancestral singularity. These traits, like language, are no more than interesting curiosities, outgrowths or appendages of expression that have arisen "within" the human family. They are novelties derived through varied environmental influences, experiences and cognitive processes over a protracted period of time. These characteristics are non-essential barriers that can be overcome and therefore it follows that any particular culture is potentially accessible to any other. Comparing one culture against another with the objective of determining separate identities is, therefore, flawed: the exercise is equivalent to examining two aspects of the same "essence" in order to discover a basic difference. The surprising conclusion is hereby reached that only one human culture actually exists; the variety of cultural expressions we find within the human

---

250 Even so-called "identical twins" may not have identical DNA sequences at the outset; besides epigenetic changes in both are unlikely to be similar < http://www.scientificamerican.com/article/identical-twins-genes-are-not-identical/ > (August, 2015)

family—despite their apparent wide diversity—are appendages or outgrowths of that one culture.

By focusing on our collective human identity we avoid the danger of creating artificial barriers that cloud the essence of what makes us who we are. Put differently; it is more revealing to contemplate our essential nature, like our ability to think, to speak, to share conscious thoughts and so forth than expend energy trying to rigidly classify the results emanating from these processes, which are transient. Focusing on the essence of our nature does not imply that we should put aside or ignore all our differences, our histories, our inward and outward cultural trappings and plunge to the deeper meaning of "humanness" to create an amorphous world culture. However, it does necessitate the discarding, within our understanding of identity, of anything that is construed to be external to the "persisting core" that makes us human.

But, in a world where identity is subjective we struggle to define who we are. The tools of the trade include a huge list of traits and characteristics such as: ethnicity; religion; location; social class; sexual orientation; political outlook; level of acculturation and assimilation; inclusion; exclusion; intellectual capacity; roles; careers; achievements; possessions; relationships. The list goes on and on, but all components are not of the same magnitude. Besides, many traits are in conflict with one another; would not change the essence of the person if they were modified; or are expressions that are at one or more removes from the core of the individual.

In many cases the word "identity" is confused with how it manifests itself. What we normally mean is the set of characteristics by which we recognise someone. But, at times, "identity" is more akin to "belonging". We can belong to a club; a tribe; a country. Equally, we can decide that we no longer wish to participate within these groupings; this does not change the essence of who we are—which never changes. At other times use of "identity" is analogous to "role" (e.g. employment). When we lose a job we may feel decidedly uncomfortable, but we don't lose our identity.

Rogers Brubaker of the University of California and Frederick Cooper of the University of Michigan quoting George Orwell state: *The worst thing one can do with words is to surrender to them.* They claim that the humanities have surrendered to the word "identity".[251] As a result of being used subjectively, it is in runaway mode gathering a plethora of meanings to itself, thus becoming overused and misused, rendering it no longer useful as an analytical tool.

To overcome the problem it is necessary to confine identity—rigorously and specifically— to its objective definition. Unfortunately, it is difficult to root out imprecise habits. We will go on using "identity" in a slovenly manner because it is part of common usage. But, to avoid confusion, I will refer to *"Personal Identity"*, *"Communal Identity"* (or simply *"Identity"*) in their objective forms by applying upper-case initial letters and emphasising the terms in italics. Our *Personal Identity* and our *Communal Identity* (*Common Human Identity*, *Universal Identity* or *Identity*) describe the essence of who we are.

---

251 Brubaker and Cooper, 2000; p. 1.

When referring to *Personal Identity* or *Communal Identity* we can no longer talk in terms of "identities" in the plural. *Identity* is essentially singular at these levels. It is false to say we have many identities depending on our circumstances. Some say we have one work identity; another family identity; another sports identity. These are loose and subjective applications of the term. Our *Identity* is not schizophrenic; it is, by definition, undivided and unique. Indeed, the definition of *Identity* cautions against use of words like "inventing" one's identity or "reinventing" oneself; these are totally artificial constructs. No one can "invent", "create" or "recreate" their essence. Our *Personal Identity*—or *Communal Identity*—are truisms; not fabrications.

We may usefully combine the objective application of *Identity* with the suggestion, by Brubaker and Cooper to corral all loose uses of the word to several alternative groups of meanings (e.g. identification and categorisation; self-understanding and social location; commonality, connectedness, groupness). This provides a harmonized solution to the current dilemma over inappropriate usages of the term. The main initial obstacle to the acceptance of this proposal may not be one of logic, but reluctance, on the part of the academic world and the media, to undertake the major shift in direction that is now required. The challenge of overcoming deeply embedded habits should not be minimised, even though they are practiced by academics that have to justify their actions in rigorous professional terms. Sadly, I foresee a long and thorny intellectual battle ahead because so many in the humanities have become comfortable with a non-objective fluid approach to the subject. Despite the difficult road facing us, in time objectivity is sure to trump the confusion caused by loose and subjective uses of "identity".

Turning to the topic of human interrelations; it is unfortunate that although cultural characteristics provide richness and diversity to our existence, they have often been used and are used to create enormous rifts, resulting in deep strife and hatred. With regards to intercultural relations, it is clearly more difficult to accept any notions of underlying unity where two factions are at war. In other words, it would be foolish to ignore the fact that cultural intermixing has not always been harmonious. The rosy picture of friendly interconnections between peoples rapidly derails where mutual respect is missing. Consider those who are in conflict with each other because of their different sets of cultural characteristics. How can they embrace the notion of accessibility to an opposing culture? Or consider those who are being unjustly treated because of who they are; how can they adopt the concept of *Universal Identity*? Is it not totally naïve, therefore, to expect that any kind of unification can ever be achieved between entities that have been starkly divided through the whole of history and pre-history?

Our *Common* or *Universal Identity* is independent of the emotions we have towards each other. However, the realisation of its reality or existence can help to enlighten the perspectives we have of one another and see ourselves in a fresh light. When I examined the two principal sets of opposing cultural groups—the Gael and Old English—in my own makeup against the universal view, I realised that the clashing traits that drove my quest arose from the residues of conflict between two distinct human cultural appendages derived, essentially, from the same foundation. This oft-repeated story, reproduced around our planet, is the blueprint of most cultural conflicts. The British had advanced faster in technological terms and took advantage of the developmental phase of the Gaelic tribes, which was at an earlier point along the social evolutionary trajectory. The two groups emerged from different territorial niches that were closer to or more remote from the sources of new technological developments. Those who happened to be closest to the springs of new knowledge advanced more rapidly than those who were more remote and their newfound knowhow gave them, for a time, the upper hand over those who were disadvantaged. An exact parallel was found in my ancient ancestors—the men who carried the R1b haplotype—who spread out from the Middle East, dominating all before them through new technologies.

In relation to my Gaelic and Old English backgrounds, I knew what it was ... *to be born and live on the brink, between two worlds, knowing and understanding both of them and to be unable to help explain them to each other and bring them closer.*[252] But, now I see the apparent contradictions between the two components in my makeup as accidents of history, location and knowhow; not of essence. As such, I can acknowledge—with or without disagreeable emotions—the differences between each set of memes and the history of conflict caused by them. I delve to the deeper level where the essence of underlying human communality reconnects my separate parts. At this point, and for the first time in my life, my sense of *Identity* becomes whole. I now see the barriers that we have erected between us in the terms we use like "Irish", "English" and "British", as flags of convenience. These expressions cannot sustain the weight of meanings assigned to them. Their collective or traditional meaning, where this implies total separation and uniqueness, is bogus and obsolete.

Nothing has changed; yet everything has changed. I am still known by the names I have always been known by. But my *Identity* defies confinement by them. My cultural base has three dimensions in space; a fourth dimension in time and multi-dimensions in its many pathways out of the past. I can delight equally in each, even though, at times, they intertwined uneasily. I can delight in my Gaelic ethnicity. I can celebrate the Old English dimension too. I approach English culture with hesitation because I am awkward and a total stranger, even though it is an intimate part of my ancestral past. I must give myself the opportunity to become accustomed to it. At the time of writing I know that a new adventure starts here though I have only a vague notion of how it might evolve. I begin this adventure with encouraging words from Dr. Bryan Sykes, who states, in relation to our neighbouring islands: *However we may feel about ourselves and about each other, we are genetically rooted in a Celtic past. The Irish, the Welsh and the Scots know this, but the English sometimes think otherwise. But, just a little way beneath the surface, the strands of ancestry weave us all together as the children of a common past.*[253]

Many believe that the only way to ultimate peace is to neutralise our differences. For this reason modern societies increasingly try to ignore or remove any suggestion of disagreeable distinctions between us—at least in the public square. But this stifling approach is totally counterproductive because it is likely to prevent rather than assist in the evolution of healthy societies. It tries to avoid apparent contradictions, which are vital elements in driving human progress. It is better to recognise, for example, that historical and contemporary cultural differences do exist and make an effort to understand the base

252 Wheatcroft, 2004; p. 267.
253 Sykes, 2007; p. 287.

of our dissimilarities and divisions, not avoid them. "Neutering" differences will achieve exactly what that word implies: it will sterilise our futures and abort potential and exciting cultural developments. The welfare of future human cultural appendages will depend on the depth and richness of their underlying worldviews; our societies should not, therefore, cultivate restricted group-think outlooks but encourage the widest possible exploration of the nature of truth itself.

We can rely on our great possibilities for social interaction rather than hide behind polite and artificial surfaces that really cloak fears to confront our dissimilarities. We can admit that we are a pluralist society; that we are white, yellow, black or red. We can portray ourselves as Atheist, Buddhist, Catholic, Hindu, Jew, Muslim, Protestant or whatever. We should not be shy of who we are and who our people have been. We can delight in the different paths of our ancestors and celebrate our diverse routes out of history. Therefore, we can be frank; and disagree; and argue with vigour. We can attempt to convert the other to our strongly-held beliefs and not withdraw into politically-correct postures that prevent exchange of deeply-held convictions. We can choose to walk forward boldly or frustrate our progress as we dance and tip-toe round egg shells. All is acceptable, provided we maintain a deep mutual respect for one another.

The March of a Nation

A debate on identity arose in association with the ninety-year celebration of the 1916 Rising and is resurfacing round its centenary. Identity is sure to become a dominant issue on the anniversary of Irish independence. Clearly, a modern concept of Irishness is being advocated, but there is no agreement about its definition. How—it is often asked—can the disparate spectrum of cultures found in Ireland be accommodated within a single "national identity"? It seems that the country as a whole is facing the same challenges that I faced as an individual. The notion of our *Common Identity* offered me a way to connect what I saw as separate and conflicting "identities". Can it offer the same at the national level?

With the object of adhering to a strict definition of *Identity*, "national culture" is, perhaps, a more appropriate term for the present discussion than "national identity". However, old habits are difficult to break and, because of this, both these terms are regarded here as being equivalent or interchangeable. The nation has already become aware of the inadequacy of its traditional national identity which was fabricated during the Irish Renaissance in the late nineteenth century. The myth was enhanced on an inflated sense of connectivity of all Irish men and women to Gaelic Ireland during the independence movement. Even today the noble virtues of the Gael that were lauded when Ireland became the Free State are officially regarded as sacred precepts, though most who maintain this outlook are reluctant—perhaps embarrassed—to admit aloud to harbouring such sentiments.

Although the romantic perception of an ancient and glorious Irish past are viewed by many as nothing more than the quaint musings of old poets, which have little or nothing to offer contemporary society, few have gone to the trouble of exploring the manner in which our national identity arose and how it came to be rejected—or at lease shelved. Links with the Gaelic past have been left aside in a type of group-acceptance: no discussion needed or accommodated. All that is left of traditional identity are the trappings. Scepticism has won the day. Meanwhile, at least in the Irish Republic, many acquiesce to traditional sentiments when patriotism is called for on state occasions. In this we have a glaring double-think.

In early modern Irish society, understanding of self *tended to be the sum of regional histories and their interaction rather than the product of 'national' movements*.[254] "Irish identity" in the modern nationalistic anti-English sense began as a reaction to the belligerent Tudor State and lasted throughout the most oppressive period of British colonisation and well into the twentieth century. Unwelcome external British intrusions into Irish affairs have largely disappeared and older forms of Irish nationalism are inevitably melting away in the absence of strife, which explains why Ireland is seeking, consciously or unconsciously, a new concept to fill the void.

Around the time of independence Gaelic symbols were used to identify the band of brothers and sisters who came together to cast out the British. But they have lost their significance in a situation where no one is fighting. Now the state is left awkwardly and self-consciously holding outdated emblems, but at the same time is reluctant to ditch them. Surly it would be irreverent to do so because of their stubborn association with the heroic fight for freedom? Would our "national culture" not evaporate by so doing? What might

---

254 Ellis, 1998; p. 17.

replace our state symbols and who would be responsible for making this decision? The reality is: our official national identity is so unyielding that it would require a radical change in attitude to replace it institutionally, at least in the short-term, particularly in southern Ireland.

The core problem with the Gaelic flavour of the Irish Republic's national view of itself is that its ethos is not a reality for many of its citizens. Its derivation was an anathema to my mother's people and many more besides. Knowing the depth of feeling of one segment of Irish society, I could never accept the official form of Irish nationalism which was being advocated for the entire country. Those who did embrace it pretended that other entities didn't exist. For example, it is ridiculous to imagine the descendants of English conquerors accepting the proposition that Irish is "their" language, yet the state declared it to be the language of all its citizens and made it compulsory for every school-going child to learn. Consider the many families in this country of English planter background; should they pretend Irish is their language? This would be equivalent to suggesting that Sioux is the national tongue of the offspring of eighteenth- and nineteenth-century European settlers in Dakota.

Earlier I quoted Finola Keogh, who put forward the suggestion that Protestant landlords became involved in the Irish Renaissance movement, probably as ... *an insurance policy for the gentry to draw upon once the Irish people attained their freedom*.[255] The approach may have been expedient at the time. But why should anyone have to conform to an official view of oneself? In modern democracy there is no room for pretence and no requirement for different cultures, or sub-cultures, to conform to a derived national perspective. Disparate entities are what they are. As such, there can be no singular cultural form (i.e. singular cultural appendage) on the island of Ireland unless by agreement.

Today a youthful Irish society, which has ever-reducing contact with the vestiges of older social orders, is taking over and the speed of this transformation is unprecedented. Perhaps, then, the best solution for Ireland's out-dated official view of itself is to ignore it; the problem will disappear of its own accord. But, there is a danger, in adopting a laissez-faire attitude, of creating discontinuity with the past, resulting in a loss of cultural consciousness in the individual. There is also the imminent danger that the cultural dimension of the country will become more shallow leading to a dominance of consumerism and materialism, even though economic recession may put a temporary break on this process.

An outside observer could be excused for thinking that a cultural reverse has, in fact, already happened. As far back as 1967 Michael Viney warned that the Irish are becoming more selfish as standards improve.[256] Frequent media reports on racism; joy-riding; binge-drinking; drug-taking and pushing; feuds; stabbings; murders; gangland-violence; bullying; suicide; the sex trade; corruption; obesity; endless scepticism; incessant moaning and other disagreeable aspects of Irish society appear to confirm a continuing and deepening of undesirable trends in contemporary Ireland. To be honest, the whole overarching sum of cultural appendages is responsible for such impoverishment; the blame cannot be laid fully on to the shoulders of "an inferior sort".

---

255 Keogh, 1992; p. 61.
256 Ferriter, 2005; p. 6.

Further loss of our cultural consciousness may lead to an even greater breakdown of social order in future. It is highly unlikely that inappropriate behaviour will find expression in a people who are intensely conscious of the value of their culture and harbour aspirations and visions of their individual roles and responsibilities in society and their society's role in the world based on deep-seated convictions. Therefore, aspiration, conviction and vision—beyond mere mercenary or economic levels—continue to be as important to modern and future society as they were in the past, irrespective of how our overall culture changes.

There is little doubt that the concept of our *Common* or *Universal Identity* can provide contemporary society a holistic, modern and accommodating view of itself, out of which there is the potential for the emergence of new visions of who we are in cultural terms. The concept is particularly appropriate for an island like Ireland, which has so many diverse cultural backgrounds, many of which were developed outside the island. The universal view of *Identity* embraces an unlimited notion of cultural "inclusiveness" that is not confined to our fixed geographic borders. Within the paradigm, the cultural attributes found across the total spectrum of the peoples within the island of Ireland can be accommodated. As such, they include the most rural representative to the most entrenched urbanite and from committed nationalist to staunch loyalist. Everyone is accommodated, whether they trace themselves back to the old Gaelic first-nation stock, to the Vikings, the Anglo-Irish, the Old English or invaders who came to Ireland under Cromwell or King William, or to other professionals and soldiers who conquered the island at other times. In like manner, the concept embraces all recent arrivals in Ireland. This ragbag of *liquorice allsorts* is "who" and "what" we are in cultural terms as a people.

In the light of our *Common Identity*, cultural entities are more like the components of a conglomerate rock—than a homogeneous massif—with old and new veins of magma crisscrossing the mass, some of very new origin. These imagined veins and the base-rock itself defy artificial borders. In cultural terms, the family from Beijing that finds itself living in Castlebar is as much a part of "New Ireland" as I am with my roots in Gaelic Leinster. For those who are conscious of our *Universal Identity*, this makes sense. For those who are not, it can lead to dread of cultural loss, fear of the erosion of traditions and, ultimately, xenophobia. The trepidation that is generated by a restricted notion of identity results in entrenched cultural views and detrimental divisions within society.

To acknowledge ourselves as part of our *Common Identity* does not demean the cultural richness of any region or locality, but it allows natural intermixing to take place that enhances the core of human cultural expression. Such mental liberation permits exciting possibilities to evolve as human cultures freely mix and weave together along a path of continual change, which is—and always has been—part of the nature of culture itself.

Nineteenth-century Irish politician Parnell said: ... *no man has the right to fix the boundary to the march of a nation. No man has the right to say to his country, 'Thus far shalt thou go and no further'.*[257] These words, crafted for Ireland at the end of the nineteenth century, constitute the mantra for changing the national paradigm by interpreting them in the light of *Universal Identity*, which embraces multiculturalism in society in the twenty-first century.

---

257 Lyons, 2005; p. 264.

Considering the widespread feeling that we lack a common culture, Ireland is in a unique position to make a radical move. It can let go its obsolete national insignias and trust its citizens to come to a new understanding of themselves on their own. As regards forging a new "national identity", the best thing that the state can do is not to try. Ordinary people must take over the role of thinking and expressing their feelings for themselves and not depend on politicians, or even journalists and academics to do it for them. This will ensure a greater participation of individuals and communities in civil society. The state's role in the process is facilitator; the journalist's role is reporter and the academic is interpreter.

It becomes inescapable that the concept of our *Common Identity* is not only relevant to Ireland but to every nation on earth. A universal perspective of *Identity* is particularly appropriate for the times in which we live. It suits us, as humans, who are in the process of overlapping with each other in ever-increasing numbers on our finite planet. It suits an increasingly globalised world that connects with itself through the internet. It is relevant for contemporary society in which the state is becoming an administrative convenience for increasing numbers of people rather than a cradle of warm-blooded human belonging. "State", as a concept, is tending to be diminished in status; or reduced to the place where we vote, pay our taxes and obtain our passports. The role of the state is not to tell us who we are.

I can sense a wave of resistance from some quarters with questions arising like: What of patriotism now? How can I be part of a nation and embrace the notion of *Universal Identity*? I counter these questions with another: Why would patriotism not extend itself beyond the artificial limits of the nation-state? Any artefact that stands between us has to be treated with suspicion and an over-identification with a rigid culture or nationalism has to be suspect.

The illusion of national identities or rigid cultures as block forces against each other are weakening and will continue to weaken as real and penetrating links develop across these artificial frontiers and as a deeper understanding of our *Common Identity* is realised and embraced. Given this change in paradigm, we will eventually come to a more mature and realistic vision of ourselves on a global level. *Universal Identity* takes each of us for what we are and accommodates a diverse society; its scope is all-embracing. And, as our notion of "separateness" or "uniqueness" weakens, our "collectiveness" strengthens.

The beauty of the notion of our *Common Identity* lies in the fact that it can be conceptualised at the level of the individual without recourse to any organisation; at the same time it is real. Everyone can awaken to its reality and, by so doing, revolutionise their sense of belonging within the human family. This revolution takes place in the mind; thus, we all have power to create a new "identity landscape" that correlates perfectly with our human condition rather than our artificial frontiers whether physical or imagined. We don't need to create new institutions or political parties or shift national borders to make its influence felt. It can be realised instantaneously. When enough people awaken to its reality, the world will change immeasurably for the better.

However, a real danger in our contemporary world is that we will forget our ancestral past and become dull and amorphous. But, we can combat this trend by developing our knowledge of our varied cultural roots, thus creating intriguing personal mental tapestries that I described earlier, where there is always something new and refreshing to see in them.

Besides, there will always be the prospect of fresh perspectives arising as new information comes to light about our individual cultures through historical analysis, genetics, genealogy, and other disciplines, irrespective of whether we were born in Dublin or come originally from Kerala, Lagos or Beijing. The descendants of John M. Keogh in the United States can access their Gaelic past; derive pride and pleasure from it; and delve into its story just as I can. Distance and time does nothing to erase their Irish roots; ocean and time cannot dampen the enchantment of their varied pathways out of the past. The Polish who are living amongst us should remember and enjoy their origins. Getting to know our collective cultural roots has the power to become a living and growing subject of fascination that spreads itself into every aspect of our lives. There is no way in which this could possibly lead to an amorphous global culture; real life is not dull and boring unless we make it so.

Each of us will become more enriched by getting to know the deeply-felt views of alternative—especially—opposing cultures, providing that there is a mature will on all sides to find the truth and to acknowledge that stark and contradictory mental views actually "do" exist, rather than be insulted by them or try to eliminate or ignore them. Frankness, a growing respect and willingness to learn from each other's cultures is a large challenge. But, interconnectedness between cultures has, possibly, the greatest power to change us. Within the conceptual freedom of our *Common Identity* no one is threatened by the prospect of cultural change. This universal perspective is a key factor that will help to ensure that modern and future cultural developments will be based on sound foundations. New and exciting cultural expressions can develop of their own accord through openness.

I believe that if sufficient numbers of representatives from different Irish cultures openly examine their pathways out of the past and make these public, we will come to interesting new conclusions about who we are—in cultural terms—as a collective people on the island of Ireland and beyond. I desire to read documents from the descendants of Ascendency Protestants, Orange Unionists or any other competing or conflicting cultures. I desire to read the experiences of newcomers, too. I cannot imagine a more appropriate way to face the anniversary of Irish independence than by implementing a self examination of this sort throughout the whole of Ireland. With such documents to hand we will begin to see new ways forward. We will be able to reflect on the reality of our own cultures as appendages of our *Common Identity*. And there is nothing stopping us from extending this exercise to our neighbouring island.

These are some of the most prominent thoughts that come to mind in relation to the practical application of the concept of our *Common* or *Universal Identity* on the wider national and international platforms. There are many other ideas that could be considered but they would need a much-extended book to contain them. However, before closing the discussion, I have one more point to make. When examining *Universal Identity*, in context with genetics and human reproduction, an issue that must be given at least a cursory mention is the domain of human ethics. Not being a lawyer, I dare not tread too far into this complex and controversial minefield. On the other hand, one fundamental principle— that no legal system or state can or should infringe—stands out.

Conception can be viewed from three points of view: the male parent, the female parent and the offspring. Given our understanding of the deep-seated impact that ancestral knowledge can have on the individual's sense of self, access to information about one's biological parents, and their history, is an inalienable right. Reproduction is a private act that has the most public of social consequences, with potential repercussions for generations to come. It is grossly selfish and ethically inadmissible to deliberately deprive a child of the awareness of his or her parents and ancestral knowledge. Everyone has a right to know "their" truth.

I would encourage everyone who has followed my journey to undertake their own enriching quest to find their own story, whatever their ancestral histories have been. Perhaps I am repeating myself, but it is an important repetition. The only compass and map required are truth and humility. In the end it is the truth that will set us free; not an evasion of the truth. Humility will allow us to accept the powerful lessons that truth will bring us. Truth and humility have the power to change us; they have the power to heal the wounds of humanity.

A vision comes to me. Imagine you are lying at fixed point on an immense crystal sphere and peering into the dim inner core. Others are distributed all around the sphere with you and are, likewise, peering inside. Assume there is a fixed and solid cylinder in the centre. This represents truth. Depending on the position on the surface of the sphere, each will perceive something different. If you are directly over or under the cylinder you will distinguish a circle. The person that is at right angles to the cylinder and at its midpoint will observe a rectangle. Others will see something else or may see nothing. If each one tries to come to the truth alone no one will ever find out what the real nature of the object is; the whole effect will appear to be an exercise in contradiction. However, if each communicates his or her version of the truth to the rest and is prepared to listen to the others, sooner or later the true nature of the object will emerge beyond all apparent contradictions.

Each one of us is peering into the centre of meaning from our own perspective. We may take the view that we recognise the whole truth. But, we can also accommodate the perspective that everyone else has "something" of the truth; they cannot be fully wrong. Our minds do not allow us the luxury of zero doubts. No matter how strong our convictions are each of us has a healthy disquiet about our own position. These doubts are positive in that they keep us open to new ideas, prevent arrogance and, ultimately, can prevent irreversible divisions between us. We may use these doubts as links to our fellows on our hypothetical sphere. It is through humility that the real glory of universal truth shines through. If we are holders of the truth we have nothing to concern us—the nature of truth can only be strengthened. In adopting this inclusive view the way opens to limitless fascination, delight and deep empathy with our fellow creatures.

Universal Reunion

The jading heat of day subsides. Temperatures reach levels of perfection and induce tranquillity and contemplation as the evening light angles towards its setting. I am alone in the shade of an *almendro* tree outside the house of Don Tadeo—Maria's father. Cocoanut stems rise high towards the blue canopy; they rise above lemon and mandarin bushes. Yellow *platanillo* flowers and crimson bougainvillea are stark colours in open patches. Roofs of terracotta tiles are held up by twisted wooden posts. Women hover about open fires and prepare the evening meal under a fog of smoke and babble of conversation.

Carts pulled by oxen trundle their iron-rimmed wheels on dust roads that lead to the village. The way is bordered on either side by lines of fence posts and trees connected by strands of barbed wire. The carts pass houses hidden behind bamboo and mango trees. Courtesies are exchanged by men returning from the fields. They trade friendly gestures; talk briefly of the day's events; then move on.

When I first arrived in La Paz it was to the old house I came, a building of adobe, wood, and clay tiles. The new house has concrete walls and a tin roof. Previously there was no running water; it was common, then, to see women carrying water jars on their heads. This image is gone. Now old and new elements live side by side. The plate or *comal* on which maize *tortillas* are heated is still in use. The ancient *piedra de moler* or grinding stone has only recently been confined to the status of a museum piece. The dogs, the devilish cat, the proud cock and his harem still conserve old-world visions and sounds. Straw hats, leather saddles and machetes freely mix with plastic chairs and iPods. The wooden cart and battered pickup truck are now companions. Children wear runners and baseball caps with the peak to the back. The North American influence is strong and getting stronger. Many years ago the old buses that arrived in the village from San Salvador carried hens and roosters in baskets on the roof and the onboard radios sang songs in Spanish. Now they are modern and blare English music. The essence of Latin America is echoed in La Paz, just as the entire sub-continent contains a flavour of its individual parts. And everywhere, immense changes are taking place as human cultures freely mix and weave together along a path of continual change.

Chicken soup, and fried plantain, and rice with cinnamon in milk are traditional tastes of the country and remind me of my first introduction to the village many years ago. I have learnt much since I first came to El Salvador. My adult life is marked by this place; it is now within me. Cultural shock is a thing of my remote past. Nephews come and call me *Tío*—uncle. I am content to be part of this; greatly content. I will always be regarded as a foreigner; yet, I am as much a part of this land as an exotic teak plant from Burma. And I am part of the change that is taking place.

Of a sudden, I visualise Maria's ancient ancestors exiting from Africa by way of the Middle-East and the great *Mammoth Steppe* of Asia and trudging on to the New World across the Bering Straits into America where they move south from the Arctic and eventually reach La Paz. This reality is reflected in the indigenous features of the female ancestors of her mother and her grandmother. As I contemplate, I see my own ancestors spread out from Africa and the Middle-East into modern-day Italy, Spain and France before reaching Ireland on the western edge of Europe. The golden threads of our lives separated from our ancestral singularity and spread and enveloped the world and met and became united again. I see our union in the light of a global amalgamation after tens of thousands of years of separation and the product of this union is our children.

The tapestry of my mind grows ever-more complex. This global reunion physically liberates our *Identity* from dependency on nation; race; culture; tribe; class; pigmentation; language; place; history or ecology. A new social order is created. It is but one fresh blend on the planet's surface where many similar combinations are being forged. The future shape of human culture is dimly visible in the fruits of our union.

*

I was thinking on these things when quietly slouched in a chair alongside the wooden house, which was my dwelling for a few days. The only way to the beach resort, on the northern tip of Panama, was by sea round the coast from Portobelo. My friend, who had invited me here, urged me to go snorkelling and inspect the reef, a good example of some of the best inshore reefs in the Caribbean. I was somewhat lethargic, but followed his suggestion and put on a mask, flippers and snorkel, then lowered myself into the water from a nearby jetty.

The first thing I saw were three fish hovering together around a seaweed-covered anchor chain. They looked like flat fish turned sideways, or squashed balloons with brown striations on their grey-white skins. I swam away from the jetty and watched as the smooth sandy bed of the shallow sea gave way to coral. I wove through ancient uprights of deposited lime and observed a wealth of marine life pass underneath. I explored the reef on my own and, as I did, I was glad that I had been persuaded to overcome my inertia. I had plunged into a world I could not have imagined when on the shore.

I became aware of my ability to move easily in any dimension. I swam along an erratic course that twisted like the weave of good conversation and I resisted no enticement. When I dived to the dappled shadows on the sandy bed amongst the vertical coral, bright shafts of sunlight pierced the surface and plunged beams of colour through soft green water like light streaming through stain-glass windows. A shoal of fish appeared, then, all together, turned in a flash of silver before darting away. More fish followed in surprises of yellows and blues and forms. The scene transformed itself as more novelties of life, colour, shape and sheen appeared and disappeared.

A blood-red fish is before me. In a peculiar way I feel his display is for me alone. I am an intimate part of a primeval seascape. As I peer at ever-smaller organisms and elements I wonder: Could it be that "smallness" is infinite? As I glance up through the water towards the light I realise that height is not restricted except by imagination; it goes on forever. I am suspended between two extremes of space betwixt the past and future. I hear contradictory voices and can no longer answer all the questions that bubble upwards, but I linger for a moment, as a child struck dumb with wonder. I remember the distance I have travelled on my journey and perceive the limitlessness of future time. I sense that the visible is only a small fraction of what exists; it is infinitesimal compared to the unspeakable, untouchable reality it springs from. For a brief moment I awaken to a deeper realisation of the nature of existence than I have hereto imagined, but it is a fleeting glimpse, yet enough to indicate that there is always a next stage in our quest to awaken fully to who we are.

References

Allison, C. E. 1896. *The History of Yonkers*. Wilbur B. Ketcham. New York.

Bardon, J. 2012. *The Plantation of Ulster*. Gill and Macmillan. [2011]

Bartlett, T. (Ed.). 1998. *Life of Theobald Wolfe Tone*. The Lilliput Press. Dublin.

Bateson, R. 2010. *They Died by Pearse's Side*. Irish Graves Publications. Dublin.

Berresford Ellis, P. 2000. *Hell or Connaught*. The Blackstaff Press. Belfast. [1975]

Brady, J. 2002. *Dublin at the Turn of the Century*. In: Brady, J. and Simms, A. (Eds.). *Dublin Through Space & Time;* pp. 221-281. Four Courts Press. Dublin. [2001]

Breen, C. 2004. *The Maritime Cultural Landscape in Medieval Gaelic Ireland*. In: Duffy, P. J., Edwards, D. and FitzPatrick, E. (Eds.). *Gaelic Ireland, c. 1250- c. 1650* ; pp. 418-435. Four Courts Press. Dublin. [2001]

Brown, D. 1991. *Bury my Heart at Wounded Knee*. Vintage. London. [1971]

Brubaker, R. and Cooper, F. 2000. *Beyond "Identity"*. Theory and Society. Vol. 29: 1-47.

Canny, N. 2009. *Making Ireland British 1580-1650*. Oxford University Press. Oxford. [2001]

Carnahan, J. W. 1899. *Manual of the Civil War*. US Army and Navy Historical Association. Washington D.C.

Clarke, A. 2009. *The Irish Economy, 1600-60*; pp. 168-186. In: Moody, T. W., Martin, F. X. and Byrne, F. J. (Eds.). *A New History of Ireland*. Volume III. *Early Modern Ireland 1534-1691*. Oxford University Press. [1976]

Colfer, B. 2002. *The Ethnic Mix in Medieval Wexford*. History Ireland. Vol. 10 (1): 19-23.

Commissioners, 1826. *Second Report of the Commissioners of Irish Education Inquiry*.

Condic, M. L. 2008. *When does Human Life Begin? A Scientific Perspective*. Westchester Institute White Paper Series. The Westchester Institute for Ethics and the Human Person, Thornwood, NY.
< http://bdfund.org/wordpress/wp-content/uploads/2012/06/wi_whitepaper_life_print.pdf > (August 2015)

Corish, P. J. 2009 (a). *The Rising of 1641 and the Catholic Confederacy, 1641-5*. In: Moody, T. W., Martin, F. X. and Byrne, F. J. (Eds.). *A New History of Ireland*. Volume III. *Early Modern Ireland 1534-1691*; pp. 289-316. Oxford University Press. [1976]

Corish, P. J. 2009 (b). *The Cromwellian Regime, 1650-60*. In: Moody, T. W., Martin, F. X. and Byrne, F. J. (Eds.). *A New History of Ireland*. Volume III. *Early Modern Ireland 1534-1691;* pp. 353-386. Oxford University Press. [1976]

Cullen, L. M. 2009. *Economic Trends, 1660-91*. In: Moody, T. W., Martin, F. X. and Byrne, F. J. (Eds.). *A New History of Ireland*. Volume III. *Early Modern Ireland 1534-1691* ; pp. 387-407. Oxford University Press. [1976]

Cullen, L. M. 1990. *Catholic Social Classes under the Penal Laws*. In: Power, T. P. and Whelan, K. (Eds.). *Endurance and Emergence. Catholics in Ireland in the Eighteenth Century*; pp. 57-84. Irish Academic Press. Dublin.

Cullen, L. M. 1983. *Princes and Pirates*. The Dublin Chamber of Commerce 1783-1983. Dublin.

D'Alton. J. 1855. *King James' Irish Army List (1689)*.

Dickson, D. 2008. *New Foundations Ireland 1660-1800*. Irish Academic Press. Dublin. [1987]

Dickson, D. 1990. *Catholics and Trade in Eighteenth-Century Ireland: An Old Debate Revisited*. In: Power, T. P. and Whelan, K. *Endurance and Emergence. Catholics in Ireland in the Eighteenth Century*; pp. 85-100. Irish Academic Press.

Dudley Edwards, R. 1990. *Patrick Pearse. The Triumph of Failure*. Poolbeg Press. [1977]

Duffy, P. J. 2004. Social and Spatial Order in the MacMahon Lordship of Airghialla in the Late Sixteenth Century. In: Duffy, P. J., Edwards, D. and FitzPatrick, E. (Eds.). *Gaelic Ireland, c. 1250- c. 1650; pp. 115-137* Four Courts Press. Dublin. [2001]

Duffy, P. J., Edwards, D. and FitzPatrick, E. (Eds.). 2004. *Gaelic Ireland, c. 1250-c. 1650*. Four Courts Press. Dublin. [2001]

Dutchen, S. 2014. Neanderthals' DNA Legacy Linked to Modern Ailments. Harvard Gazette. < http://news.harvard.edu/gazette/story/2014/01/neanderthals-dna-legacy-linked-to-modern-ailments/ > (August, 2015).

Edwards, D. 2004. *Collaboration without Anglicisation: The MacGiollapadraig Lordship and Tudor Reform*. In: Duffy, P. J., Edwards, D. and FitzPatrick, E. (Eds.). *Gaelic Ireland, c. 1250-c. 1650; pp. 77-97. Four Courts Press. Dublin. [2001]*

Ellis, S. G. 1998. *Ireland in the Age of the Tudors* 1447-1603. Longman. UK.

Ellmann, R. 1983. *James Joyce*. Oxford University Press. [1959]

Fagan, P. 1991. *The Population of Dublin in the Eighteenth Century with Particular Reference to the Proportions of Protestants and Catholics*. Eighteenth-century Ireland / Iris an dá chultúr, Vol. 6: 121-156.

Fawcett, P. H. 1968. *Exploration Fawcett*. Arrow. London. [1953]

Ferriter, D. 2005. *The Transformation of Ireland 1900-2000*. Profile Books. London. [2004]

Fleming, P. 1957. *Brazilian Adventure*. Penguin. Great Britain. [1933]

Floyd, F. C. 1908. *History of the Fortieth (Mozart) Regiment, New York Volunteers*. < http://www.archive.org/stream/cu31924030909752/cu31924030909752_djvu.txt > (August, 2015)

Foster, R. F. 1989. *Modern Ireland 1600-1972*. Penguin. UK. [1988]

Frazer, J. 1996. *The Golden Bough*. Penguin. London. [1922]

Galaty, J. G. 1993. *Maasai Expansion & the New East African Pastoralism*. In: Spear, T. & Waller, R. (Eds.). *Being Maasai*; pp. 61-86. Eastern African Studies. James Currey Ltd. London.

Gardner, N. 2003. *Trial by Fire: Command and the British Expeditionary Force in 1914*. Praeger.

Gefter, A. 2010. *Touching the Multiverse*. New Scientist. 6th March; pp. 28-31.

Geoghegan, P. M. 2008. *King Dan*. Gill and Macmillan. Dublin.

Glendinning, V. 1999. *Jonathan Swift*. Pimlico. London. [1998]

Goff, H. 2001. *English Conquest of an Irish Barony. The Changing Patterns of Land Ownership in the Barony of Scarawalsh 1540-1640*. In: Whelan, K. and Nolan, W. (Eds.). Wexford: History and Society; pp. 122-149. Geography Publications. Dublin. [1987]

Gwynn, D. 1928. *The Struggle for Catholic Emancipation (1750-1829)*. Longmans, Green & Co. London.

Haddick-Flynn, K. 2003. *Sarsfield & the Jacobites*. Mercier Press. Cork.

Hansard, T. C. 1812. *The Parliamentary Debates from the Year 1803 to the Present Time*. Vol. XI. Comprising the Period from the Eleventh Day of April to the Fourth Day of July 1808. Fleet Street.

Hayes, W. J. 2011. Holycross. Lisheen Publications. Roscrea County Tipperary.

Hayes, W. J. 1973. *Holy Cross Abbey*. Kamac Publications. Dublin.

Heath, I. 2008. *The Irish Wars 1485-1603*. Osprey Publishing. Oxford. [1993]

Herrera, B. 2006. *Mestizaje y Cultura en América Latina*. En: Araujo Aguilar, P. (Ed.). *Palabra y Cultura. Reflexión y Creación en América Latina*. Comunicación y Lenguaje. Escuela de Estudios Generales. Universidad de Costa Rica. pp. 13-23. [2003]

Hogan, R. and O'Neill, M. J. (Eds.). 1967. *Joseph Holloway's Abbey Theatre*. Southern Illinois University Press.

Huish, R. 1836. *The Memoirs, Private and Political, of Daniel O'Connell*. W. Johnston. London.

[The] Irish News and Belfast Morning News. National Library Ireland 9A 6323.

Johnson, J. (Ed.). 2000. *James Joyce. Dubliners*. Oxford University Press.

Kearns, K. C. 1996. *Stoneybatter Dublin's Inner Urban Village*. Gill & Macmillan. Dublin. [1989]

Kelly, J. 2004. *Keogh, John*. In: Matthew, H. C. G. and Harrison, B. (Eds.). Oxford Dictionary of National Biography. Vol. 31: 356-357. Oxford University Press.

Kennedy, K. A., Giblin, T. and McHugh, D. 1988. *The Economic Development of Ireland in the Twentieth Century*. Routledge. London.

Kenyatta, J. 1991. *Facing Mount Kenya*. Heinemann. Kenya. [1938]

Keogh, F. 1992. *Lifting Lady Gregory's Skirts*. Summer Edition. Theatre Ireland: 59-67.

Keogh, R. M. 2015. *The Emergence and Growth of Gaelic Merchants and Traders in Dublin 1660-1911*. Dublin Historical Record. Vol. 68 (2): 149-162.

Keogh, R. M. 2009. *Well Dressed and from a Respectable Street*. History Ireland. Vol. 17 (2): 32-33.

Keogh, R. M. 1995. *St Patrick's Letter to Prosper*. Paulines Publications. Africa.

Kiberd, D. 1996. *Inventing Ireland*. Vintage. UK. [1995]

Kildea, J. 2007. *Anzacs and Ireland*. Cork University Press. Ireland.

Kostick, C. and Collins L. 2004. *The Easter Rising*. The O'Brien Press. Dublin. [2000]

Lennon, C. 2008. Dublin Part II, 1610 to 1756. Irish Historic Towns Atlas No. 19. Royal Irish Academy. Dublin City Council.

Lyons, F. S. L. 2005. *Charles Stewart Parnell*. Gill & Macmillan. Dublin. [1977]

McCabe, D. 2009. Ó *Gormáin, Muiris*. In: McGuire, J. and Quinn, J. (Eds.). Dictionary of Irish Biography. Cambridge University Press. Vol. 7: 495-496.

MacDermotRoe, K. (nd) The MacDermots Roe and the French Revolution.

< http://www.macdermotroe.com/MDRandFrenchRevolution.html > (August, 2015)

McGlinchey, C. 1987. *The Last of the Name*. The Blackstaff Press. Belfast. [1986]

McMahon, A. (Ed.). 1980. *The Celtic Way of Life*. O'Brien Educational. Dublin. [1976]

McManus, A. 2006. *The Irish Hedge School and Its Books, 1695-1831*. Four Courts Press. Dublin. [2002]

Mac Niocaill, G. 1980. *Ireland before the Vikings*. Gill and Macmillan. Dublin. [1972]

Maginn, C. 2005. *'Civilizing' Gaelic Leinster*. Four Courts Press. Dublin.

Mahon, W. (Ed.). 2000. *The History of Éamonn O'Clery*. Seán Ó Neachtain. Cló Iar-Chonnachta. Indreabhán. Conamara.

Malcolm, E. 1989. *Swift's Hospital*. Gill & Macmillan. Dublin.

Mitchell, F. 1977. *The Irish Landscape*. Collins. London. [1976]

Morash, C. 2004. *A History of Irish Theatre 1601-2000*. Cambridge University Press. Cambridge. [2002]

Murphy, J. 1902. Taken from: *Final Report on the Battlefield of Gettysburg (New York at Gettysburg)* by the New York Monuments Commission for the Battlefields of Gettysburg and Chattanooga. Albany, NY: J. B. Lyon Company. <http://dmna.ny.gov/historic/reghist/civil/infantry/40thInf/40thInfHistSketch.htm > (August, 2015).

Murphy, M. and Potterton, M. 2010. *The Dublin Region in the Middle Ages*. A Discovery Programme Monograph. Four Courts Press. Dublin.

Mytum, H. 1992. *The Origins of Early Christian Ireland*. Routledge. London.

NCSE, 2008. *What is Old Growth?* In: *Beyond Old Growth*. National Council for Science and the Environment. USA. < http://andrewsforest.oregonstate.edu/pubs/pdf/pub4524.pdf > (August, 2015)

Nicholls, K. W. 2005. *Gaelic and Gaelicized Ireland in the Middle Ages*. Lilliput Press. Dublin. [2003]

Ní Mhurchadha, M. 2008. *Early Modern Dubliners*. Dublin City Public Libraries.

O'Byrne, E. 2005. *One World: the Communities of the Southern Dublin Marches*. History Ireland. Vol. 13 (3): 17-21.

O'Byrne, E. 2003. *War, Politics and the Irish of Leinster, 1156-1606*. Four Courts Press. Dublin.

Ó Ciardha, E. 2004. *Ireland and the Jacobite Cause, 1685-1766*. Four Courts Press. Dublin. [2001]

O'Leary, D. J. 1998. *Passion for the Possible*. The Columba Press. Dublin.

Oppenheimer, S. 2004. *Out of Eden*. Robinson. London. [2003]

Ó Siochrú, M. 2008. *Confederate Ireland 1642-1649*. Four Courts Press. Dublin. [1999]

O'Sullivan, A. 2008. *The Western Islands: Ireland's Atlantic Islands and the Forging of Gaelic Irish National Identities*. In: Noble, G., Poller, T., Raven, J. and Verrill, L. (Eds.).

Scottish Odysseys: The Archaeology of Islands. Tempus. Stroud; pp. 172-190.

< http://www.academia.edu/4448807/The_Western_Islands_Irelands_Atlantic_islands_
and_the_forging_of_Gaelic_Irish_national_identities > (August, 2015)

Ó Tuathaigh, G. 2003. *Cultural Visions and the New State: Embedding and Embalming.*
In: Doherty, G. and Keogh, D. (Eds.). *De Valera's Irelands;* pp. 166-184. Mercier Press.
Cork.

Prunty, J. 2002. *Improving the Urban Environment.* In: Brady, J. and Simms, A. (Eds.).
Dublin Through Space & Time; pp. 166-220. Four Courts Press. Dublin. [2001]

Redmond-Howard, L. G. 1916. *Six Days of the Irish Republic.* John W. Luce & Co.
Boston.

Reynolds, J. J. 1926. *Four Courts and North King St. Area.* An t-Óglách. Vol. IV (18):3-
6.

Russell, C. W. and Prendergast, J. P. 1877. Calendar of the State Papers, Relating to
Ireland, of the Reign of James I. 1611-1614. London.

Shiga, D. 2007. *The Universe Before Ours.* New Scientist. 28th April; pp. 28-33.

Spear, T. & Waller, R. (Eds.). 1993. *Being Maasai;* pp. 137-139.Eastern African Studies.
James Currey Ltd. London.

Stout, M. 1997. *The Irish Ringfort.* Irish Settlement Studies No. 5. Four Courts Press.
Dublin.

Sykes, B. 2007. *Saxons, Vikings, and Celts.* W. W. Norton & Co. [2006]

Taaffe, M. 1959. *Those Days are Gone Away.* Hutchinson & Co. London.

Wall, M., 1989 (a). *The Rise of a Catholic Middle Class in Eighteenth-Century Ireland.*
In: O'Brien, G. and Dunne, T. (Eds.). Catholic Ireland in the Eighteenth Century:
Collected Essays of Maureen Wall; pp. 73-84. Geography Publications. Dublin.

Wall, M. 1989 (b). *John Keogh and the Catholic Committee.* In: O'Brien, G. and Dunne,
T. (Eds.). Catholic Ireland in the Eighteenth Century. Collected Essays of Maureen Wall;
pp. 163-170. Geography Publications. Dublin.

Watts, J. R. 1981. *Na Fianna Eireann: A Case Study of a Political Youth Organisation.*
PhD thesis. University of Glasgow. <http://theses.gla.ac.uk/1907/1/1981wattsphd.pdf >
(August, 2015)

Welch, R. 2003. *The Abbey Theatre 1899-1999.* Oxford University Press. [1999]

Wheatcroft, A. 2004. *Infidels.* Penguin. London. [2003]

Wren, J. 2015. *The GPO Garrison Easter Week 1916. A Biographical Dictionary.*
Geography Publications.

Wright, R. 2001. *Nonzero.* Vintage. USA. [2000]

Relevant Dates in History

1169	Beginning of the Norman (or Anglo-Norman) conquest
1348	The Black Death appears
1394	First visit of King Richard II; agreement made with Leinster tribes
1530	Protestant Reformation under English King Henry VIII starts in England
1601	Battle of Kinsale
1607	Flight of the Earls
1610	Beginning of New English and Scottish plantations
1641	Rebellion of the combined Gaelic and Old English forces
1649	Oliver Cromwell lands in Ireland
1660	Restoration of the English monarchy
1667	Birth of Jonathan Swift
1690	Battle of the Boyne
1756	Foundation of the Catholic Association
1793	Catholic Relief Act
1798	Rebellion of the Irish
1800	The Act of Union
1817	Death of John Keogh of the Catholic Committee
1829	Catholic Emancipation
1845	Beginning of the Great Famine
1861	Outbreak of the American Civil War
1879	Parnell's tour of the US begins
1891	Death of Parnell on 6th October
1899	Foundation of the Abbey Theatre
1904	James Joyce begins writing *The Dubliners*; completed it in 1907
1914	Outbreak of World War I in Europe
1916	Easter Rising
1922	Irish independence (Free State set up)
1953	Discovery of DNA in the UK
1966	Dismantling of protective economic barriers in the Irish Republic
1972	Bloody Sunday killings in Northern Ireland on 2nd February

Author

Raymond M. Keogh is a graduate of agricultural science, University College Dublin. He is est known for his international work with teak, which began in the 1970s when he joined the UN in Central America. His extensive experience in tropical forestry; his involvement with local communities; his marriage into Salvadorian society and a lifetime dedicated to exploring his own family's complex social histories, became the ideal blend in which to develop the original concept of our *Common* or *Universal Identity*. The adventure that led to the discovery of this revolutionary idea is outlined in *Shelter & Shadows*. Raymond's other writings include peer-reviewed scientific publications, family history and the novel, *Letter to Prosper*.

Follow on Twitter @ourownidentitys

Follow on Facebook https://www.facebook.com/ourownidentity/

Website http://ourownidentity.com